Collaboration in Space and
the Search for Peace on Earth

Collaboration in Space and the Search for Peace on Earth

Andrew L. Jenks

ANTHEM PRESS

Anthem Press
An imprint of Wimbledon Publishing Company
www.anthempress.com

This edition first published in UK and USA 2026
by ANTHEM PRESS
75–76 Blackfriars Road, London SE1 8HA, UK
or PO Box 9779, London SW19 7ZG, UK
and
244 Madison Ave #116, New York, NY 10016, USA

First published in the UK and USA by Anthem Press in 2022

Copyright © Andrew Jenks 2026

The author asserts the moral right to be identified as the author of this work.

All rights reserved. Without limiting the rights under copyright reserved above,
no part of this publication may be reproduced, stored or introduced into
a retrieval system, or transmitted, in any form or by any means
(electronic, mechanical, photocopying, recording or otherwise),
without the prior written permission of both the copyright
owner and the above publisher of this book.

British Library Cataloguing-in-Publication Data
A catalogue record for this book is available from the British Library.

Library of Congress Control Number: 2025947346

ISBN-13: 978-1-83999-840-9 (Pbk)
ISBN-10: 1-83999-840-7 (Pbk)

Cover credit: Apollo-Soyuz test project with experimental joint flight of the
Soviet spaceship Soyuz-19 and the American spaceship Apollo, elements of this
image furnished by NASA - 3D render, By Elenarts / Shutterstock.com

This title is also available as an eBook.

CONTENTS

List of Illustrations   vii

Introduction: An Alternative History of the Space Age   1

1. Handshakes in Space and the Cold War Imaginary   11

2. Transnational Identity and the Limits of Cosmic Collaboration   41

3. Androgynous Coupling, Technological Fixes, and the Engineering of Peace   75

4. Securitization and Secrecy in the Cold War: The View from Space   117

Conclusion: Cooperation and ASTP's Enduring Legacies   149

Bibliography   161
Acknowledgments   167
Index   169

ILLUSTRATIONS

0.1	The joint US-USSR crew for the Apollo-Soyuz	2
1.1	Aleksei Leonov, ever light on his feet, joins a belly dancer in San Antonio, TX	30
1.2	A Space-suited Mickey Mouse welcomes the Apollo-Soyuz crew to Florida's Disney World	40
2.1	Aleksei Leonov welcomed by Shoshone tribal leaders during one of his many trips to the United States during Apollo-Soyuz training	58
3.1	A drawing of the APAS design	89
3.2	The cosmonauts and astronauts assemble the commemorative plaque in orbit	101
3.3	The ASTP handshake in space	107
3.4	The American astronauts eat borscht soup from tubes with Soviet vodka labels	111
4.1	The ASTP news center for the world's press	132
5.1	Putin meets the ASTP crew in Moscow in July 2010	153

INTRODUCTION: AN ALTERNATIVE HISTORY OF THE SPACE AGE

The shorthand "space race" has dominated popular and academic understandings of space exploration.[1] Yet the history of space has also been marked by extensive episodes of international collaboration, including the linkup between the Apollo and Soyuz capsules on July 17, 1975, the Soviet Interkosmos crewed missions of the 1970s and 1980s, the Mir space station and Shuttle couplings of the 1990s, and the launching of the International Space Station on November 22, 1998. The Soviet Union developed an extensive program of collaboration, reaching across the so-called Iron Curtain in the 1960s and 1970s to work with France on a number of different joint engineering and scientific projects. Beginning in 1978, the Soviets initiated the first of many international crewed missions that would launch individuals into space from Czechoslovakia, Poland, East Germany, Bulgaria, France, Cuba, Hungary, Vietnam, India, Syria, Mongolia, Japan, the United Kingdom, Austria, and many others. With every mission, the map of space exploration became more diverse ethnically, racially, and politically (though not so much in terms of gender). While the United States was less focused on international collaboration until the end of the Cold War, it, too, worked with the Soviets and the European Space Agency on various collaborative ventures.

This book tells the early history of collaboration in space, focusing on the Apollo-Soyuz Test Project (ASTP). ASTP was a showcase of the policy of détente and the dividing line between the earlier phase of the space race and the new period of space collaboration (1970–present).[2] The chapters that follow

---

1 For the typical view of space exploration as a race driven by superpower competition: Deborah Cadbury, *Space Race: The Epic Battle between America and the Soviet Union for Domination of Space* (New York: HarperCollins, 2007); Paul Dickson, *Sputnik: The Shock of the Century* (New York: Walker, 2011).
2 Among the works that discuss collaboration: Matthew J. von Bencke, *The Politics of Space: A History of U.S.-Soviet/Russian Competition and Cooperation in Space* (Boulder, CO: Westview, 1997), discussed collaboration but its focus was primarily on ideological competition. Gerson S. Sher's *From Pugwash to Putin: A Critical History of U.S.-Scientific Cooperation* (Bloomington: Indiana University Press, 2019) covers a broader time period and focuses primarily on scientific exchanges rather than joint engineering projects. Naomi Oreskes

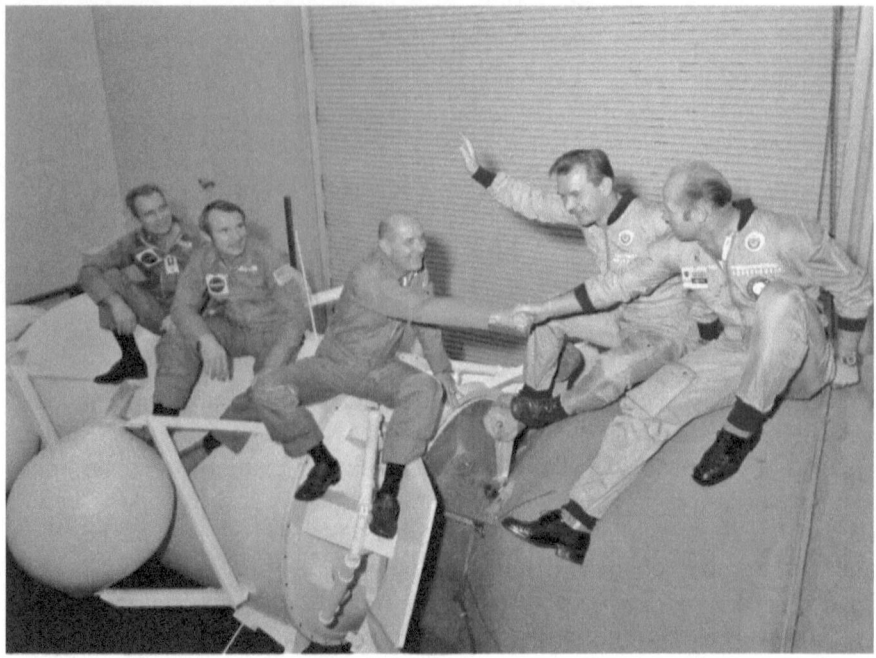

Figure 0.1 The joint US-USSR crew for the Apollo-Soyuz
Source: NASA

discuss ASTP and its aftermath. They provide a thick description of the foundational acts of collaboration among the superpowers of the Cold War and interrogate the historical significance of cooperation in space, which is often dismissed as a symbolic gesture, at best, and at worst as a colossal waste of money with little political, cultural, scientific, or technological significance. The history of collaborative space investigation illustrates the many competing forces—military and civilian, transnational and national, technological and political—that have driven space engineering since its military origins in the Nazi V-2 rocket program of World War II. That program provided much of the initial expertise, human resources (e.g., Wernher von Braun) and technology that jumpstarted the space age. The story of space collaboration also provides an alternative view of the political and cultural dynamics of the Cold War, analyzing episodes of scientific, technological, cultural, and political interchanges to challenge the idea of two opposed ideological camps, and in the process complicating notions

---

and John Krige, eds., *Science and Technology in the Global Cold War* (Cambridge, MA: MIT Press, 2014), discusses technology in the context of Cold War competition.

of the United States as collaborative and open to the world and the Soviet Union as closed and secretive.³ The pages that follow will reveal that the Soviet Union was not so walled off as is often assumed, and the United States not nearly so accessible. In short, regimes of secrecy and openness, as well as conclusions regarding which historical actors were open to compromise and peace initiatives, did not map neatly onto the ideological divisions of the Cold War, especially in the areas of space technology and engineering.⁴

A Tale of Two Tales

In telling the story of space exploration, participants and observers often interpreted the Space Age in two ways. One vision—dubbed "cosmopolitics" by a space policy analyst—viewed space exploration as an extension of national power on Earth, just as "the great maritime powers of the past used specific means and instruments, such as navy and naval bases, to achieve and maintain their power position."⁵ According to this narrative, forays into the cosmos served a national and military purpose, extending military prerogatives—and national economic growth—into outer space, just as European powers in the nineteenth and early twentieth centuries had expanded their political, military, and economic reach into Asia, Africa, and the open seas. This interpretive framework emphasized the dictates of Cold War politics and

---

3 Christine Evans has explored the collaborative impulses in the Soviet satellite communications arena, which also set precedents that contributed to crewed space exploration: "Dividing the Cosmos: INTELSAT, Intersputnik, and the development of transnational satellite communications infrastructures during the Cold War," in Mari Pajala and Alice Lovejoy, eds. *Remapping Cold War Media: Institutions, Infrastructures, Networks, Exchanges* (Bloomington: Indiana University Press, forthcoming 2022).
4 For an excellent analysis of the way that ideology affected US perceptions of the Soviet space program: Thomas Ellis, "Reds in Space: American Perceptions of the Soviet Space Programme from Apollo to Mir 1967–1991," PhD diss., University of Southampton, 2018.
5 Stephan F. von Welck, "Outer Space and Cosmopolitics," *Space Policy* 2, no. 3 (1986), 202. On international cooperation in space from the American standpoint: John Krige, Angelina Long Callahan, and Ashok Maharaj, eds., *NASA in the World: Fifty Years of International Collaboration in Space* (New York: Palgrave Macmillan, 2013), and on the post-1970s malaise: Alexander Geppert, ed., *Post–Apollo: Outer Space and the Limits of Utopia* (New York: Palgrave Macmillan, 2018). On the Soviet Union in the 1970s: James T. Andrews and Asif A. Siddiqi, eds., *Into the Cosmos: Space Exploration and Soviet Culture* (Pittsburgh: University of Pittsburgh Press, 2011). See also Siddiqi's *Challenge to Apollo: The Soviet Union and the Space Race, 1945–1974* (Washington, DC: National Aeronautics and Space Administration, 2000); *The Soviet Space Race with Apollo* (Gainsville: University of Florida Press, 2003); and *The Red Rocket's Glare: Space Flight and the Soviet Imagination, 1857–1957* (New York: Cambridge University Press, 2010).

various national programs for economic growth and strategic nuclear capability, including the use of rockets as nuclear weapons delivery vehicles. In this interpretation the pursuit of scientific goals through space exploration or utopian projects for unifying people across ideological and national barriers were secondary to military and strategic imperatives. As Foy D. Kohler (1908–1990), US ambassador to the Soviet Union during the Kennedy administration noted, "Whatever else may be said of America's motivations in embarking on its great space undertaking, certainly a compelling reason was to deny to the Soviet Union a monopoly of the benefits—political, strategic, and psychological—that went with the forward surge of science-technology in the conquest of space."[6] Ayn Rand, in a letter to President Richard Nixon on September 3, 1969, expressed an unvarnished view of cosmopolitics, reducing the problem of space exploration to an apocalyptic struggle between freedom and tyranny:

> There are in technology no evasions of such magnitude as the present chorus of slogans to the effect that Apollo 11's mission should somehow lead men to peace, good will and the realization that mankind is one big family. What family? With one-third of mankind enslaved under an unspeakable rule of brute force, are we to accept the rulers as members of the family, make terms with them and sanction the terrible fate of victims.

Nixon's Direction of Communications, Herbert Klein, told Nixon that Rand's comments were "most perceptive."[7]

But Nixon ultimately embraced an alternative and increasingly popular view of space exploration as something potentially opposed to Cold War politics. According to this interpretation, the Cold War and geopolitical considerations should play a subordinate role in the history of spaceflight. Instead, these observers focused on the scientific and utopian potential of space-age discovery. The colonization of space, in this view, signaled the final stage of history leading to a perfect global community. Ecological awareness occupied center stage in the new global consciousness of the space age emerging in response to the cosmic view of Earth as a unified yet fragile ecological system. The iconic 1968 Earthrise and 1972 Blue Marble images of Earth,

---

6 Dodd L. Harvey and Linda C. Ciccoritti, *U.S.-Soviet Cooperation in Space* (Miami, FL: Center for Advanced International Studies, University of Miami, 1974), x.

7 Nixon Presidential Library and Archives, OS Outer Space Box 2, 1969–1970, Ayn Rand's letter to Nixon on September 3, 1969, which includes a clipping of her article in the *Objectivist*, vol. 8, no. 9 (September 1969).

like bookends around the first Earth Day in 1970, would inspire people to be far better stewards of the home planet and to unify against the militarization of space and nuclear war. Those images, and the dramatic stories of the first space travelers, linked environmental science and an emerging ecological consciousness to space travel and to visions of new transnational communities. Crewed space flight was thus "a foundation for building a galactic and eventually a universal civilization [...] beyond national and ideological barriers."[8] Typical of this point of view was a letter to Nixon on November 28, 1969, from a man in Moses Lake, Washington. "We feel our space program is a wonderful thing," he wrote, in a letter that appeared among many right after the letter from Ayn Rand in the Nixon Library archival file.

> It will provide an excellent replacement for war as it is phased out and the space program and domestic needs increased. Hopefully too, we can have cooperation with Russia and other countries in building a space station [...] [Yet it] appears again that the military is gaining control and perverting the program to their purposes. We stand for the peaceful use of space. [...] The arms race must stop if Earth is to survive.[9]

This letter reflected an increasingly enthusiastic view of the potential of space collaboration in the 1970s. Previously separate strands of thinking began to migrate across the ideological borders of the Cold War and to merge. Those strands included ecological perspectives, the traditions of utopian thinking about space in Russia called cosmism, ideas about global integration, and Western notions of astrofuturism, which linked human progress to the human colonization and exploration of the cosmos.[10]

Meanwhile, if the Cold War encouraged "cosmopolitics," the threat of nuclear annihilation fueled quixotic visions of unification and global peace through space exploration. The signing in 1967 by the Soviet Union and the United States of a United Nations treaty banning nuclear weapons from space was one watershed moment, prompting paeans "to cooperation and mutual understanding" from Soviet foreign minister Andrei Gromyko and President

---

8 Hoover Institution Archives, Association of Space Explorers (ASE), Folder 3, September 10, 1984, Paris press release; September 6, 1984, draft of press release; Frank White, *The Overview Effect: Space Exploration and Human Evolution* (Boston, MA: Houghton Mifflin, 1987), 100, 108.
9 Nixon Presidential Library and Archives, OS Outer Space Box 2, 1969–70, November 28, 1969, letter from Mr. James Pritchard to Richard Nixon.
10 Douglas De Witt Kilgore, *Astrofuturism: Science, Race, and Visions of Utopia in Space* (Philadelphia: University of Pennsylvania Press, 2021).

Lyndon Johnson.[11] Seeking an exit from the path of self-destruction, space powers in the 1970s and 1980s occasionally joined forces to overcome the very national military and strategic prerogatives that had launched them into space in the first place. The cosmonaut Oleg Makarov remarked, "Unconsciously, you look for the lines that are usual on such maps, the parallels and meridians; it is strange not to see the markings on the living map."[12] The East German Cosmonaut Sigmund Jähn said that "when it takes 90 minutes to go around the world, there is no need for borders."[13] That statement reflected a common view—even among those in charge of national space programs—that space travel would encourage broader identities that would eventually supersede national affiliations. The idea of space as a collaborative venture, and of people acquiring a global consciousness and identity through space flight, seemed to promise connections outside the reach of the nation state. Satellite images of Earth constantly pushed people's imaginations beyond the boundaries on political maps, making space technology a key moment in the history of transnationalism—a popular idea in historical studies but one often lacking a concrete chronological, institutional, or cultural emphasis. This book thus connects transnationalism to ways of thinking that came out of the practices of space collaboration.

Secret versus Open Science

While national security imperatives drove many technological programs—from nuclear and space to computers and telecommunications—they also produced one of the distinctive features of the scientific and technological enterprise of the twentieth century and in particular of the Cold War: The phenomenon of secret science was funded and operated by the national security state. Given the increasing perception of science and technology as central to the acquisition and projection of global power, states with global ambitions began to construct elaborate scientific infrastructures that were cut off from the scientific systems and people on the other side of ideological and national borders. During World War II, the Manhattan Project, the German V-2 Rocket program, and the Soviet Gulag section for scientists and engineers known as the "sharashka" provided templates for national security science and

---

11 Harvey, *U.S.-Soviet Cooperation in Space*, 172–73.
12 Kevin W. Kelley, ed., *The Home Planet* (London: Queen Anne Press, 1988), unnumbered page in Oleg Makarov, "Preface."
13 "Club's Entry Requirement: Orbit Earth," *Houston Chronicle*, January 27, 1986, 4.

engineering.¹⁴ At the same time, earlier traditions of science and technology as transnational activities that united people across ideological, religious, and national borders continued. The secret and open worlds of science and technology intersected in messy and unexpected ways. Many scientists and engineers lived in both the closed and open worlds, devoting their labors to national security and at the same time collaborating with colleagues in the countries designated as competitors and national security threats. Perhaps they entered gated and key-coded office buildings located behind checkpoints guarded by men in khaki, but they often also published articles and attended conferences in open, international journals and associations.

If secret science emerged out of the chrysalis of world wars and the Cold War, the open and collaborative model had its roots in the scientific revolution of Early Modern Europe and the networks of exchanges of research and ideas between the various academies of sciences throughout Europe. The Enlightenment had produced the utopian vision of a transnational Republic of Letters, which would unite adversaries and competitors in a common quest for knowledge and progress. And while it is undoubtedly true that institutions of secret and national security science clearly came to dominate research and engineering during the Cold War, especially in the United States and the Soviet Union, the older Enlightenment idea of science and engineering as a collaborative effort did not simply disappear but lived on in popular consciousness and professional identity. As one American journalist noted in 1966, "Russian and American space scientists, guided by a tradition that scientific research belongs to all men, have been even more eager to cooperate [...] the great space adventure goes beyond national rivalries."¹⁵ The spirit of cooperation asserted itself in international law regarding the exploration of Antarctica, the oceans, and the moon, even as the United States planted its flag on the moon's surface. And it asserted itself in the collaborative projects described in the chapters to follow, though not without profound and sometimes fatal challenges from those same national rivalries.

---

14 I discuss the earlier phase of the space race and the importance of secrecy in the Soviet crewed space program in Andrew Jenks, *The Cosmonaut Who Couldn't Stop Smiling: The Life and Legend of Yuri Gagarin* (Dekalb, IL: Northern Illinois University Press, 2012). Asif Siddiqi's forthcoming *Behind the Wire: Soviet Experts and the Making of Stalin's Gulag* (Oxford: Oxford University Press, 2023) examines secrecy and science in the Soviet context. A recent oral history shows the complex position of Soviet scientists as both isolated from and connected to the broader world outside the Soviet Union: Maria A. Rogacheva, *Soviet Scientists Remember: Oral Histories of the Cold War Generation* (New York: Lexington Books, 2020).

15 "An Open Letter: Can We Get These Two Space Men Together?," *Parade*, January 9, 1966, 3–4.

For outside observers, the meaning of landmark events in space exploration, such as Aleksei Leonov's first human spacewalk in March 1965, could be interpreted in cosmopolitical terms or as an expression of a common human achievement. One American journalist noted that Leonov, on a visit to the United States in May 1965, was said to be "reborn" by his crew partner Pavel Belayev, though reborn into just what was not clear. Leonov's response to one journalist suggested that his rebirth was into an internationalist and peacemonger. Regarding the possibility of a joint trip with Americans, he said, "We'll invite them to climb aboard and have a cup of tea together. We have never objected to friendship in our common task. All earthlings are members of one family." His words were prescient: Just ten years later he would be Soviet commander of the ASTP and invite his American colleagues into the Soyuz for a drink and a meal, displaying all the qualities of hospitality (*gostepriimstvo*) for which Russians are justly famous. Others, however, detected in Leonov's banter an element of gloating and something threatening and humiliating for Americans. The *Washington Post* titled its spacewalk article: "Russian Exercises, Gloats in Stay Outside of Craft." The Soviets, it noted, were rubbing it in, distributing video of the feat to the United States and Western Europe. One British tabloid called the feat, "the greatest circus act in the history of the universe." *Newsweek* noted the ambiguous meaning of the spacewalk, which could tip humanity further in the direction of dangerous superpower competition or, conversely, bring both sides together. "To talk of a space race has meaning only in terms of a goal. [...] Or is the real goal scientific understanding, the extension of man's domain into space? In this race all mankind wins. When Leonov stepped out last week into the 'dark, unbottomed infinite abyss,' it was a human, as well as national achievement."[16]

While onlookers debated the many possible meanings of space exploration, a number of factors drove the forces of collaboration that are explored in the pages that follow. The first was momentum from the tradition of collaboration itself, established as part of the ethos and culture of science and engineering communities and professions for centuries. To be engaged in advanced theoretical and practical work in space exploration was thus to belong to a national military-industrial complex but also to a longer tradition of international conferences, communications, journals, and joint research projects. The second factor was the growing awareness in the Atomic Age that secret science was leading humanity down the path toward self-destruction. It was hoped that collaboration across ideological and cultural barriers could bring humanity

---

16 "Rebirth Conveyed by 'The Man Who Walked in Space,'" *Evening Bulletin*, May 17, 1965, 1; "Russian Exercises, Gloats in Stay Outside of Craft," *Washington Post*, March 19, 1965, 1; "Take a Giant Step—into Space," *Newsweek*, March 29, 1965, 13–16.

back from the brink of nuclear war. Such acts of collaboration were viewed as critical confidence-building measures, as opposed to intercontinental ballistic missiles (ICBMs), that would be the first step toward building the trust needed to put the weapons down and find solutions to joint problems—environmental destruction, poverty, disease, the development of new devices and technological systems—common to all. The belief that science and technology represented supposedly neutral and apolitical spheres helped ideological enemies find common ground. It was a convenient fiction that served both the interests of the narrower project and the broader desire to transcend the limitations and dangers of ideological conflict. The search for technical solutions to political problems—the technological fix—would push political differences into the background of international and professional relations, or so it was hoped. Faith in technocracy and expertise was therefore the essential fuel that fired visions of collaboration.[17]

By divorcing science and technology from politics, by depicting space exploration and engineering as supposedly neutral and disinterested activities, the dramatis personae of this study ultimately succeeded, paradoxically, in showing their political utility: as a way to unite people across ideologies and cultures and to replace the zero-sum politics of the Cold War with the win-win politics of collaboration. The tension between the two competing meanings was captured in 1984, in response to Ronald Reagan's Strategic Defense Initiative (SDI), by Hawaii Senator Spark Matsunaga:

> It is conceit carried to the point of sheer absurdity, if not madness, to assume that the Cold War will simply march out from our tiny microbe of a planet into the infinite reaches of the cosmos. That sort of video game version of the future has no place in mature councils [...] no matter how futuristic our costumes and our machines, civilization is doomed if its advance into space is to be guided by tribal drumbeats.

He called for a policy of "aggressive cooperation" in space to counter SDI and to reset superpower relations back on the path of peaceful coexistence and of science and technology–driven political harmony.[18] What follows is the story of how aggressive cooperation in space began and its many ambiguous political, cultural, and technological legacies.

---

17 On the political function of numbers and expertise in modern public life: Theodore M. Porter, *Trust in Numbers: The Pursuit of Objectivity in Science and Public Life* (Princeton, NJ: Princeton University Press, 1996).

18 "Cooperative East-West Ventures," *Congressional Record – Senate*, October 11, 1984, S14018.

Chapter 1
HANDSHAKES IN SPACE AND THE COLD WAR IMAGINARY

The Cold War, unlike the very hot war that preceded it, first emerged as an imaginary conflict. There were no tank battles, aerial bombings, formal declarations of war, or direct military clashes between the United States and the Soviet Union. Reversing the more conventional understanding of causality—from the concrete event to its representation—assumptions about the existence of a state of war between the two countries intensified ideological and military confrontation in the late 1940s, transforming the Cold War from an imagined event (an iron curtain that never existed except as a metaphor in Churchill's mind) into a seemingly objective reality ("Eastern Europe," NATO, and the Warsaw Pact) and turning former allies into nuclear-armed enemies poised for war.[1]

The terrifying next step to direct military confrontation was nearly complete when both superpowers fought proxy wars in Korea and Vietnam and faced off over Berlin and the Cuban missile crisis. The history of the space program seemed to be a direct result of that confrontation, initiated in October 1957 by Sputnik and driving both sides to go higher and further into the cosmos as a way to measure political, technological, and, above all, military superiority. The military implications of rocket technology—that launching a satellite, dog, or person into space also proved the ability to heave an intercontinental ballistic missile (ICBM) against your enemy—was not lost on anyone.[2] However, what could be imagined as an expression of military superiority could also be unimagined, thereby reducing the potential for military confrontation.

---

1 Masuda Hajimi, *Cold War Crucible: The Korean Conflict and the Postwar World* (Cambridge, MA: Harvard University Press, 2015).
2 For the history of technology as a measure of national superiority: Michael Adas, *Machines as the Measure of Man: Science, Technology, and Ideologies of Western Dominance* (Ithaca, NY: Cornell University Press, 1990).

This chapter examines the use of joint space technology programs to imagine an alternative to war. It focuses on the political history of the first major collaborative space engineering project between the Soviet Union and the United States, the Apollo-Soyuz Test Project (ASTP) in July 1975. While ASTP marked the transition from the space race to the age of space collaboration, it also built upon earlier precedents of cooperation. These efforts (admittedly half-hearted at times) grew out of broader scientific exchanges and cooperation between the two superpowers since the late 1950s, which had been conceived as a way to reduce tensions and create bridges across ideology.[3] Both sides claimed that their space programs served the interests of scientific progress and world peace, and this was more than mere political smokescreen. Sergei Korolev, the father of Soviet rocketry, was as interested in the romance of human space exploration as in explicitly military and national goals, and the devastation suffered by the Soviets during World War II made the goal of peace a very concrete and compelling goal for him.[4] As a Soviet brochure at the 1958 Brussels Universal and International Exhibition put it, "If humanity would once and for all abandon war and direct all its energy to the solution of peaceful scientific problems, the day when Man would set foot on the surface of the Moon and Mars would be considerably closer."[5] On the second anniversary of his flight on April 12, 1961, Yuri Gagarin told global radio audiences that

> space is eternal and infinite. There is enough room for everyone. For us, for the Americans, and the British, and the French, and the Germans— all, in general who want to go there. [...] The main thing is that outer space should serve humanity. The Soviet government raises the question: let's not dominate each other in space, but let's cooperate, cooperate closely.[6]

Meanwhile, the enabling act in 1958 that created NASA envisioned space exploration as "an arm of American diplomacy" and a vehicle for promoting

---

3 For an overview of scientific exchange program and agreements during the Cold War: Gerson S. Sher, *From Pugwash to Putin: A Critical History of U.S.-Scientific Cooperation* (Bloomington: Indiana University Press, 2019).

4 On the mix of motives that inspired the Soviet space program, see Asif Siddiqi, *The Rocket's Red Glare: Spaceflight and the Soviet Imagination, 1857–1957* (Cambridge: Cambridge University Press, 2010).

5 "Facing the Cosmos," Brochure handed out at the USSR Section: Brussels Universal and International Exhibition. Author's personal collection.

6 Thanks to Victoria Milanova of the RT news service for providing me with the transcript of Gagarin's radio address on April 12, 1962.

international collaboration and scientific progress.[7] True, military imperatives and ideological competition often eclipsed visions of peaceful collaboration in the early years of space conquest, but that did not stop President John F. Kennedy from making overtures toward the Soviet Union about cooperation. With Kennedy's assassination and the increasing focus on the military challenge of fighting communism in Vietnam, collaborative efforts were largely limited to the exchange of satellite meteorological data, and even then Soviet obsessions with secrecy made it seem unlikely that collaboration would ever be possible, at least to many American observers.[8]

It was in the late 1960s, following a period in which collaborative efforts with the Soviet Union took a backseat to beating the Soviets to the moon, that both sides again viewed cooperation as a serious possibility. Among the factors that changed attitudes was the American triumph of the moon landing, which was accompanied by an increasing sense of waning economic resources and the need to refocus NASA on its original collaborative mission, even while finding a stopgap program to keep crewed spaceflight busy between the anticipated end of the Apollo missions and the new Shuttle launch system.[9] On the Soviet side, in the wake of their own failed effort to get to the moon, there was a growing commitment to low-earth-orbit docking systems and a new focus on forging scientific and technological partnerships with foreign countries, and of reaping the political benefits that those links would supposedly create. By 1970, both sides were thus considering joint missions with the former enemy as a way to kill two birds with one stone or, as the Russians say, kill two rabbits all at once: pool resources for space exploration and create a new dynamic of peaceful collaboration between the Cold War rivals.[10] Returning to the

---

7 On the complicated and difficult attempts by NASA to realize the international, collaborative part of its mandate: John Krige, Angelina Long Callahan, and Ashok Maharaj, eds., *NASA in the World: Fifty Years of International Collaboration in Space* (New York: Palgrave Macmillan, 2013); Matthew J. Von Bencke, *The Politics of Space: A History of U.S.-Soviet/Russian Competition and Cooperation in Space* (Boulder, CO: Westview, 1997); and Dodd L. Harvey and Linda C. Ciccoritti, *U.S.-Soviet Cooperation in Space* (Miami, FL: University of Miami, 1974).

8 John Logsdon, *John F. Kennedy and the Race to the Moon* (New York: Palgrave Macmillan, 2010); and on the American and Soviet agreement on June 8, 1962, to exchange satellite weather data following the Cuban missile crisis: Angelina Long Callahan, "Sustaining Soviet-American Collaboration, 1957–1989," in John Krige, Angelina Long Callahan, and Ashok Maharaj, eds., *NASA in the World: Fifty Years of International Collaboration in Space* (New York: Palgrave Macmillan, 2013), 135–37.

9 On the post-Apollo malaise: Alexander Geppert, ed., *Post–Apollo: Outer Space and the Limits of Utopia* (New York: Palgrave Macmillan, 2018).

10 Nixon Presidential Library Research Files, National Security Study Memorandums, NSSM 70 to NSSM 76, Box H-162, "Cooperation between the U.S. and USSR in

original vision of space exploration as an international enterprise, the two sides thus set the stage for détente—the policy pursued by President Richard Nixon and General Secretary Leonid Brezhnev in the early 1970s to transcend ideological tensions and to build a relationship based on shared interests—and embarked on one of the first serious peace initiatives of the Cold War.[11]

The ASTP, started in 1970 and completed on July 17, 1975, embodied the shift from competition and confrontation to cooperation in space and in politics. As such, it was a critical event in challenging the Cold War imaginary: a way of thinking that represented the ideological enemy as an existential threat that could only be countered with a commitment to total military preparedness and mobilization. As the 1950 National Security Council 68 (NSC-68) policy document put it in its imagined conception of the Soviet Union, the Soviets, according to the NSC, viewed the United States as "the principal center of power in the non-Soviet world and the bulwark of opposition to Soviet expansion [...] [and thus] the principal enemy whose integrity and vitality must be subverted or destroyed by one means or another if the Kremlin is to achieve its fundamental design." With such an enemy, "a despotic oligarchy" hell-bent on "world domination," there could be no peace but only a permanent state of preparation for war.[12] The Soviets, meanwhile, increasingly imagined the United States as an implacable foe that had essentially replaced the Nazis as the destructive force gathering at its borders in preparation for an invasion.[13]

Space Activities, Prospects and Opportunities," April 8, 1970. The key Soviet docking engineer on ASTP, Vladimir Syromiatnikov, in his memoirs discussed the broader implications of the technical act of docking in changing political and diplomatic relationships between the United States and Soviet Union, which is explored in more detail in Chapter 3. Vladimir Syromiatnikov, *100 Stories about Docking and Other Adventures in Space, Vol. 1* (Moscow: Universitetskaia kniga, 2005), 11–13. This is Syromiatnikov's own translation of his Russian language memoir: *100 Rasskazov o stykovke i o drugikh prikliucheniakh v kosmose i na zemle, Chast' 1* (Moscow: Izd. "Logos", 2003).

11 Cold War historians contributed to a three-volume series on the history of the Cold War in which vol. 3 in particular deals with détente. The idea of scientific and technological collaboration, however, is not discussed, though the volume does examine science and technology as spheres of competition. Melvyn P. Leffler and Odd Arne Wested, eds., *The Cambridge History of the Cold War*, Vols. 1–3 (Cambridge: Cambridge University Press, 2010).

12 "NSC-68," https://www.mtholyoke.edu/acad/intrel/nsc-68/nsc68-1.htm, accessed July 24, 2019. On the mobilization of US politics and public opinion in accordance with the image of the Soviet enemy created by NSC-68: Steven Casey, "Selling NSC-68: The Truman Administration, Public Opinion, and the Politics of Mobilization, 1950–51," *Diplomatic History* 29, no. 4 (2005), 655–90.

13 For examples of anti-American poster propaganda that shaped the Soviet Cold War Imaginary, in which the U.S. was increasingly represented as a replacement for the Nazis: https://www.rbth.com/history/329103-15-soviet-anti-american-posters,

A lead engineer for the ASTP remembered the propaganda images that greeted him during his first visit to Moscow in October 1970: "There were great billboards, and they showed this picture of Uncle Sam, and Uncle Sam had big canine teeth sticking out and blood was running out of his mouth, and he's got a Vietnamese baby in one hand, killing the baby, and he's stomping on the baby's mother."[14]

On both sides of the ideological divide, then, the Cold War imaginary was fueled in the late 1940s and early 1950s by what recent scholarship has called the process of "securitization," which suggests that conceptions of security are as much social and political constructions, dependent on ideological and cultural biases, as they are the result of ongoing events or objective factors.[15] The social process of securitization—encouraged by hostile speech acts by political leaders, media representations, and objective events such as a nuclear bomb test—exploited a feeling of vulnerability that was accentuated and amplified in the Soviet case by the bloodbath of World War II, producing a state of permanent military preparedness on both sides, constantly reinforced by the clichéd images of the enemy other as irredeemably evil and duplicitous.

ASTP countered the Cold War imaginary with images of enemies shaking hands, smiling in each other's presence, and designing a technology to enhance the security and safety of space exploration. The central goal of ASTP was to test a safety system that would allow the Soviets and Americans to survive a catastrophic failure in orbit by docking with each other and using the other's capsule as a safe haven.[16] Collaboration in space was, as the cosmonaut Vitalii Sevastianov put it, an escape hatch in both a literal sense but also in the sense of escaping the madness of the nuclear doctrine of mutual assured destruction (MAD), and the first step toward sanity and security was to see each other as friends and partners rather than enemies and adversaries.[17]

ASTP was therefore a physical event—the docking of two orbiting space ships—but it was also an imagined project that was intended by both Nixon and Brezhnev as a way to deconstruct the Cold War and lay out a vision of

---

accessed July 24, 2019; and http://www.oldmagazinearticles.com/article-summary/cold-war-cartoons#.XTnOyC2ZPGI, accessed July 25, 2019.

14 Interview with Caldwell Johnson, May 12, 1998, League City Texas, NASA Johnson Space Center Oral History Project, 51. The interviews with Johnson cited in this book are located online at: https://historycollection.jsc.nasa.gov/JSCHistoryPortal/history/oral_histories/JohnsonCC/johnsoncc.htm.

15 Michael C. Williams, "Words, Images, Enemies: Securitization and International Politics," *International Studies Quarterly* 47, no. 4 (2003), 514.

16 Syromiatnikov, *100 Stories*, 615.

17 V. I. Sevastianov and V. F. Priakhin, *Rescue: avariinyi vykhod. Kosmonavtika i novoe politicheskoe myshlenie v iaderno-kosmicheskuyu eru* (Moscow: Mezhdunarodnye otnosheniia, 1989).

politics based on peaceful scientific and technical collaboration and of creating a technology that enhanced global security rather than threatened it. That vision, in the Soviet context, drew on the traditions of Russian cosmism, as well as the Soviet emphasis on friendship of peoples, that saw the collaborative conquest of space as a common task (*obshchee delo*) that would unite people across ideology, nationality, and religion. The Russian traditions of cosmism had begun in the late nineteenth century and involved a vision of space exploration as a Russian-led effort that would unite humanity in a common struggle against disease and war. By the 1970s, the ideas of cosmism provided a planetary perspective with which many cosmonauts and Soviet space industry officials came to understand the meaning of their professional endeavors.[18] ASTP—whose most dramatic moment was the handshake in space between Aleksei Leonov and Thomas Stafford—thus helped the Soviet Union and the United States to construct an alternative to the Cold War, creating a new dynamic in superpower relations that spread outward from the scientific and technological realm and into the political, diplomatic, and social worlds. Or so it was hoped.

The use of ASTP as an instrument of diplomacy and as a catalyst for détente has received little attention in either the general literature on the Cold War—which has only recently begun to address the political significance of science and technology—and in the literature on space history, which has focused mostly on the earlier space race but little on collaboration in space that has dominated crewed space missions from the 1970s and leading up to the International Space Station.[19] This analysis thus connects two previously separate spheres of study—space history and diplomatic history—to shed light on the importance of space exploration in the bigger story of Cold War

---

18 See the following for an attempt to integrate Soviet space exploration into the cosmist traditions: V. I. Sevastianov and A. D. Ursul, *Era Kosmosa: obshchestvo i priroda* (Moscow: Znanie, 1972). On cosmism: George M. Young, *The Russian Cosmists: The Esoteric Futurism of Nikolai Fedorov and His Followers* (New York: Oxford University Press, 2012).

19 The technical details of how both sides engineered this project—on time and with few technical problems in July 1975—have been ably told by NASA itself in the official history of ASTP: Edward Clinton Ezell and Linda Neuman Ezell, *The Partnership: A History of the Apollo–Soyuz Test Project* (Washington, DC: NASA, 1978). For the Russian story of ASTP, which relies on interviews with all the principal Soviet players, from cosmonauts and engineers to managers and scientists. K. D. Bushuev, ed., *Soyuz i Apollon: rasskazyvaiut sovetskie uchenyi, inzhenery, y kosmonavty – uchastniki sovmestnykh rabot s amerikanskimi spetsialistami* (Moscow: Izd. Politicheskoi literatury, 1976). For the American popular response to ASTP: Thomas Ellis, "'Howdy Partner!' Space Brotherhood, Detente and the Symbolism of the 1975 Apollo–Soyuz Test Project," *Journal of American Studies* 53, no. 3 (2019), 744–69.

diplomacy.[20] Seen in this combined perspective, ASTP exemplifies the concept of technopolitics, which historians of technology use to explain the mutual and simultaneous construction of technological systems and new political regimes.[21] As a technopolitical system operating in the domain of international relations, ASTP involved both the design of a docking interface between the Soviet and American space programs and, simultaneously, the building of an alternative, less adversarial, less militaristic, and safer relationship between the Soviet Union and the United States. Advancing an alternative to the Cold War imaginary, ASTP involved what the historians of technology Sheila Jasanoff and Sang-Hyun Kim refer to as a "sociotechnical imaginary"—the projection of ideas about social and political progress through scientific and technological projects—which in the case of ASTP conveyed a radical new understanding of Soviet-American relations based on peaceful technical and economic collaboration.[22]

Where Pragmatism Meets Idealism

A mutually reinforcing combination of pragmatic and idealistic considerations culminated in the ASTP project, the deconstruction of the Cold War imaginary and the launching of the age of space collaboration. Faced with the prospects of budget cuts in the post-Apollo era, NASA administrator Thomas Paine in March 1970 noted that NASA simply could not fund its many crewed and uncrewed missions. Collaboration would help to defray the costs of space exploration, extend the life of the Apollo technologies beyond the planned moon missions, and challenge claims that the American space program was "largely a selfish effort run for purposes of national prestige and to compete with the Russians." The Apollo 8 astronaut Frank Borman, in a note to the White House in December 1969, wrote that foreign cooperation would lead "hopefully to more direct financial participation from the other countries of the world," including the Soviet Union. Taking advantage of the popularity of the Apollo 8 mission that produced the famous "Earthrise" photograph,

---

20 For recent works that integrate the history of science and technology into Cold War history: Egle Rindzevicute, *The Power of Systems: How Policy Sciences Opened Up the Cold War* (Ithaca, NY: Cornell University Press, 2016); and Audra J. Wolfe, *Freedom's Laboratory: The Cold War Struggle for the Soul of Science* (Baltimore, MD: Johns Hopkins University Press, 2018).
21 On the concept of technopolitics and the simultaneous construction of engineering systems and political regimes: Gabrielle Hecht, *The Radiance of France: Nuclear Power and National Identity* (Cambridge, MA: MIT Press, 1998).
22 On sociotechnical imaginaries: Sheila Jasanoff and Sang-Hyun Kim, eds., *Dreamscapes of Modernity: Sociotechnical Imaginaries and the Fabrication of Power* (Chicago: University of Chicago Press, 2015).

Nixon had made Borman his point man for floating ideas about collaboration when the Apollo hero became the first American astronaut to visit the Soviet Union and its formerly secret space facilities in July 1969.[23]

Nixon also believed that closer relations with the Soviet Union in space might produce the breakthrough necessary to move beyond the bloody stalemate of the Vietnam War. Meanwhile, as the United States was mired in a costly military and ideological struggle with Soviet proxies in Southeast Asia, US allies in Europe were imagining a new kind of relationship with their Eastern European neighbors. German chancellor Willy Brandt in 1969 redirected West German foreign policy toward closer relations with East Germany and the Soviet Union with his policy of *Ostpolitik*. French president Charles de Gaulle had visited the USSR on June 30, 1966, followed by Soviet premier Alexei Kosygin's return visit to France on December 9, 1966. The Soviets were especially impressed by the French willingness to propose collaborative science and technology projects across a range of applications—from meteorology to space physics—and they saw the political utility of closer ties with France as a way to extend Soviet influence in Western Europe. De Gaulle's successor Georges Pompidou visited the USSR in July 1967 and again in October 1970, while Brezhnev traveled to France in October 1971 to solidify the ever-expanding relationship. These visits initiated a Franco-Soviet collaboration across a broad range of science and technology fields, creating a vibrant and enduring exchange of knowledge and personnel that challenged Cold War divisions.[24] It is telling that in the Russian Academy of Sciences archive devoted to Soviet international collaboration in space, files describing French contacts through the late 1960s and 1970s far outnumber those about fellow "friendly" socialist countries in Eastern Europe.[25]

The Franco-Soviet alliance deeply impressed Nixon with its emphasis on scientific and technological collaboration, which he conceived of, like Brezhnev and the French leadership, as a starting point for a broader relaxation of tensions. As the president learned from one NSC briefing paper,

---

23 Nixon Presidential Library and Archives, OS Outer Space Box 1, 1969–70, 1 of 2, March 26, 1970, memorandum from Thomas Paine to the White House; December 2, 1969, memorandum from Frank Borman to Peter Flanigan.

24 Archive of the Russian Academy of Sciences (ARAN), f. 1678, d. 108m, l. 14 (the agreement signed by both sides in Moscow on June 30, 1966, and preparatory discussions during Soviet-French meetings in October 1965 in Paris). On the Soviet satisfaction with French willingness to collaborate: ARAN, f. 1678, o. 1, d. 108m, l. 80.

25 On the deepening scientific and technological collaboration between the Soviets and the French: ARAN, f. 1678, o. 1, d. 182, ll. 1–46; d. 307, l. 10 (about collaborative efforts in 1974 in nuclear energy, space exploration, and the development of satellite color television).

In this connection the [Soviet and French] sides referred to the important achievements in cooperation in the fields of space exploration, peaceful uses of atomic energy, as well as high energy physics, in particular the installation of a French laser reflector on the moon surface, the commissioning of the French bubble chamber Mirabelle at the Soviet proton accelerator in Serpukhov, [and] the Soviet-French contact on enriching French natural uranium in the Soviet Union.[26]

Nixon's policies of détente—which began with a focus on scientific and technological collaboration—thus owed a debt to the innovative policies of Cold War deconstruction initiated by the French, who, along with their Soviet partners, viewed science as a supposedly objective enterprise that could transcend the zero-sum mentality of Cold War ideological confrontation. For both the Soviets and the French, science and technology had entered into the political arena as a supposedly neutral ground upon which to ease tensions and transcend ideological differences.[27] Their shared technocratic mindset provided a convenient cover that allowed otherwise hostile powers to meet in an atmosphere of reduced ideological and political tensions, providing a "track-two" alternative to more traditional diplomacy, which was grounded in the assumption "that actual or potential conflict can be resolved or eased by appealing to common human capabilities to respond to good will and reasonableness."[28]

For the Soviets, meanwhile, Franco-Soviet collaboration was just one piece of a broader program of cooperation that gained momentum in the late 1960s and coincided with the growing US interest under Nixon in enacting the rhetoric of space collaboration. In the mid-1960s the Soviets created a formal institutional mechanism by which to connect the formerly secretive Soviet space industry to open, collaborative ventures with communist and noncommunist partners. Known as Interkosmos, the program dovetailed with cosmist notions about the common, unifying task of space exploration as well as long-standing traditions of Soviet internationalism, based on the idea of using science and technology to advance both socialism and the human condition. It also was an expression of soft power and track-two diplomacy that relied on coopting rather than coercing enemies and friends (as the Soviets had done so disastrously

---

26 Nixon Presidential Library and Archives, NSC HAK Files-Europe-USSR Box 67, Sonnefeldt Papers [1 of 2] 5.
27 Isabelle Gourne, "Dépasser les tensions Est-Ouest pour la conquête de l'espace. La coopération franco- soviétique au temps de la Guerre froide," *Cahiers SIRICE* 2, no. 16 (2016), 49–67.
28 William D. Davidson and Joseph V. Montville, "Foreign Policy According to Freud," *Foreign Policy*, no. 45 (Winter 1981–82), 155.

in the invasion of Czechoslovakia in 1968).[29] The idea for Interkosmos originated with a letter Kosygin had sent in April 1965 to fellow communist countries about scientific collaboration.[30] It was formally put into effect on April 12, 1967—International Cosmonaut Day celebrating the day Yuri Gagarin became the first human in space. The organization, which was attached to the Soviet Academy of Sciences, became the formal body responsible for coordinating negotiations with foreign partners as well as Soviet design bureaus in the Soviet aerospace industry to conduct joint crewed missions and scientific experiments. By the mid-1970s it handled partnerships with communist and noncommunist countries such as France, and in November 1975 Interkosmos invited the United States to participate in the Soviet Cosmos satellites devoted to biology and medicine.[31]

The Soviets were eager also to build upon another precedent, namely the 1967 UN space treaty's formal declaration of space as a demilitarized zone, signed by both the United States and the Soviet Union.[32] Immediately afterward, Mstislav Keldysh, the Soviet Academy of Sciences president and front man for civilian Soviet space ventures, began floating the idea of collaboration in the Western press, inspired by the example of the Antarctic Treaty of 1961, which grew out of the International Geophysical Year of 1957 and had set aside the Antarctic as a demilitarized region devoted exclusively to international science.[33] Trained as a mathematician, Keldysh in the late 1960s had taken an increasingly active role as an international spokesperson for the civilian and peaceful uses of science and space collaboration, replacing Anatoly Blagonravov in this role. Soviet space managers remembered Keldysh as a critical figure in the history of Soviet space exploration following the untimely death of the father of Soviet rocketry, Sergei Korolev, in 1966.[34] In the wake of Korolev's sudden death, which deprived the Soviet space industry of one of its most effective advocates for funding and political support, Keldysh reoriented Soviet space exploration away from the super-secret world of Soviet missile command, creating a public and civilian function

---

29 Joseph S. Nye, "Public Diplomacy and Soft Power." *Annals of the American Academy of Political and Social Science* 616, no. 1 (2008), 94–109.
30 ARAN, f. 1678, o. 1, d. 108m, l. 13.
31 V. I. Kozyrev and S. A. Nikitin, *Polety po programme 'Interkosmos'* (Moscow: Znanie, 1980), 9–10, 64; and Krige, *NASA in the World*, 143.
32 *Soyuz i Apollon: rasskazyvaiut sovetskie uchenyi, inzhenery, y kosmonavty*, 15.
33 "Soviet Space Aide Interested in Joining With U.S.," *New York Times*, October 13, 1967, 1. For a general history of Antarctica: Gordon Elliott, *A History of Antarctic Science* (Cambridge: Cambridge University Press, 1992).
34 On the importance of Keldysh following Korolev's death: A. S. Eliseev, *Zhizn': Kaplia v more* (Moscow: Aviatsiia i kosmonavtika, 1998), 100–101.

for the vast infrastructure of Soviet space technology and in the process providing the Soviet Academy of Sciences with a visible and important role in space exploration and diplomacy.[35] Technically, then, Keldysh was the Soviet Union's most important scientific bureaucrat, but in fact he was playing the role of diplomat and politician, using the authority of his scientific position to reach out to the ideological enemy just as the astronaut Borman, following Apollo 8, was essentially working for Nixon on diplomatic assignment to the Soviet Union. Equally important, Keldysh also acted as intermediary between the Soviet political leadership and Soviet space industry engineers, many of whom were eager to learn about foreign space capabilities and work with their American colleagues. As Aleksei Eliseev, the Soviet flight director of ASTP, put it, Keldysh prepared Brezhnev and other political leaders for "the psychological reorientation" of sharing technology and collaborating with the ideological enemy, skillfully arguing for the political utility of technological cooperation and countering resistance from the Soviet military-industrial complex to the various efforts at declassification that would be necessary to make joint missions possible.[36]

The "Chief Theoretician of Space," as Keldysh was known, thus urged joint projects with socialist and nonsocialist countries, heading Soviet delegations to England, France, and Japan, where he described space exploration and science as something that "transcends nationalism."[37] In August 1969 he told Frank Borman that he was interested in bilateral agreements to limit the development of space-based offensive strategic weapons. Keldysh (who in 1973 traveled to the United States for a six-hour heart operation with the famous American surgeon Michael DeBakey, perhaps aware that Korolev had died at the hands of an incompetent Soviet surgeon) suggested the joint tracking of space probes and the "complete advance publication of all scientific probes, manned and unmanned," as well as joint meetings of cosmonauts and training personnel. Keldysh thought the latter was particularly important, given "the public awareness of the cosmonauts and astronauts," who would symbolize the new relationship between the superpowers. Borman, in a letter to Henry Kissinger, said that Keldysh had told him that "the publicity focused on cosmonauts and astronauts looking at common problems in a field that

---

35 Library of Congress, Thomas O. Paine Papers, Box 25, Folder 4, various correspondence between NASA and Keldysh in 1970 illustrates the active role that Keldysh played in connecting the formerly secret Soviet space program to the outside world.
36 Eliseev, *Zhizn'*, 100.
37 "Unorthodox Soviet Science Chief Mstislav Vsevolodovich Keldysh," *New York Times*, October 19, 1967, 32; "Scientific Internationalist: Mstislav Vsevolodovich Keldysh," *New York Times*, July 19, 1969, 10; and "Soviet Reveals Keldysh Is Chief Space Planner," *New York Times*, May 31, 1971, 32.

offers no direct threat to either country's national interests would be favorable and conducive to closer relations in all fields."[38]

As for the idea of a cosmonaut and astronaut flight, Nixon instructed Borman to explore the possibility of a joint mission on his European and Soviet tour in the summer of 1969 and to emphasize points Nixon had repeated in public speeches since his inauguration in January 1969. In that speech and elsewhere Nixon described the Apollo missions as a common human achievement devoted to scientific progress and "all mankind," emphasizing NASA's role in the spirit of the international collaborative mandate of the 1958 National Aeronautics and Space Act. Following his Soviet trip, which many in the Nixon administration had earlier advised against, Borman told the president that he encountered a "tremendous response to my assertion that the space program may eventually draw people of the earth together. References to the fact that national boundaries and political differences were not visible from 240,000 miles inevitably drew enthusiastic applause." He also received an enthusiastic response to the idea of managing moon stations in the same way as Antarctica—as an international scientific collaborative project. Said Borman in a memorandum to Peter Flanigan at the White House, "The time to take the initiative in this field is ripe," and while he was unsure if the Soviets were ready for such a venture—which turned out to be incorrect—keeping lines of communication open was the best strategy. By 1970, the political leadership of both sides had come to see science and technology—and in particular space exploration as a supposedly neutral sphere—as an ideal way to begin a reset of their relationship that would become known as détente in the United States and "peaceful coexistence" in the Soviet context.[39] As the lead docking engineer on ASTP, Vladimir Syromiatnikov, put it in his memoirs, referring to the supposedly nonideological nature of technology: "A rocket delivers a satellite not only beyond the atmosphere and Earth's gravity, but also beyond political activity."[40] A consensus thus seemed to be emerging that if the United States and the Soviet Union were to be at peace with each other, the new relationship would have to begin in a technical area seemingly divorced from ideological entanglements. The high-profile successes of the Apollo missions and Soviet space program fit the bill, appearing to

---

38 Nixon Presidential Library and Archives, OS Outer Space Box 1, 1969–70, 1 of 2, August 5, 1969. Frank Borman's letter to Henry Kissinger.
39 Nixon Presidential Library and Archives, OS Outer Space Box 1, 1969–70, 1 of 2, December 2, 1969, Frank Borman memorandum to Peter Flanigan; WHCF FO 8 International Travel, January 24, 1969, NASA memorandum to the White House; and 6 March 1969 Borman letter to Nixon.
40 Syromiatnikov, *100 Stories*, 373.

the political establishments of both countries as leading fronts in the détente peace initiative.

Earthrise and the New Imaginary

The experience of space flight, meanwhile, had triggered the emotional response that allowed many of the military officers in both space programs to think like doves. During the first space walk in 1965, the Soviet officer Aleksei Leonov said he became more acutely aware that "earthlings are members of one family" and that space exploration should solve "scientific problems having purely peaceful purposes." Recounting his experience before the UN in 1968, he said that space flight would be critical in "expanding the point of view of people" and in overcoming "psychological and social barriers between people."[41] The view of the earth from space—the "Earthrise" image from Apollo 8 on Christmas Eve of 1968 or the view that cosmonauts earlier had experienced since Yuri Gagarin's first trip into space in 1961—was splashed across the front pages of newspapers, on television, in artistic representations, and on the cover of the *Whole Earth Catalog*, where it became the banner of a newly emerging environmental and planetary consciousness in the United States.[42]

Space exploration and satellite imagery thus encouraged visions of a global community united by a shared commitment to peace, science, and the preservation of the planet (an idea explored in more detail in the next chapter). The transnational individual, whose identity emerged from a cosmic perspective, was thus a byproduct of the space age and a direct challenge to the Cold War imaginary as represented in Soviet propaganda images of the United States or in NSC-68. And just as newly emerging national identities in the nineteenth century had made the modern nation-state possible, so, too, had new transnational communities given birth, first in space and then on earth, to a new kind of person: the post–Cold War subject, conceived in an act of peaceful scientific and technological collaboration.

A number of factors thus converged to encourage a policy shift toward space collaboration on both sides of the Cold War: the Earthrise image from Apollo 8,

---

41 "Rebirth Conveyed by 'The Man Who Walked in Space,'" *Evening Bulletin*, May 17, 1965, 1; NASA Historical Reference Collection, A. A. Leonov, "The First Egress into Space," paper presented at the XVI International Astronautics Congress, Athens, Greece, September 13–18, 1965; A. A. Leonov, "Vospriatie prostranstva v kosmose," Konferentsiia Organizatsii Ob'edinennykh Natsii po issledovaniiu i ispol'zovaniiu kosmicheskogo prostranstva v mirnykh tseliakh," June 14, 1968, LEK 1/10/3, Leonov (Post Voskhod 2 to ASTP); and "Astronauts Find God in Space," *San Diego Union*, May 19, 1973, 9.
42 Robert Poole, *Earthrise: How Man First Saw the Earth* (New Haven, CT: Yale University Press, 2008), 8.

the ever-deepening Franco-Soviet collaboration, Soviet eagerness to cooperate, and, finally, bipartisan support for collaboration at a time in American politics when bipartisanship was considered the norm toward which both parties should strive. Senator William Fulbright, on January 23, 1969, wrote to Nixon that the image of Earthrise had "made people everywhere acutely aware of the reality that this is indeed one world." The democrat wanted Nixon to "capitalize on that spirit by taking steps toward closer cooperation with the Soviet Union in future space activities." Fulbright thought it unfortunate that national competition had driven space exploration. "There are already all too many areas where our interests and those of the Soviet Union conflict." He noted that both sides, with the International Space Treaty of 1967, had formally rejected

> the use of outer space for military purposes. [...] The beginning of your Presidency, coupled with the recent successes of Apollo 8 and Soyuz-4 and 5, make this an especially appropriate time for new approaches to the Soviet Union concerning closer cooperation in space activities. I am sure that the world would applaud such a move on your part.

It was a point echoed in letters to Nixon from other major national figures of both parties, including the Pennsylvania governor William Scranton, who thought that the Apollo successes offered an ideal opportunity to display "American leadership [...] in advancing technology and understanding," along the lines of Eisenhower's Open Skies proposal as well as the Communications Satellite Act of 1962, which offered US "satellite know-how to world communications."[43] Right before Nixon assumed the presidency, he received a memorandum that claimed that the Apollo successes had bolstered the national image and in so doing had also improved the US "international negotiating position" and provided a potentially unifying goal, internationally and domestically, at a time of increasing social tensions between races, countries, and generations.[44] Meanwhile, a bipartisan Congressional delegation, called the "Members of Congress for Peace through Law," sent Nixon a letter in October 1970 echoing Keldysh's emphasis on the 1967 Outer Space Treaty, which committed both the United States and the Soviet Union to make space "the province of all mankind." Nixon did not hesitate to follow that advice, responding warmly to

---

43 Nixon Presidential Library Research Files, OS Outer Space Box 1, 1969–70, 1 of 2, January 23, 1969, William Fulbright letter to Richard Nixon; and August 20, 1969, William Scranton letter to Nixon.

44 Nixon Presidential Library Research Files, OS Outer Space Box 1, 1969–70, 1 of 2, December 8, 1968, White House memorandum on the National Conference of Aerospace Companies.

the Congressional delegation, which also dovetailed with Leonid Brezhnev's own wish to be remembered in world history as a "man of peace."[45]

The Fig Leaf of Scientific Objectivity

The Soviet willingness to collaborate surprised many US officials in the Nixon administration and ultimately challenged their assumptions about the Cold War as an objective and unalterable fact. Even as late as July 1970, just half a year before the United States and Soviets signed a series of space exploration agreements that would produce ASTP and prepare the way for the broader policy of détente, Kissinger had expressed doubts about the potential for collaboration, noting that "the prospects for expanding cooperation with the Soviets, in contrast with other countries such as Germany, continue to be limited." The Soviet space program, he continued, was "controlled by the military and there is undoubtedly great reluctance within the leadership to risk compromise of military space programs."[46] One White House security memorandum in April 1970 noted:

> We doubt that the Soviets will readily undertake substantial programs of space cooperation with us in the near future. Because of U.S./USSR differences [...] they probably wish to avoid direct cooperation with the U. S. Further, their program is encumbered by security to a far greater degree than our own.[47]

NASA's director Thomas Paine persisted, however, sending a letter to Keldysh in July 1970 (against the recommendations of the Pentagon) in which he invited two Soviet engineers to examine US docking technology in Houston. He reiterated that he had Nixon's authority to negotiate directly with the Soviet Union.

> If we indeed can agree on common systems, and I foresee no technical difficulty, we will have made an important step toward increased safety and additional cooperative activities in future space operations. This is

---

45 Nixon Presidential Library Research Files, FG 221-18 Space, 1969–70, October 1, 1970, letter to the White House from "Members of Congress for Peace through Law"; and Donald J. Raleigh, "'Soviet Man of Peace': Leonid Il'ich Brezhnev and His Diaries," *Kritika: Explorations in Russian and Eurasian History* 17, no. 4 (2016), 837–68.
46 Nixon Presidential Library Research Files, OS 6-1-70 to 7-7-70, July 6, 1970, Kissinger memorandum to Nixon.
47 Nixon Presidential Library Research Files, National Security Study Memorandums, NSSM 70 to NSSM 76, Box H-162, "Cooperation between the U.S. and USSR in Space Activities, Prospect and Opportunities," April 8, 1970.

particularly timely in my view as we proceed toward the initial experiments leading to the orbiting space station.⁴⁸

Keldysh, for his part, made it clear that he also had the support of the Soviet leadership in negotiating a collaborative project. In response to Paine's July letter, he urged his NASA counterpart to accept a final agreement for a docking project:

> I want to assure you that the leadership of the USSR Academy of Sciences understands the entire importance and timelines of this problem. There is no doubt that a positive solution of this question would constitute an important contribution in the interests of world science and the progress of all mankind.

He reiterated that the Soviets were ready to enter into final talks immediately and form technical working groups to work out the details. Behind the scenes in October 1970, the Soviets were developing a number of different possible docking proposals with the Americans. Keldysh impressed NASA's Robert Gilruth, director of human spaceflight, as a "powerful" and "bright" leader who was determined to "make the project a reality. Keldysh went out of his way to treat us Americans well, thus showing his subordinates that he and his superiors were squarely behind the effort." NASA's Arnold Frutkin described Keldysh as "extremely intelligent, very constructive, very sensitive, and responsive to our requirements, and very forthright in putting his own problems on the table." Keldysh, who "seems head and shoulders" above other Soviet space managers NASA had contacted, told NASA administrators that he was also facing budgetary constraints and that collaboration was essential to maintaining and expanding upon the gains made by both space programs.⁴⁹

As it became apparent that the Soviets were serious about collaboration, the real challenge, it turned out, was internal to the US national security state.⁵⁰ Imagined visions of communist bogeymen grew out of deeply embedded

---

48 Nixon Presidential Library Research Files, WHCF EX OS-3, 31 July 1970, Thomas Paine's letter to Mstislav Keldysh.
49 Nixon Presidential Library Research Files, WHCF EX OS-3, September 11, 1970; NASA Historical Reference Collection, Keldysh's letter to Paine; "Gilruth, Robert K. (Bio)," 1/6/2, March 25, 1975 interview by E. C. Ezell; NASA Historical Reference Collection, ASTP Inception-1971, Memorandum, "Moscow Negotiations, January 1971"; and ARAN, f. 1678, o. 1, d. 207, l. 15, on internal Soviet discussions of possible docking systems in the fall of 1970.
50 Chapter 4 explores in more detail the challenges that the national security state and classification posed to both sides in the ASTP project.

attitudes that space was a territory to be conquered for national power and in the name of American political values—despite the collaborative mandate of the National Aeronautics and Space Act of 1958. Still steeped in the spirit of the Cold War imaginary contained in NSC-68, the Pentagon was against collaboration of any sort, reasoning that it would be a waste of time, at best, and dangerous give-away of technology at worst. Their recommendation in the summer of 1970, regarding collaboration with the Soviet Union, was to "cold-shoulder the Soviets because they have not been responsive to our past efforts seeking to develop a closer working relationship."[51]

It is surprising, then, that Nixon was able to overcome opposition and reach the historic agreements that would culminate in ASTP. Partly, that was a result of a surprising Soviet willingness to cooperate. But it also had to do with the allure of scientific objectivity, which suggested that science and technology transcended ideological and national borders. The technocratic way of thinking reduced ideological and political tensions and provided an alternative to more traditional diplomacy.[52] The Franco-Soviet science and technology agreements of 1966, which produced a deep and sustained collaboration in a number of fields, established an important precedent in this regard, suggesting that space exploration was devoted to scientific progress rather than Cold War competition. The Soviets had recognized the utility of space technology with their Interkosmos program, which provided a soft-power alternative for building relationships with other countries in the name of universal scientific progress.[53]

Nixon similarly viewed space exploration as a powerful tool for pursuing the broader politics of collaboration and détente that would be "for the benefit of all mankind," as he was fond of saying after Apollo 8.[54] In July 1969, he instructed Apollo 11 astronauts to carry Russian medals honoring the late cosmonauts Gagarin and Komarov during their visit to the Soviet Union. Nixon noted in a White House press announcement:

---

51 Nixon Presidential Library Research Files, National Security Study Memorandums, NSSM 70 to NSSM 76, Box H-162, June 19, 1970, NSC memorandum to Henry Kissinger; and April 10, 1970, "Second Report of the NSSM-72 Committee."
52 Davidson and Montville, "Foreign Policy According to Freud," 155.
53 "Before the Meeting in Orbit," *New Times*, no. 1 (January 1975), 20; and on the creation of Interkosmos to solidify Soviet relations with socialist and nonsocialist countries: ARAN, f. 1678, op. 1, d. 1, and fond 1678, op. 1 more generally.
54 On the shift in the US space program from competition to portraying "space accomplishment as a global accomplishment," see Teasel Muir-Harmony, "Project Apollo, Cold War Diplomacy and the American Framing of Interdependence," PhD diss., MIT, 2014, 36.

> This adds to the historic mission of Apollo 11 the aspect of cooperation between the people of the Soviet Union and the people of the United States. We trust that this reach across national boundaries, demonstrating good will between the Russians and Americans closest to exploration of space, bodes well for mutual peace and progress in the future.

The astronaut Frank Borman, meanwhile, was warmly received at all levels when he traveled to the Soviet Union just before the Apollo 11 mission in July 1969.[55] He encountered the Russian tradition of hospitality, which without fail impressed US officials and negotiators in their many trips to the Soviet Union.[56]

Meanwhile, since May 1967, when Michael Collins, David Scott, and Pavel Belaev drank a vodka toast together to peace and collaboration at the Paris Air Show, official and unofficial visits and meetings of cosmonauts and astronauts helped to create the goodwill that made both sides less fearful of making additional proposals for cooperation. What both sides discovered in these get-togethers was that they could get along and that ideology mattered much less than a shared technocratic mindset and commitment to problem-solving. This shared sense of professionalism allowed them to transcend their ideological differences and to view space as a "universal language," in the words of the astronaut David Scott.[57] The Russian émigré and veteran US translator for Apollo-Soyuz project, Alexander Tatistcheff, recalled that ASTP was among the most effective US–USSR encounters he had witnessed in his long career in US diplomacy precisely because it featured problem-solving as its central purpose. It was a

> bunch of American engineers, scientists, sitting down with a bunch of Soviet scientists and engineers, discussing some very unprecedented and difficult engineering problems, trying to find a solution, not in terms of political advantage but in terms of joint interest in a successful flight. The result of it is a friendship, a comraderie, a relationship developed which is very heartening. [...] And after the meeting, slapping each other on the back [...] having cokes, having vodka, of course, visiting in their houses and swimming together in the swimming pool, and in general

---

55 Nixon Presidential Library Research Files, OS 3-1 Astronauts 7/31/69, "Proposed White House Press Release to be Issued on July 17"; and Library of Congress, Thomas O. Paine Papers, Box 22, Folder 1, January 23, 1969, letter from Thomas Paine, NASA Director, to Academician A. A. Blagonravov.
56 "Soviet Hospitality," *Aviation Week and Space Technology*, August 5, 1974, 62. On a post-trip mission tour of the Soviet Union, the US astronauts received half a ton of gifts.
57 "Astronaut Scott 'Eager' to Join Russian in Flight," *Baltimore Sun*, August 24, 1971, 2.

behaving like normal human beings. I think that such programs as this are extremely important and I hope to God that this thing continues in some way, shape, or manner.[58]

The feelings of comraderie that Tatistcheff described produced what the historian of emotions William Reddy has referred to as an "emotional regime." The emotional regime of scientific and technological collaboration constructed a reality for its participants—a willingness to collaborate grounded in a technocratic commitment to problem-solving—that ultimately challenged the Cold War imaginary and the feelings of fear and mutual distrust that fueled negative images on both sides of the ideological divide.[59]

Each meeting produced more momentum for further meetings, leading both sides to an image of each other as potential allies. On October 21, 1969, the cosmonauts Georgii Beregovoi and Konstantin Feoktistov met with Nixon in the White House. The ASTP cosmonaut Valerii Kubasov remembered that the cosmonauts' visit with the president and with space officials and politicians left an important and positive impression in Soviet political and technical leadership circles that greatly aided the advocates of collaboration on both sides.[60] Attending also were Kissinger and Borman, who had invited Beregovoi during his July 1969 trip to the Soviet Union, in which the cosmonauts praised American friendliness and ingenuity, with "receptions, food and wine everywhere." Beregovoi and Feoktistov, after a visit to Disneyland and photo ops wearing Mickey-Mouse hats, stayed in Hollywood at the house of the famous Hollywood actor Kirk Douglas, who hosted a Hollywood party that included two other actors of Russian heritage, Goldie Hawn and Natalie Wood (who spoke Russian and who was the only movie star the Soviets recognized at the gathering). Feoktistov greeted reporters and declared an end to the space race and the beginning of a new era of cooperation—though he was apparently completely baffled by an American professional football game they had watched, which his colleague Beregovoi described this way: "All fall down. All get up. All fall down." Feoktistov, in particular, wrote a detailed account of his impressions, praising American organization and hospitality and noting a particularly fruitful conversation with NASA administrator Thomas Paine in

---

58 NASA Historical Reference Collection, ASTP July 1975, "Interview with Alex Tatistcheff by E. Z. Ezell," April 30, 1974; and Stafford, Thomas P. (1976–79), "Transcript of Interview with Major General Thomas P. Stafford by Edward Ezell."
59 Mark Steinberg and Valeria Sobol, *Interpreting Emotions in Russia and Eastern Europe* (DeKalb: Northern Illinois University Press, 2011), 5–6.
60 T. A. Golovkin and A. A. Chernobaev, eds., *Kosmos. Vremia moskovskoe. Sbornik dokumentov*, 2nd ed. (Moscow: Russian State Humanitarian University, 2018), 494.

which they discussed collaboration, philosophy, the state of the world, and the future of space exploration. The two-week visit was a modest but important step in the ongoing thawing of relations.[61] It provoked an immediate response from NASA administrator Thomas Paine, who wrote heartfelt letters to Keldysh, Beregovoi, and Feoktistov in which he also included a copy of his report to the president on NASA's new strategy of international collaboration.[62]

Figure 1.1 Aleksei Leonov, ever light on his feet, joins a belly dancer in San Antonio, TX

Source: NASA

---

61 Nixon Presidential Library Research Files, EX OS 3-1 [through 12/70], October 21, 1969, "Visit of the Cosmonauts" memorandum; Yuri Karash, *The Superpower Odyssey: A Russian Perspective on Space Cooperation* (Reston, VA: American Institute of Aeronautics and Astronautics, 1999), 78–89; K. P. Feoktistov, *Sem' shagov v nebo* (Moscow: Molodaia gvardiia, 1984), 182–204; "Visiting Cosmonauts Assert Space is for Science and Not for War," *Washington Post*, October 24, 1969, A3; "Cosmonauts Ending 2-Week U.S. Visit," *Evening Star*, November 4, 1969, A2; "Cosmonaut Sees Football: 'All Fall Down, All Get Up,'" *Washington Star*, October 27, 1969, A5; and "Disneyland 'Blastoff': Cosmonauts 'Fly' to the Moon," *Washington Star*, October 25, 1969, A3.
62 Library of Congress, Thomas Paine Papers, Box 24, Folder 1, November 21, 1969, letter from Paine to Feoktistov.

A year later, in October 1970, the courting ritual continued as the cosmonauts Andrian Nikolayev and Vitalii Sevastianov, with the Soviet leadership's calculated blessing, visited the U.S. to reiterate wishes for cooperation. Shortly thereafter, Robert Gilruth, director of NASA's human spaceflight, traveled to Moscow for more negotiations and took with him a plaque from NASA honoring Yuri Gagarin and presented it to the Soviet cosmonaut corps. "It was an emotional moment, and it was obvious that they were pleased at the recognition by us of their being first in space," noted Deputy NASA administrator George Low. "The plaque was just perfect in every way." Six months later, on the tenth anniversary of Gagarin's flight, Low sent a letter to Keldysh to "honor the achievement of this brave man"—Borman had emphasized the importance of the Soviet cult of Gagarin after his Soviet visit—and to express his desire for "increasingly significant cooperation between our two countries in space research and exploration."[63]

Helping to pave the way for closer collaboration was the exchange of condolences when cosmonauts or astronauts passed away. That tradition began with the death of three American astronauts in January 1967, and was followed by sympathies for the deaths of the cosmonaut Komarov in April 1967 and Gagarin in March 1968. Similarly, both sides began offering aid when the other side experienced some difficulty, as when Apollo 13 ran into problems on its lunar mission in April 1970. Kosygin on April 15 wrote to Nixon that

> with alarm we are following the flight of the space ship Apollo 13, which finds itself in an emergency situation. I want to inform you that the Soviet government has commanded all civil and military aviation of the Soviet Union to use all means, if necessary, to lend aid in the saving of the American cosmonauts. In the name of the Soviet government I express my hope for the safe return of the brave cosmonauts Lovell, Schweickart, and Hays.[64]

That offer put into stark relief the horrific death of three cosmonauts during reentry in the Soyuz 11 mission of June 1971. Thomas Stafford, the future commander of ASTP, attended the funeral of the three cosmonauts on behalf of Nixon. The Soviets treated him as one of their own ("as though he were a

---

63 NASA Historical Reference Collection, 1/612, "Gilruth, Robert R. (Bio)," January 27, 1971, George Low letter to Robert Gilruth; and "Foreign Relations and Keldysh," April 12, 1971, letter from Low to Keldysh.
64 Nixon Presidential Library Research Files, WHCF EX OS 3/#/13, April 15, 1970, letter from Kosygin to Nixon; and "Kosygin Offers Apollo Help as Ships Move into Position," *Baltimore Sun*, April 16, 1970, 1.

member of the cosmonaut group"), placing him alongside other cosmonauts, including his future Russian colleague on ASTP, Leonov, as a pallbearer. Later he was thanked personally by Brezhnev, Kosygin, and Defense Minister Grechko. The dangers of space travel evoked feelings of shared human sacrifice—an emotional regime based on the "anguish of their tragedy," as Nixon put it with regard to Soyuz 11—and produced a sense of common humanity that transcended the national security mindset. The American side followed up in July 1971, during the Apollo 15 mission, by filming the placement of a ceremonial plaque on the moon in honor of all Soviet and American space travelers who had lost their lives. The Soviets received a copy of the film in a diplomatic pouch through the auspices of the US embassy in Moscow. These moments of commemorating the other side's sacrifice gave additional momentum to the ASTP project, which was seen above all as a test of emergency docking procedures that would allow either side to come to the aid of the other in the event of a mishap in Earth's orbit. As such, the project involved a critical shift in both space exploration and politics from risk-taking and brinkmanship to a new focus on safety, in the narrower technical sense and in the broader political context. The docking engineer Vladimir Syromiatnikov, for example, conceived of ASTP as an attempt to insure the survival of cosmonauts and astronauts in space as a well as human "survival in any political climate" on Earth. By foregrounding the problem of safety and survival, ASTP thus provided an alternative to the Cold War imaginary, and in the process, according to the ideology of scientific objectivity, advanced the cause of science and universal human progress.[65]

Enemy Imaginaries and Bureaucratic Resistance

Resistance within the US government constituted the last major barrier to collaboration. Since the Manhattan Project, bureaucratic structures such as the Coordinating Committee for Multilateral Export Controls, designed to protect the supposed US technological advantage, created seemingly insuperable barriers to international cooperation. A June 18, 1970 memorandum from the Nixon's Office of General Counsel reviewed the complex issues involved in technology transfer. The central question was "what authority does NASA and its contractors have to disseminate technical information to foreign countries." The question had rarely been asked with regard to space technology

---

65 Nixon Presidential Library Research Files, WHCF EX OS 3-1, Department of State Telegram, April 17, 1970; Department of State Telegram, June 30, 1971; ARAN, f. 1678, o. 1, d. 147, l. 65; Vladimir Syromiatnikov, *100 Rasskazov o stykovke i o drugikh prikliucheniakh, Chast' 2, 20 let spustia* (Moscow: "Logos," 2010), 80.

because up until the Nixon administration there had been little emphasis on internationalizing the space program. The memorandum noted that "purely scientific data is treated more leniently" than data "relating to technological applications." Control over the export of technical data was realized "through a series of statutes, Executive orders and comprehensive regulations, placing the responsibility for prior approval of exports within several government agencies. There is a certain amount of overlap and it is not always clear which agency has primary jurisdiction." One thing was clear in this tangle of bureaucratic control, and that was that "any release of technical data [...] exported from this country is controlled." That presented a challenge, said the memo, to NASA's enabling legislation, which mandated foreign collaboration and stipulated that, "it is the policy of the United States that activities in space should be devoted to peaceful purposes for the benefit of all mankind" and toward "international collaboration." The fact that many of the basic technologies of space travel had potential military applications made collaboration a potentially treasonous activity because the same peaceful technologies could be converted "to strategic delivery applications." In short, open exchanges of scientific and technical information were a policy goal, but that policy was undermined by national security considerations. As the memorandum noted, practically everything NASA did had "direct or indirect military potential or applicability."[66]

Meanwhile, the Soviet system lacked the legal and bureaucratic system of technology transfer control that had often thwarted the desires of even the most powerful political leaders in the United States. To be sure, the secretive Soviet space industry was often divided by bitter internal politics, but the authoritarian structure of the Soviet Union also gave the Soviets more flexibility in collaborating with foreign powers in science and technology, once the political leadership gave its approval.[67] Strong managerial personalities such as Keldysh, armed with the approval of the political bosses, could cut through red tape in ways that NASA colleagues envied. As a NASA delegation to Moscow later observed, "strong, dynamic personalities can have an influence on events and programs orders of magnitude beyond what an equivalent person can do in the U.S. [...] On a day-to-day basis it means that there is actually more flexibility in their system [...] than in ours." Managerial cults of personality were aided by the Leninist legacy of democratic centralism, so that "once a general policy is decided or

---

66 Nixon Presidential Library and Archives, WHCF, FG 164 NASA, Box 1, "Dissemination of Technical Information Abroad," June 18, 1970.
67 Nixon Presidential Library Research Files, National Security Study Memorandums, NSSM 70 to NSSM 76, Box H-162, "Cooperation between the U.S. and USSR in Space Activities, Prospect and Opportunities," April 8, 1970.

elaborated, there is virtually no discussion and it serves as a guiding light for a wide range of discussions (and entrepreneurs!)."[68] The upshot was that once leaders on both sides decided that they were willing to collaborate, as they did by the end of 1969, the Soviets faced far less internal resistance than the Nixon administration.[69]

Well aware of the bureaucratic challenges, Nixon in November 1969 had his aide Peter Flanigan send a letter to Kissinger, Borman, and NASA administrator Paine reiterating his personal commitment to "multi-national participation in our future space flights." He was dismayed by the "technical difficulties he had encountered," but also wanted them to know that he was determined to "press" the idea of collaboration whenever possible and requested updates from everyone regarding efforts to cut through the thickets of red tape in the technology-transfer bureaucracy.[70] He also formed an interagency group to deal with "the technical data exchange between the United States and foreign governments and agencies desirous of entering into cooperative arrangements with us," as he put it in a memorandum to the NSC in July 1970.[71] But even with Nixon's prodding, the White House discovered that cooperation "turns out to be more difficult than might be expected."[72] When Thomas Paine left NASA for the private sector in September 1970, he seemed less than optimistic about the prospects for collaboration, despite positive Soviet responses to his last hurrah: a September 1970 proposal for a joint docking system.[73]

Meanwhile, as the Nixon administration continued to work back channels to confront the technology-transfer challenge, George Low, deputy NASA administrator, traveled to Moscow in late 1970 to hash out details of Paine's proposed docking system that would become ASTP. The NSC characterized the meeting as "unexpectedly productive." After finalizing most of the details

---

68 NASA Historical Reference Collection, "Field Trip Report for the NASA Advisory Council International Relations Task Force, Moscow, USSR, April 11–17, 1987," 10/14/4, 15591.
69 NASA Historical Reference Collection, February 14, 1972, NASA Memorandum from George Low, 10/14/4, 15590.
70 Nixon Presidential Library and Archives, WHCF, EX OS-3, November 25, 1969, Peter Flanigan's memorandum to Kissinger, Paine, Borman, and DuBridge; and November 24, 1969, Nixon's memorandum to Flanigan.
71 Nixon Presidential Library and Archives, OS Outer Space Box 1, 1969–70, 1 of 2, July 17, 1970, memorandum to the NSC.
72 Nixon Presidential Library and Archives, OS Outer Space Box 1, 1969–70, 2 of 2, March 6, 1970, White House memorandum.
73 Nixon Presidential Library and Archives, OS Outer Space Box 1, 1969–70, 1 of 2, September 15, 1970, Paine's letter to Kissinger.

of the docking system, and despite his initial expression of grave doubts before his trip, Low was enthusiastic, privately invoking the lofty rhetoric of Earthrise that Nixon had taken up in his public pronouncements. "No other human activity has so captivated the imagination of peoples everywhere," wrote Low in a January 1971 letter to Kissinger. Space, he wrote, was "not a frontier of one nation or another but of man himself. Here there are no boundaries." A joint docking system, he wrote, would be a keystone in a growing relationship of "mutual trust and regard" that would "contribute toward a broader confidence for working together on earth."[74] Meetings between NASA and Soviet space working groups in August 1971 honed a long list of recommendations and areas for collaboration that both sides had endorsed by the beginning of 1971—making ASTP a linchpin of the broader science and technology agreements that Nixon consummated with his May 1972 visit to Moscow. With ASTP as the centerpiece, those science and technology agreements represented a critical testing ground for the newly imagined relationship of cooperation embodied by détente.[75] The lead ASTP docking engineer from NASA, Caldwell Johnson, later remembered the importance of Nixon's decision to build ASTP through personal connections, beginning with his relationship with Brezhnev and on down through the engineers, as a way to transcend the Cold War political impasse. "Nixon [...] agreed that it was going to be on a person-to-person level, that as long as there were not political overtones involved in this thing, it was going to be engineer to engineer, and that's the way it turned out. It's hard to believe."[76]

Androgyneity and the Handshake in Space

By the end of 1972, the administration had developed a formal statement about the docking agreement that satisfied the technology transfer control bureaucracy. The docking technology would be a "clean interface," meaning that both sides would only be involved in the linkups between the Soyuz and Apollo aircraft and not in sharing basic information that did not directly pertain to the creation of the docking mechanisms. The docking system was to

---

74 Nixon Presidential Library and Archives, OS Outer Space Box 1, 1/1/71, 1971–72, 1 of 3, November 19, 1970, NSC memorandum to Kissinger; and January 29, 1971, George Low's memorandum to Kissinger.
75 Nixon Presidential Library and Archives, WHCF, FG 164 NASA Box 1, August 11, 1971, George Low's letter to Nixon. One historian called ASTP the "star of the show" for broader science agreements: Sher, *From Pugwash to Putin*, 26.
76 Interview with Caldwell Johnson, May 12, 1998, League City Texas, NASA Johnson Space Center Oral History Project, 36.

be "androgynous," meaning that neither side would have to be the male or the female in the linkup, a matter of some importance to the macho engineers in the space programs of both nations; instead, both sides would jointly design the interface to which they would attach their separate capsules in an interlocking rather than penetrating fashion, creating a neutral territory of contact between the Apollo and Soyuz capsules—a kind of Switzerland in space (Chapter 3 investigates the engineering of the androgynous docking mechanism and its relationship to gender and Cold War politics).[77] While in space, one crew would enter the docking chamber between the two capsules to adapt to the air and different pressure environments of the host capsule (the Soviets had an atmosphere that was more like Earth's whereas the US side used pure oxygen) before social visits to the other side for proclamations of peace and friendship. To further assuage concerns about technology transfer, NASA officials rightly pointed out that information about the Apollo technology was largely available in the public domain, whereas the Soviet technology was mostly a secret, so there was nothing to lose and everything to gain for the American side. From the perspective of the NSC, there were now few downsides to ASTP—a remarkable shift in attitudes from just two years earlier, and certainly from NSC-68, suggesting just how much the Cold War was grounded in imaginary as well as real conflicts.[78]

One of the more surprising aspects of cooperation on the US side was that it turned out to be far easier to collaborate with the Soviets than with European allies. The main reason was that the plan for Western European collaboration would involve the direct participation of Europeans in developing any post-Apollo flight system, and Western European partners were expected to pay NASA for their participation even while accepting their status as junior partners.[79] In the case of Soviet collaboration, ASTP involved a limited exchange of technologies, both sides already had their own fully developed space-transportation systems, the United States recognized the Soviets as equal partners, and the two countries needed only to construct the "androgynous" interface for docking in space. Each side, moreover, funded its own efforts. Thus, while attempts to collaborate with Western Europeans went nowhere in the summer

---

77 See Chapter 3 for more details on the challenges engineers faced in overcoming the sexually charged problem of domination and submission in docking: Syromiatnikov, *100 Stories*, 340, 395, 421–22.
78 Nixon Presidential Library and Archives, NSDM 187 [1 of 2], National Security Defense Memorandum 187, August 30, 1972.
79 Nixon Presidential Library and Archives, OS Outer Space Box 1, 1/1/71, 1971–72, 2 of 3, August 13, 1971, draft letter to the European Space Conference; and 3 of 3, December 13, 1971, draft of President's report to Congress on space activities for 1971.

of 1971, the ASTP project experienced, according to Low, "definite forward movement [...] in terms of levels of detail, the extent of commitment, and the immediacy of exchanges which they are prepared to accept."[80]

The final science and technology agreements—which formalized work that had been done for nearly two years—came in May 1972, when the Soviets informed NASA that they were ready to sign an agreement for the joint crewed mission, which NASA also supported and which the Office of Management and Budget had approved with a budget of $250 million. Both sides, moreover, were clearly excited about the prospects for expanding collaboration from ASTP to joint projects, crewed and uncrewed, to explore Venus and Mars.[81] As for ASTP, the Soviets and Americans agreed

> that rendezvous and docking systems of future generations of manned spacecraft of both countries will be compatible, to permit rendezvous, docking, rescue, and possible joint experiments in space. It is further agreed that the first flight to test these future systems will be carried out in 1975, using specially modified Apollo-type and Soyuz-type spacecraft. In this flight the two spacecraft will rendezvous and dock in space, and cosmonauts and astronauts will visit each other's spacecraft.[82]

Subsequently, the "rapport and understanding" of both sides improved with every meeting, according to the astronaut David Scott, creating a project "on firmer ground than any in recorded history" and inspired by "an obvious desire by both sides at all levels to insure the project gets off the ground on July 15, 1975."[83] True, there were challenges at first as engineers from both sides encountered very different technological and managerial systems. Those barriers were linguistic, as both programs had developed their own specialized vocabulary and jargon. They were also cultural, as the Soviets had to adapt to working in a far more open and less secretive way, including allowing the American press and space officials to visit the many formerly closed training, production, and launch sites of the Soviet space industry (the topic

---

80 Nixon Presidential Library and Archives, OS Outer Space Box 1, 1/1/71, 1971–72, 2 of 3, August 11, 1971, George Low's letter to Nixon; and August 9, 1971, Peter Flanigan's memorandum to Nixon.
81 ARAN, f. 1678, o. 1, d. 383, Ll. 6–7 on post-ASTP proposals by the US and Soviet sides.
82 Nixon Presidential Library and Archives, OS 1, 1971–74, May 17, 1972, Memorandum for the president. On plans to expand collaboration into other areas: NASA Historical Reference Collection, George Low and Keldysh communications from September 7, 1972 to April 3, 1974, 14/10/4, 15590.
83 NASA Historical Reference Collection, ASTP 1972–73, LEK 7/14/1, memorandum, "ASTP Mission to Moscow, June–July 1973."

of secrecy is explored in Chapter 4). Yet Soviet engineers and managers, like their American counterparts, were surprised at how easy it was to work with American colleagues, which they attributed in part to a shared commitment to technical problem-solving but also to the revelation that, "Americans in many respects turned out to be similar to us."[84]

From 1971 through the culmination of the mission in July 1975, technological and diplomatic regimes were mutually constitutive. The Soviet engineers and designers quickly adapted the American term "interface" to describe the human and technical connections that were required to make the project a success. Both sides began to build these interfaces between engineers, managers, and politicians. Those interfaces linked two fundamentally different systems at the personal, technical, and political levels, as noted elsewhere in the book. Teams of designers and engineers met in Houston, Moscow, and outside Los Angeles to hash out problems and coordinate docking mechanisms, retreating afterward to their respective systems to overcome bureaucratic, political, and technical barriers and to spread their own transformed understanding of the "other." The lead Soviet docking engineer Syromiatnikov remembered that it was a "unique experience, for which precedents are rarely found in the history of technology," where a technological project was transformed into an instrument for radically changing the relationship between two military rivals and enemies. Boris Chertok, one of the founding fathers of the Soviet space program, noted that "even space engineers do not fully realize that such a single piece of space technology as the docking system [...] is only the visible tip of the iceberg." The invisible part "includes the process of space system development itself, and the activities of many people [...] sometimes so distant from the field of engineering."[85]

ASTP's Place in History

ASTP in the narrowest sense was a docking test of proven launch systems and crewed spaced-flight capsules on both sides. It went off with only a few minor hitches, producing the docking mechanisms that ultimately became a universal space docking standard with far-reaching implications for space exploration (see Chapter 3 on the significance of this accomplishment). If ASTP marked an important advance in the history of space technology, it also represented a "moral and ethical" achievement, according to Kurt Vonnegut and the Soviet

---

84 Eliseev, *Zhizn'*, 102.
85 Syromiatnikov, *100 Stories*, 8, 429.

writer Chingiz Aitmatov.[86] ASTP brought two separate systems together in a way that enhanced feelings of mutual security and safety, and that opened up previously unimagined opportunities for exchange and communication on both sides of the docking site.[87] ASTP, moreover, had played a seminal role as a catalyst in Brezhnev's and Nixon's historic policy of détente, using the supposedly objective realm of science and technology to pave the way for the policy's broader cooperative agreements in science, technology, and business, and in the process developing a compelling alternative to the previous Cold War imaginary in which both sides had constructed images of each other as implacable enemies incapable of cooperation. History, of course, can't be written in the conditional tense, but it seems clear from the evidence that both sides saw ASTP as jumping off point for détente (and what the Soviets called peaceful coexistence). The "frankness, confidence and personal working relationship" of Keldysh and George Low, and of the technical directors Glynn Lunney and Konstantin Bushuyev, helped to bring this project to a successful close, as did the dynamic personality of Leonov, a fan of double-breasted suits who was a "remarkably wise choice" as Soviet commander, according to the ASTP US translator. Leonov got along with everyone and especially with his equally outgoing American counterpart Thomas Stafford. "When they walk into our offices in Houston," said Stafford about the cosmonauts, "they carry very businesslike briefcases. Then they grin and open them up and you see black bread, sturgeon, caviar, crabmeat and, naturally, vodka." Leonov, meanwhile, was an "extrovert [...] an outgoing man [...] he will conquer you, heart and soul, because he is that kind of man. And any audience, he will have it in his hand in a minute." Ultimately, the most important achievement of ASTP was to destroy Cold War stereotypes at the highest levels of government and among thousands of program managers and engineers and to forge professional and personal relationships that transcended the militant and mutual hostility of the two collaborating superpowers.[88]

---

86 "Vstrecha nad planetoi," *Literaturnaia gazeta*, July 23, 1975, 21; "Cosmos: Arena dlia sotrudnichestva," *Sotsialisticheskaia industriia*, November 17, 1973, 4; "Soyuz y Apollon," *Sovetskaia Rossiia*, June 28, 1974, 3.
87 Syromiatnikov, *100 Stories*, 391.
88 NASA Historical Reference Collection, ASTP July 1975, "Interview with Alex Tatitscheff by E. Z. Ezell," April 30, 1974; NASA Historical Reference Collection, ASTP-73, 7/14/1, "U.S./USSR July Working Group Meeting," July 24, 1973; and NASA Historical Reference Collection, Thomas P. Stafford (1976–79), "Transcript of Interview with Major General Thomas P. Stafford by Edward Ezell." On the importance of trust and friendship in overcoming Cold War hostilities: A. A. Leonov, B. F. Lomov, and V. I. Lebedev, "K probleme obshcheniia v internatsional'nykh kosmicheskikh poletakh," *Voprosy filosofii*, no. 1 (1976), 56–69.

Figure 1.2 A space-suited Mickey Mouse welcomes the Apollo-Soyuz crew to Florida's Disney World

Source: NASA

The next chapter builds upon and elaborates the ideologies of collaboration that inspired ASTP, but it also probes the limits of the socio-technical vision of peace that politicians and space engineers had constructed. From the perspective of July 1975 everyone seemed to be a winner, but the Cold War imaginary endured, maintaining superpower politics as a zero-sum game, reducing the momentum of collaboration started by ASTP, and frustrating the emerging peace imaginary.

Chapter 2
TRANSNATIONAL IDENTITY AND THE LIMITS OF COSMIC COLLABORATION

Space exploration, as noted in the introduction, was driven by tensions between cosmopolitics and utopian visions of a new global community. In the words of the Dutch astronomer H. C. van de Hulst, recipient of the 1990 Planetary Award at the Association of Space Explorers annual conference in the Netherlands: "When a system without frontiers, such as science, meets a system with frontiers, such as politics [...] a dialogue between the political and scientific systems must take place in order to minimize the turbulence which could be encountered."[1] The world was at the center of this turbulence zone, transformed into a staging ground for Cold War military competition. Yet the same processes of militarization also created the sense of urgency that inspired new experiments in cosmic and terrestrial collaboration. The first part of the chapter discusses early ideas about global forms of consciousness and their connection to space travel, pacificism, and transnational utopias. It then turns to two areas that became launching pads for further acts of collaboration. The first was a joint US–USSR moon-mapping project and the second the formation in 1985 of a nongovernmental organization in Paris called the Association of Space Explorers (ASE), founded by many of the principal actors of the Apollo-Soyuz Test Project (ASTP). ASE considered itself to be a vanguard of a peace-loving and ecologically aware transnational community to which all people, they hoped, would soon belong.

The Cosmic Perspective

Historian Robert Poole has commented on the iconic image snapped on Christmas Eve 1968 from Apollo 8. "Looking back," wrote Poole, "it is possible to see that Earthrise marked the tipping point, the moment when the

---

1 Speech of H. C. Van de Hulst at the 1990 Association of Space Explorers 6th Congress: http://www.space-explorers.org/congress/congress6.html, accessed October 1, 2017.

sense of the space age flipped from what it meant for space to what it meant for the Earth."[2] Yet even before the Earthrise moment of the late 1960s, competing urges to escape into space (as a way of transcending human limitations) and to recognize the need to confront those challenges on Earth had a long pedigree. Like the astrofuturist ideal pursued in the West by science fiction writers such as Arthur Clarke and engineers like Wernher von Braun, the Russian cosmists at the beginning of the twentieth century believed the survival of the species required the colonization of other planets. Space colonization, in their view, was both the solution to terrestrial problems and the culminating point and rationale for human development.[3] Russian science fiction writers (*fantastika* in Russian) began representing aviation and space flight "as the catalyst for abolishing all concepts of the national, linguistic, ethnoracial and religious identity." Combining ideas about social revolution and aerospace technology, they imagined that "democratic internationalism [...] would pervade the world when everyone had free access to the sky," a belief later integrated into Soviet representations of the space age.[4]

Borrowing from the ideas of the Frenchman Pierre Teilhard de Chardin, the cosmist Vladimir Vernadskii by the 1940s was contemplating Earth as an integrated planetary system. His breakthrough in the 1930s involved a radical shift in perspective that anticipated later satellite imagery: imagining Earth from the vantage point of space. Integrating the increasingly fractured disciplines of geology, biology, chemistry, and physics, he believed that a description of an organism (including mankind and the earth itself as a "biosphere") was not possible without an analysis of the environment within which the organism lived. Toward the end of his life he developed the idea of a "noosphere." The noosphere was the stage of cosmic development that followed the biosphere. In this final stage of cosmic evolution the accumulation of scientific knowledge about the physical environment had allowed people to manipulate the natural world and to produce technologies that could destroy the planet. Vernadskii, ever the optimist, nonetheless believed a greater sense of collective moral responsibility for the fate of the cosmos would emerge along with the ability to dominate nature. Moral development would catch up with technological and scientific development, putting science into balance and allowing humans to live in harmony with each other and with their

---

2 Robert Poole, *Earthrise: How Man First Saw the Earth* (New Haven, CT: Yale University Press, 2008), 8.
3 On a key figure in Russian cosmism: see James T. Andrews, *Red Cosmos: K. E. Tsiolkovskii, Grandfather of Soviet Rocketry* (College Station: Texas A&M University Press, 2009).
4 Anindita Banerjee, *We Modern People: Science Fiction and the Making of Russian Modernity* (Middletown, CT: Wesleyan University Press, 2012), 48–49.

natural environment. He anticipated the dark implications of nuclear physics, dying seven months before the dropping of atomic bombs on Hiroshima and Nagasaki. Yet somehow, amid the ruins of Nazi devastation in Russia, he saw the silver lining in the looming mushroom clouds. Echoing the ecological consciousness later associated with Rachel Carson's 1962 *Silent Spring*, he wrote during the Second World War:

> The planet's face—the biosphere—is consciously and mainly unconsciously being chemically and physically changed by Man. As the result of the growth of human culture in the twentieth century, the coastal seas and parts of the ocean are changing more and more dramatically. Man must take more and more steps now to preserve the riches of the sea for future generations.[5]

Vernadskii's cosmic perspective evoked a heightened sense of the planet's vulnerability as well as demands for global collaboration to prevent its destruction.

The International Geophysical Year of 1957 (when scientists from around the globe pooled resources to study the earth as a unified system) marked a key moment in the conception of space exploration as a collaborative venture, drawing on Enlightenment ideas about science as an inherently international and cooperative endeavor. One scientific participant in that venture noted that space's, "electromagnetic fields, particles, and radiations has no palpable appeal to nationalism or power politics [...] Copernican astronomy not only achieved a revolution in science but also changed man's concepts of man and of earth. The onset of the space age affords the possibility of a comparable impact."[6] But it was the ability to actually see the earth from space—and reproduce that image for mass consumption—that provided the most powerful stimulus to the imagination. When Yuri Gagarin became the first human in space on April 12, 1961, his gaze shifted almost immediately from outer space to the home planet. He commented on the fragility of the earth and on the need "to preserve and multiply this beauty and not destroy it." That statement, set against the backdrop of an angelic image of Gagarin's helmeted head with his charismatic smile, and the earth below, was reproduced in an iconic propaganda poster that dominated Soviet public space as thoroughly as the Beatles in the capitalist West. Ultimately, Gagarin's flight, as a RAND

---

5 Vladimir Vernadsky, *Geochemistry and the Biosphere* (Santa Fe, NM: Synergetic Press, 2007), 416.
6 Hugh Odishaw, "International Cooperation in Space Science," in Lincoln P. Bloomfield, ed., *Outer Space: Prospects for Man and Society* (Englewood Cliffs, NJ: Prentice-Hall, 1962), 106–7, 121.

political scientist put it in 1963, had "an emotional appeal for people at large, regardless of their political attitudes. Here is a Soviet success that can be presented as a success for all mankind."[7] The irony was lost on most observers that Major Gagarin, a fighter pilot whose job it was during his flight to test the viability of intercontinental ballistic missile (ICBM) technology, represented a project managed by strategic nuclear rocket forces. Said another RAND analyst, "Space exploration, to adapt a Maoist formulation, grew out of the nose cone of the ICBM."[8]

Gagarin's simultaneous status as both a representative of a military-industrial complex and a messenger of global peace captures a key paradox of space flight. In the realm of politics and popular culture space technology had the potential to both unite and to separate, to appear as a catalyst for world peace and harmony or, alternatively, as an instrument of global self-destruction. As Robert Poole noted, this was true both of space technology and air travel in general: "In a swords-into-plowshares movement, long-range air travel with its potential for peaceful interchange was the product of the bomber technology of the war, just as space travel was to be the product of the intercontinental ballistic missile technology of the Cold War."[9] New satellite images and communication technologies constantly pushed people's imaginations beyond the boundaries on political maps, just as earlier technological innovations had given rise to the idea of the nation-state. Benedict Anderson famously pointed to the vital role of print capitalism and newspapers in helping people to imagine themselves as members of the modern nation-state.[10] The nation was a community of millions of people who physically could never see each other but who nonetheless imagined themselves (through newspapers, textbooks, and images on maps) as having a common national identity. Mary Louise Pratt suggested that new European technologies for conquering terrestrial space, starting in the eighteenth century, combined with new ways of representing distant corners of the globe and ultimately produced a planetary consciousness, a "picture of the planet appropriated and redeployed from a unified, European

---

7 The quote from the Gagarin poster is from a poster in my personal collection; Paul Kecskemeti, "Outer Space and World Peace," in *Outer Space in World Politics*, ed. Joseph M. Goldsen (New York: Frederick A. Praeger, 1963), 29. For the life and cult of Gagarin, see my biography: Andrew Jenks, *The Cosmonaut Who Couldn't Stop Smiling: The Life and Legend of Yuri Gagarin* (Dekalb: Northern Illinois University Press, 2012).
8 Arnold L. Horelick, "The Soviet Union and the Political Uses of Outer Space," in *Outer Space in World Politics*, 44.
9 Poole, *Earthrise*, 41.
10 Benedict Anderson, *Imagined Communities: Reflections on the Origin and Spread of Nationalism* (New York: Verso, 1991).

perspective."[11] Space exploration and satellite imagery of the earth marked another phase in the development of this planetary consciousness, stimulating ever-larger visions of a global human community. The transcripts of communications from Apollo during the Apollo-Soyuz mission illustrated this global view, as well as the way it combined with and facilitated a new environmental conscience. The crew was presented with the following view on its 90th revolution around the globe:

> Central America geological structures, currents and eddies in the Gulf of Mexico, the fish killing rip tide along the Florida coast, sediment and pollution plumes that are flowing out into Chesapeake Bay, a red tide along the New England coast, the confluence of the Gulf Stream, and the Labrador current, oil slicks along shipping routes and shipping lanes in the north Atlantic and finally in the bioluminescence caused by microorganisms in the Red Sea.

The view offered itself to the crew at a speed of 25,000 miles per hour, allowing them to imagine the entire globe in ways unimaginable previously, and also to encounter dramatic, visual evidence of human-made environmental destruction.[12]

While the Earthrise and Blue Marble images began to saturate popular culture in Western Europe and the United States in the early 1970s, artistic and photographic representations of the earth from space—along with messages of universal peace, brotherhood and environmental protection—dominated propaganda poster images (the communist equivalent of capitalist billboards) behind Europe's Iron Curtain. One of the Soviet Union's major artistic producers of those images was the cosmonaut Aleksei Leonov. During the 1970s his paintings of Earth from space were produced by the millions on propaganda posters, postage stamps, and in art galleries. The Soviet view of the earth from space seemed to mark the beginning of a new phase of global integration.

For some scientists the movement toward unity would begin, not on Earth, but on the moon. In sending Borman off on his Western European and Soviet tour in the summer of 1969, Nixon invoked the romantic spirit of collaboration and eschewed the cosmopolitical stance of the earlier space race. "These great discoveries," said Nixon, "[are] not limited to this Nation." He said the United States was prepared to collaborate in space exploration, "to work together with all peoples on this earth in the high adventure of exploring the new areas of

---

11 Mary Louise Pratt, *Imperial Eyes: Travel Writing and Transculturation* (New York: Routledge, 1992), 36.
12 Transcript of ASTP mission communications, Part 32 (MC 496/1–MC 510/1), https://history.nasa.gov/astp/gallery.html.

space."[13] The result of these overtures—which unexpectedly for the Americans resonated with romantic cosmist ideals in Soviet astroculture—was the agreement signed in Moscow between American Nixon and Soviet Premier Aleksei Kosygin in May 1972 to develop, among other things, the docking system between the Apollo and Soyuz capsules discussed in the previous chapter. But that agreement also made way for scientific collaborations inspired by both the Apollo lunar missions and the successful uncrewed Soviet Lunar probes. Both those programs had produced a bounty of lunar soil and rocks that were brought back to Earth and then used to build the foundations of a new international order. Conceiving of the moon as international rather than national space (despite the American planting of the flag) both the United States and the Soviet Union attempted to use the moon as a neutral territory where they could explore a new peaceful relationship with each other. This time, however, the romance quickly fizzled after much initial passion and enthusiasm.

Lunar Utopias

Following the Apollo lunar triumphs, Nixon had received thousands of letters from US citizens. Some applauded the placement of the American flag on the moon, but many others expressed outrage at the gesture, which seemed to violate the view that space exploration was a common human enterprise, as Nixon's own rhetoric often suggested. Typical of those letters was this missive from Carol Zimmer Bellamy to Nixon on January 5, 1971:

> It occurred to me as I watched the first moon landing and the planting of our country's flag on the moon surface that in reality those astronauts represented a much larger group than just those whose national symbol they saluted at that historic moment. In fact astronaut Neil Armstrong indicated that he realized the larger-than-national significance of their mission by his choice of the first words to be spoken on the moon "[...] a giant step for mankind."[14]

---

13 Weekly Compilation of Presidential Documents, Week Ending Friday, January 31, *1969*, 190 (NASA Historical Reference Collection, 1/3/1 "Borman, Frank NASA Post-Apollo 8"); "Armstrong Tells Russian Scientists U.S. and Soviet Should Cooperate in Space Projects," *New York Times*, June 4, 1970, 27C. For Nixon's embrace of Apollo 11 as something for all humankind: Teasel Muir-Harmony, *Operation Moonglow: A Political History of Project Apollo* (New York: Basic Books, 2020), especially the chapter "Making Apollo 11 for All Humankind, 1969", 179-199.
14 Nixon Presidential Library and Archives, OS Outer Space Box 3, January 1–September 30, 1971, letter from Carol Zimmer Bellamy to President Richard Nixon on January 5, 1971.

Another group from Seattle wrote to Nixon after Apollo 11:

> But why, with such a golden opportunity to exclaim to the world our desire for international cooperation and brotherhood, why, when all nations were watching us set the stage for the future endeavors of mankind, why did we confirm graphically, by planting triumphantly the American flag, the appallingly widespread apprehension in political systems different from our own that we view not only the world but the entire universe in nineteenth century colonial perspective?

How much these views influenced Nixon's policies of space collaboration is hard to say, but he clearly devoted much attention to reading these letters, and their ideas were at least reflected in his space policies and speeches. He even bothered to respond on occasion, instructing his staff assistant to send a note on his behalf to one anguished mother whose son was killed in Vietnam: "He understands the conflicting feelings this feat [the moon landing] has evoked and joins in your hope that the success of this mission into the infinite reaches of space may inspire equal triumphs in man's search for peace. This peace, when it comes, will be a monument to the courage and selfless commitment of men like your son."[15]

A number of letters came in 1971 and 1972 from longtime Republican and Nixon supporter named Barbara Marx Hubbard, who was organizing director of an organization called "Committee for the Future." The Committee had developed an initiative called "Harvest Moon" in June 1970. As a member of an influential Republican donor family, her letters caught the attention of Alexander Butterfield, deputy assistant to the president, who sent them along to the president. Nixon was intrigued enough to tell Butterfield to meet with Hubbard. The group's ultimate goal was to create a "lunar committee open to people of all nations" and concurrently "to apply in a concentrated effort the best systems and technologies [to solve] environmental problems—viewed as a whole." The organization claimed it was "having some success in converting former opponents of the 'space program' to the new worlds program—because our cause is the development of man—for which space is vital." The group informed the president that its aim was to include China and the Soviet Union in its effort. Harvest Moon was the end goal, "a citizen-sponsored lunar

---

15 Nixon Presidential Library and Archives, OS Outer Space Box 3, 6/11/1969–7/31/1969, letters from July 30, 1969 and May 18, 1969; Nixon's response July 31, 1969.

expedition—as an initiative for world unity." The group emphasized that their idea was a "non-ideological initiative for world unity." They bragged that their effort constituted "the first truly transnational effort in human history."[16]

Harvest Moon expressed a common obsession with finding technological solutions to political, social, and environmental problems. For example, it believed that political revolution was no longer necessary since "it is based on the past necessity of scarcity." Because technology had supposedly solved the problem of material want, political revolution was destined to go the way of the horse-drawn carriage. The group took issue with the popular idea promoted by the Club of Rome in 1970 and 1971, which suggested that there were profound limits to economic and population growth. "Now we can both solve Earth problems and move into an unlimited future. Pessimism in the face of this possibility is childish and old-fashioned." The ideas struck a chord with Butterfield, who summarized them in a memo to the president on February 8, 1972. "The concept of a 'peoples-of-the-earth' mission to the lunar surface is, in fact, gaining fairly wide support from globally-minded people." Most importantly, the idea was "non-ideological" and promised to become the first "transnational effort in human history [...] I do think the President should be made aware of the mere fact that the Committee exists and that the project is off and running." Telling Nixon he could count on "future-oriented support for the thrust of his policies," Butterfield also wanted to let Kissinger know that the group was traveling to a number of foreign countries "and probably selling shares in the 'Harvest Moon' lunar expedition."[17]

Other information reaching Nixon's desk indicated the potential usefulness of the moon as a tool for forging global unity. Perhaps one of the bigger surprises for Americans was the way that Soviets greeted the US moon landings as a common human accomplishment. Soviets hungered for a glimpse of human presence on the moon, even if it was American. Reflecting Nixon's emerging view of moon rocks as potent instruments of international diplomacy, the American government arranged a display in Moscow in December 1969. Thousands of Soviet visitors were so eager to get a glimpse that they smashed down a glass door and burst through a cordon of 20 Moscow cops. When the visitors crammed into a temporary 15-square-foot film-viewing room, they brought the thin walls crashing own. Despite the unanticipated shutdown, 12,000 managed to see the exhibit that day. Soviet newspaper coverage of life in the United States, according to one American journalist in

---

16 Nixon Presidential Library and Archives, White House General Files, OS 3 Outer Space Box 9, 1/1/72, folder 1 of 2, "Harvest Moon Initiative."
17 Nixon Presidential Library and Archives, White House General Files, Outer Space OS 3, Box 9, 1/1/72, folder 1 of 2.

Moscow, was almost completely negative in July 1969 except for one thing: the moon landing. Americans in Moscow noted that Soviet citizens congratulated them, often noting that the Apollo missions were an accomplishment for all humanity, and not just the United States, and a tribute also to earlier Soviet successes that had prompted the Americans in the first place.[18]

The Soviet suggestion that the moon landing was for all of humanity matched Nixon's rhetoric, of course, and also encouraged him to find other ways to use the moon to bring the two sides together. One idea was to use gifts of moon rocks as diplomatic instruments, both to solidify relations with American allies and to build good will with the Soviets. The first exchange occurred when Neil Armstrong toured the Soviet Union in June 1970 and presented a moon sample to Soviet Premier Kosygin. That sample, though, was strictly political rather than scientific, according to the *LA Times*: "The fragment, embedded in a shaft of clear plastic, was given as a gesture of goodwill, not for scientific research." The Soviet scientists were clearly eager to get their hands on more lunar samples, inspired by the success of their own uncrewed lunar probes. The Soviet Academy of Sciences had thus approved exchanges of lunar soils back in January 1971, involving an exchange of two to three grams each from the Luna 16 and Apollo 11 and 12 missions (Luna 16 landed on the Moon on September 20, 1970, about 200 miles east of where Apollo 11 landed on July 20, 1969).[19]

In February 1972 NASA associate administrator John Naugle proposed an extensive collaboration on lunar science that produced exchanges of moon rock samples collected by both sides, joint scientific conferences, and the final, triumphal product of that cooperation: a jointly produced map of the moon. A particularly important aspect of the joint mapping project was inclusion of information from the US Defense Intelligence Agency director for Mapping, Charting and Geodesy.[20] The inclusion of the classified agency meant launching lunar data from the secretive national realm and into the public, international scientific arena—a gesture hoped to generate more goodwill. It also was an act that redefined the moon from being national security territory, which the famous planting of the American flag during Apollo 11 had indicated, to an international domain akin to Antarctica and in line with UN

---

18 "Soviets Break Door Getting to U.S. Show," *Chicago Tribune*, December 1, 1969, 1; "Russians Leave Scant Space for Future U.S. Goodwill," *Philadelphia Inquirer*, July 17, 1969, 1; Nixon Presidential Library and Archives, OS Outer Space Box 6, 8/9/1969–8/15/1969, August 12, 1969 memorandum to the White House on Soviet responses to Apollo 11.
19 "U.S., Russia Will Swap Lunar Samples, Data," *Los Angeles Times*, January 22, 1971, 4.
20 NASA Historical Reference Collection, Materials on collaboration with Soviets in 1972, 10/14/4, 15580.

treaties regarding both Antarctica and the moon. As for the exchanges of lunar rocks, the United States sent them to the Soviet side for examination by diplomatic pouch, thereby indicating the combined political and diplomatic functions of collaborative lunar science and moon soils. Said Naugle at NASA in a February 4, 1972 letter to the Academy of Sciences that seemed like the negotiations for a precious gem sale. "When the core sample has been examined, we can either send you a representative sample or, if you wish, await a visit by one of your experts to negotiate the content of the third gram."[21]

However, imaginative leaps into new transnational worlds at some point were bound to clash with cosmopolitical realities, and it was precisely on the contested territory of the moon that Earthrise-ism suffered a first setback. In March 1972, the Apollo Lunar Exploration office attempted to set some ground rules for exchange of information with the Soviets. The office complained that it had already submitted materials to the Soviet Union from its Lunar Exploration Program, which were not available to the public, and it had gotten little of value in return from the Soviet side. From the American point of view, the relationship seemed to be unequal and to violate the principle of parity that had guided détente. Said the NASA official: "This means that we will enter into joint discussions with a larger information base […] To what extent should we divulge our cartographic information if our initial discussions confirm that our base of information is much larger than that of the Soviets?" The NASA official noted that their lunar mapping had been conducted under the auspices of the US Army and US Air Force and it was therefore not clear if the information could be shared for reasons of national security. It was also common practice in their mapping activities that participants be able to visit the facilities of their partners, but since those facilities were in classified, military areas it did not seem possible for Soviet partners to visit. Finally, the NASA missive noted that if the American side was worrying about the "cartographic potential" of their information, by which he meant military significance, it was safe to assume that the Soviets were as well, and thus would be "unwilling to discuss theirs."[22] The failure of the joint mapping mission was becoming a self-fulfilling prophecy.

So while the Nixon administration had endorsed the joint lunar mapping project in theory, the US side, in practice, might be forced to limit its participation to only that part of the information which was unclassified, which seemed like very little. The Soviet Union had become famous for producing maps that

---

21 NASA Historical Reference Collection, Materials on collaboration with Soviets in 1972, 10/14/4, 15580.
22 NASA Historical Reference Collection, materials on joint lunar cartographic meeting in March 1972, 10/14/4, 15590.

omitted or changed the location of whole cities that were considered military secrets, but the United States had its own secret maps that marked off territory designated as important for national security; and it was unclear how to get a territory claimed for national security redesignated as open and international, even if the political will to do so had been formed.

Both sides struggled with how to resist the common imperialist practice of declaring newly discovered territory "mine"—like teenage kids (but armed with nuclear weapons) calling shotgun before climbing into a friend's car. Seemingly simple plans to pool information for joint mapping dragged on and on, stalled by both sides, who refused to provide significant data until the other side had done so; and no one could figure out a way to meet in some neutral space and conduct a simultaneous lunar data drop. A NASA meeting with the Soviets in May 1972 left the NASA program managers for lunar exploration feeling like they were giving much more than they got. "The Soviet delegation either was not prepared for, or chose not to present data in such detail [...] Their presentations, for the most part, were 'school-bookish' in nature." While NASA felt it answered Soviet questions about US mapping procedures in detail, "our questions about the USSR systems were not answered."[23]

It was a stark contrast to the far more open and relaxed data exchanges on docking for ASTP. The mapping impasses were the result of the inability to find a way to take the discussion of lunar territory, unlike docking, outside of the national security arena that seemed to take precedence where mapping and new territories were concerned. There was no apolitical mechanism for producing Soviet-American maps: each side was only capable of producing their own maps of the moon, and they had little conception of how to put those two together in a way that would be anything other than a zero-sum game.

Another stumbling block turned out to be topography and the naming of features on the lunar landscape. NASA suggested turning to the International Astronomical Union (IAU) to form a special neutral committee to develop a naming system, or at the least through the auspices of IAU to hash out a bilateral agreement "to come up with a good system for naming features." But the Soviets rejected this idea, apparently fearing that IAU was not a neutral player and would favor the Americans. The NASA official responsible for lunar mapping at one point said that his Soviet counterpart "was new to this kind of thing" (as they all were of course!) and refused to believe that "differences in language could account for some of our difficulties in negotiating." The bigger challenge, of course, was that the technocratic idea that

---

23 NASA Historical Reference Collection, materials on joint lunar cartographic meeting in May 1972, 10/14/4, 15590.

science could be separated from politics was failing both sides. Mapping was too clearly a political as well as scientific enterprise, and this became particularly apparent through the fraught process of trying to coproduce a Soviet-American map of the moon. It would have been easier to simply split the moon in half (as Portugal and Spain once divided the Americas), have both sides produce their own maps according to their respective cartographical regimes, tape the two halves together, and call the resulting portmanteau "the Moon." But whose moon?

Negotiations over lunar cartography dragged on through 1973. During a May 1973 meeting in Constance, Germany, the United States and the Soviet Union exchanged more topographic maps. The Soviets, from the NASA perspective, seemed more confident and forthright in exchanging information. That confidence had much to do with the success of the uncrewed lunar missions, which seemed to put them on a par with the American side. But most of the meaningful data exchanges did not concern the moon. After a meeting in Moscow in October 1973, a NASA official noted that he felt a bit overwhelmed by Soviet hospitality and the Interkosmos escorts, who gave him little free time to explore on his own or just relax. He spent a lot of time worrying about the Soviet insistence on paying for his room and food expenses, since NASA's policy was that the visiting side should always pay for expenses (to avoid the appearance of being beholden to the hosts). Russian traditions of hospitality, however, required that the host take care of everything for the guest, and the Soviet hosts, as American visitors to Russia quickly discover, could be very insistent.[24]

The bustle and packed schedule made it difficult to focus during the actual meetings to discuss cartography, and the NASA selenologist felt outnumbered and greatly in need of some backup. By December 1973, both sides committed to producing a complete map of the moon, based on exchanged data, on a scale of 1:5,000,000. But other than that, there was very little progress. Negotiations dragged on for more than a year and in March 1975 one NASA official admitted it had as much to do with the American side as the Soviet side. "All activities under the task to explore possible joint efforts to produce a lunar map have not identified any potential benefit to the USA." The official was convinced the Soviets had nothing to offer and so, "under this situation it is proposed that no initiative be taken to continue the joint USA/USSR production of a lunar map."[25]

---

24 The Soviets raised the issue with NASA of reversing the US practice during exchanges of having the visiting side pay expenses, but NASA refused: NASA Historical Reference Collection, "US-USSR Cooperation Documentation, 1963–1974," 10/14/4, 15590.

25 NASA Historical Reference Collection, Materials on joint lunar cartographic meeting in May 1973, 10/14/4, 15590.

While ASTP was entering into its final and glorious culminating phase, the lunar mapping project was stuck in terrestrial thickets of national security bureaucracies, clearly indicating the limits of cartographic science in healing superpower relations – much less in producing leaps for humankind in selenology. As always, the topographical problem of nomenclature for objects on the moon provided the most difficult challenge. By April 1974 IAU had produced a working group for Planetary System Nomenclature. A meeting in Moscow led by the Soviet Academy of Sciences Vice President A. P. Vinogradov was testy and tense, according to the NASA participant. At the meeting the two sides did agree to some basic principles – above all, that extraterrestrial nomenclature should be "clear and unambiguous" and that where ever possible names "shall be international" and subject to IAU approval. They also agreed that Latin names would provide a neutral language for lunar nomenclature — Catena for crater, for example, or Labyrinthus for a complex of intersecting narrow depressions.[26]

But the devil, it turned out, was in the moon-dusty details, especially when it came to naming craters on Moon or Mars after famous people. The atheist Soviets insisted on prohibiting naming things after religious figures (especially given the American astronauts' tendency to invoke biblical verse in their proclamations from space). Also out were "military leaders, political leaders and philosophers of the 19th and 20th centuries," thus preventing the possible politicization of the Martian and Lunar landscapes in the way that both Soviet and American terrestrial space had been inscribed with the names and ideals of various historical personages. Seeking more neutral ground, both sides agreed that distinguished and deceased "artists, musicians, sculptors, and writers and poets [could] without difficulty, provide several hundred names." Other potential candidates for naming included "animals, birds, cities, first names of men and women, islands, lakes, minerals, mountains, rivers and villages." Still other names could be drawn from "deserts, fundamental particles, geographical provinces, observatories, scientific instruments, ships of discovery, and the name of the particular planet or satellite in various languages." But that was as far as the joint groups seemed to get, at least regarding attempts to play like God and name the objects of the cosmos and in the process complete the collaborative vision of lunar terrain. If ASTP had succeeded in effectively neutralizing superpower conflict on the depoliticized terrain of docking engineering, at least for a time, the seemingly simple task of joint mapping was too overtly ideological. Unlike ASTP, the challenge of joint mapping was to create an entirely new system—a jointly produced and

---

26 NASA Historical Reference Collection, Materials on joint lunar cartographic meeting in April 1974, 10/14/4, 15590.

conceived moon—and not simply a mechanism linking the two separate national territories (the American Apollo and the Soviet Soyuz). In the ASTP mission both sides therefore only needed to create "clean" interfaces between themselves, as the Nixon export controls bureaucrats put it, rather than collaboratively produce and define common space that they then planned to inhabit. And that was why the joint moon-mapping mission failed and the ASTP docking succeeded. Interestingly, NASA and the Soviet space authorities had also planned to produce jointly made films and publications about the ASTP project, but none of those materialized for all the same reasons as the failed moon-mapping project: they could not agree on how to tell a single story of the mission. Narration and mapping remained zero-sum games for the superpowers.

Cosmism in Policy and Practice

While the two superpowers attempted, with clearly mixed results, to turn the moon into a neutral zone, the Soviets pursued their quixotic quest for space peace, either with or without the capitalist world. Even as the 1968 invasion of Czechoslovakia seemed to solidify Europe's division into two armed camps, Soviets looked toward space flight as a way of realizing very different ideas about universal community, albeit with a socialist rather than capitalist emphasis. The Soviets created Interkosmos in the late 1960s, a counter to the European Space Research Organization in 1964, and Intersputnik in 1971 in response to Intelsat's creation.[27] Soviet commentators waxed philosophical about the potential for space exploration to transform Europe into a no-war zone—a belief forged in the bloody experience of World War II. The civilian cosmonaut Vitalii Sevastianov, an engineer rather than fighter pilot who also hosted a popular television science show in the Soviet Union, was a regular contributor in the English-language space industry press during the 1970s. A protégé of the ASTP docking engineer Syromiatnikov and one of his acolytes, he viewed space technology as a panacea that would lead humanity down the path toward a more perfect global community. The space age, he wrote, completed the movement from a geocentric point of view to a heliocentric one, thus ending a distinct era in modern history initiated by Copernicus. Space exploration, he concluded, "has been exerting an ever greater influence on social being and consciousness, it has been changing our traditional ideas about the world and the relationship between society and

---

27 On telecommunications during the Cold War: Mari Pajala and Alice Lovejoy, eds. *Remapping Cold War Media: Institutions, Infrastructures, Networks, Exchanges* (Bloomington: Indiana University Press, forthcoming 2022).

nature."²⁸ Such ideas—along with a desire to view the American system of technological management and production—had inspired the Soviets to work with the United States on ASTP, discussed in detail earlier. Sevastianov presented a cosmist interpretation of the project for the readers of the American space industry journal *Space World*. The high costs of space exploration, he noted, had made collaboration across ideological and national borders imperative. But even more pressing was the need to prevent the devastation of the environment and to find the resources that might solve the Malthusian dilemma, elaborated by the Club of Rome, that seemed to promise a future of resource deprivation. "We must go beyond the confines of this planet," wrote Sevastianov, whose communist ideology seemed to have morphed into cosmism, "because of the earth's limited surface and natural population growth and search for other worlds with favorable conditions for existence and development [...] we of the twentieth century must work out a global program for developing space vehicles which would ensure the emergence of human civilization outside the solar system."²⁹ A November 1975 issue of *Space World* devoted to the Soviet view of ASTP proclaimed that "the world appears to be entering the period of grandiose space ventures."³⁰ The Soviet newspaper for the Red Army declared a new era of world peace. Inspired by ASTP, Soviet commentators floated various utopian ideas about an international space platform—with broad US and Western and Eastern European collaboration—as a basis for building a new global order based on peaceful technological and scientific exchanges and inspired by ideas more akin to the Harvest Moon project (presented to Richard Nixon by a Republican donor) than Karl Marx.³¹ Far from marking an end to utopian conceptions of space flight, the 1970s, at least in the Soviet Union, stimulated the utopian imagination to go to many weird and wonderful places.

NASA, however, was entering a perilous period in its space program following the Apollo missions and until the creation of a new launch vehicle in the Space Shuttle, which would not fly until 1981. Through the 1970s American plans to collaborate in space were also stymied by cosmopolitical concerns in the US government that the nation would be giving away its competitive

---

28 Vitali Sevastyanov and Arkadi Ursul, "Space Age: New Relationship between Society and Nature," *Space World*, no. 1 (1972), 31.
29 "Russian Report," *Space World*, no. 2 (1975), 26.
30 "The Soviet Story of Soyuz-Apollo," *Space World*, no. 11 (1975), 13.
31 See "Vperedi—novye mezhdunarodnye polety (Forward to New International Flights)," July 20, 1975, 1; and "Na blago chelovechestva (For Mankind's Benefit)," *Krasnaia zvezda*, July 23 1975, 1.

edge.³² Meanwhile, the Soviets were eager to build on ASTP and promote joint ventures in space with Eastern Europeans, if not their Western counterparts. They initiated joint manned missions through the late 1970s, underwriting the costs of the launches—in stark contrast to NASA's insistence that international partners share launch costs—and promoting joint manned missions as milestones toward the creation of a new global order of peace. Similar to Antarctic exploration, space science for the Soviets was neutral space, both advancing knowledge of the cosmos and promoting peace and brotherhood. Eastern Europeans became the first Europeans other than Russians to leave Earth's atmosphere. Vladimír Remek from Czechoslovakia in March 1978 was the first. The selection of a Czechoslovakian was a symbolic gesture designed in part to patch over ill feelings from the Soviet invasion 10 years previously. Remek was followed by a Pole (to celebrate the anniversary of Copernicus) and then the East German Jähn.³³ Thanks to the Soviets, the first Western European, Jean-Loup Chrétien, flew into space on June 24, 1982.³⁴ While Chrétien was the first West European in space, his flight was the culmination of a long collaboration across the Cold War divide between France and the Soviet Union. As noted earlier, Charles de Gaulle had promoted France as a third way between the Soviet Union and the Anglo-American alliance. Those policies, in part, led de Gaulle to a visit to Moscow in June 1966 to sign a bilateral agreement on space exploration in a number of areas. The French participated in the Soviet lunar probe landings of the early 1970s. A 1973 Soviet Mars probe carried French instruments. French biological experiments were included in the Soviet space station Salyut 6 in 1978, followed by tests for satellite transmissions between the Soviet Union and France in 1981.³⁵

Europe at the Margins

It was nonetheless difficult to escape the reality that superpower competition seemed always to stymie the search for neutral space, either in the practices of science and engineering, on the moon or somewhere in Europe. The Western and Eastern Europeans were sandwiched politically and geographically between two superpowers who were armed to the teeth with nuclear weapons. Where ever the US and Soviet space programs went in search of neutral territory, they

---

32 On military concerns about space collaboration at NASA: see Nixon Presidential Library and Archives, National Security Decision Memorandums, Box H-326, NSDM-187 [1 of 2]; "NASA official gets 'a little mad' over joint space mission claims," *Houston Post*, November 7, 1977, 3.
33 "Cosmonauts Have the Right Stuff Too," *Space World*, no. 9 (1986), 19.
34 Guy Collins, *Europe in Space* (Basingstoke: Macmillan 1990), 123.
35 Ibid., 124–26; "De Gaulle Invites Soviet Science Tie," *New York Times*, June 23, 1966, 1.

seemed to bring their cosmopolitics with them. "Throughout the 1960s and 1970s Western Europe seemed condemned to the status of an also-ran in the headline-grabbing space race between Washington and Moscow," destined to be a staging ground for Cold War conflicts rather than new ideas about politics or an equal partner to the United States or the Soviet Union.[36] Tensions between the Soviets and their European partners constantly surfaced, despite rhetoric about international brotherhood and collaboration. For example, the original Soviet commander for the Franco-Soviet mission on which Chrétien flew transferred out of the mission due to personal problems with his French comrades. The United States also made it clear that it was a first among equals when it came to its Western European colleagues.[37] A NASA official in 1986 reflected the often superior attitude that irked so many Europeans: "Partners accepted NASA control because [...] they perceived themselves to be junior partners in fact, and especially because they did not have ready alternatives to working with NASA if they wished to work at the cutting edge of the space frontier."[38] Depending on whose rockets they used, Europeans were thus cosmonauts or astronauts, even though the French briefly named themselves "espationautes," just as the Chinese created the term "Yuhangyuan," thereby hoping to nationalize their own path to the stars.[39] In the tradition of cosmopolitics, the neutrality of outerspace—or its transformation into a staging ground for new types of human community—was constantly challenged by the Cold War tensions between the United States and the Soviet Union, or just old-fashioned patriotism.

As détente collapsed in the late 1970s a group of retired astronauts and active cosmonauts, led by Apollo mission veterans Russell Schweickart and Edgar Mitchell, and Aleksei Leonov on the Soviet side, came up with the idea of an Association of Space Explorers (ASE). What had failed to materialize at the highest political levels had been taken over by citizen diplomacy. Edgar Mitchell first suggested the idea in October 1973 in a letter to the White House. He proposed a committee of retired astronauts and cosmonauts "to function as goodwill ambassadors for peace and unity on a global scale." Nixon, for his part, was intrigued by the idea.[40] It was another suggestion of

---

36 Collins, *Europe in Space*, 1.
37 Niklas Reinke, *The History of German Space Policy: Ideas, Influences, and Interdependence 1923–2002*, trans. Barry Smerin and Barbara Wilson (Paris: Beauchesne, 2007), 472; "ESA Aims at 2001," *Space World*, no. 5 (1985), 26.
38 Kenneth S. Pedersen, "The Changing Face of International Cooperation: One View of NASA," *Space Policy* 2, no. 2 (1986), 129.
39 Collins, *Europe in Space*, 126–27.
40 NASA Headquarters Archive, 1/12/6 "Mitchell, Edgar D. (1966–1976)"; Nixon Presidential Library and Archives, WHCF GEN OS 3-1 Astronauts, 10 October 1973 letter from Kenneth Dam to Edgar Mitchell.

the utopian notions that Nixon had associated with space flight since his first inaugural address, which made the Earthrise image of Apollo 8 a centerpiece of his call for a new international order. Meanwhile, despite the collapse of Nixon presidency, retired Apollo astronauts, along with active Soviet cosmonauts who had met during various exchanges of the 1970s and on ASTP, kept the idea alive. The group's founders wanted the group to be open to space travelers from all countries, though the initial focus was on Soviet and US space travelers. Leonov, in particular, was inspired by ASTP's memorable "handshake in space" and by visions of a fragile planet under the twin threats of nuclear holocaust and environmental destruction.[41] ASE members had a sense of being instruments of a certain vision of historical destiny in which space travel marked an end to the conflicts that arose from national competition. They had become models of the future global citizens, ecologically aware and peace-loving, or so they believed.

Figure 2.1 Aleksei Leonov welcomed by Shoshone tribal leaders during one of his many trips to the United States during Apollo-Soyuz training

Source: NASA

---

41 Hoover, ASE, Folder 6, Russell Schweickart letter to Walter Cunningham, May 24, 1983.

Political circumstances, however, quickly shifted the Association's focus from the United States and the Soviet Union to France. Sure of the superiority of American space technology, and with a Hobbesian view of outer space as an arena for national competition rather than collaboration, American opponents of collaboration gained official support during the first Reagan administration. Space-faring peacemongers were now persona non grata on US territory. Those views were reflected in NASA's reluctance to work with Western Europeans on joint missions and payloads (whose origins went back to Nixon's initiatives) and to a refusal to renew in 1982 the agreement for widespread collaboration with the Soviet Union in space, first signed in 1972 in Moscow by Nixon and Kosygin.[42] The heightening of Cold War tensions with Reagan's Star Wars speech in March 1983, and then the downing of a South Korean civilian jetliner in Soviet airspace in September 1983, aggravated conditions further and destroyed plans for a planning meeting on US soil. Meanwhile, many within the astronaut corps considered ASE a betrayal of US national security imperatives in the wake of the Strategic Defense Initiative and US plans to upgrade nuclear arsenals in Western Europe. The Cold War Imaginary beckoned. The astronaut and ASTP crew member Vance Brand, of all people, noted that the Soviet Cosmonauts were not "free agents," supposedly unlike the American participants. Brand's resistance to ASE is particularly notable as he was a crew member on ASTP, but like a good American soldier he followed the politics of Reagan Cold Warriors and turned his back on his former Soviet crewmates. The Soviet side, he said, would invariably try to "reap any propaganda or political advantages" from the ASE group, while putting the astronauts into the uncomfortable position of opposing their own government by participating in the effort. Another astronaut, Joseph Kerwin, said he liked the idea of world peace, but he believed it was naïve to expect such an outcome in the face of military and strategic realities.[43] Kerwin's sentiments were not uncommon, as Russell Schweickart learned when he polled Apollo veterans about ASE in order to gage potential support among US space-traveling veterans.

Based on his polling data, it became apparent to Schweickart that it would be difficult to achieve his original goal, as expressed in a letter to the Soviet

---

42 "The Last Frontier for Trust, NASA Shuns Contact with Cosmonauts," *San Francisco Chronicle*, March 27, 1988, 6. On NASA frustrations with Reagan administration hostility toward foreign and Western European participation in the Space Shuttle program, see a Hans Mark memorandum from February 1983: NASA Headquarters Archives, OSX/A/2 "Astronauts, Foreign."; "First European Astronaut Criticizes Shuttle Manning," *Washington Post*, December 20, 1983, A4.

43 Hoover, ASE, Folder 3, questionnaire response from Vance Brand, Joseph Kerwin to Russell Schweickart.

cosmonaut Aleksei Eliseev: "We want to proceed in such a way so as not to criticize the views and actions of political leaders and institutions. Rather we will clarify or elucidate problems of importance for humanity, contributing to the unification of efforts toward their solution."[44] The problem was that any declaration of unified efforts to solve global problems, in the context of the Cold War, was often interpreted as a direct attack on the views and actions of political leaders and institutions in the Reagan administration and, to a lesser extent, the Soviet Union. The US refusal in 1982 to renew the program of space collaboration with the Soviets was one reflection of this ideological animosity toward joint space missions as a stepping stone to a new international order; another indication was the Reagan administration's active discouragement of attempts to celebrate the tenth anniversary of ASTP in 1985—which stood in stark contrast to prominent Soviet celebrations urging the demilitarization of space.[45] Thus, despite the impressive and growing record of international collaboration in the 1970s, beginning with ASTP and French and Soviet joint efforts, the perceived national and strategic imperatives of the Reagan administration had stopped the momentum of international space-cooperation initiatives.

France as a Neutral Zone

The NASA correspondence in the Reagan Presidential Library Archives, especially as compared to NASA records from the 1970s, reveals an obsession with injecting ideological meaning back into the US space program on two fronts: emphasizing the military and national importance of space exploration; and a dogmatic insistence on privatization as the only possible future direction for civilian space initiatives. To the extent that the Reagan administration was prepared to encourage collaboration of any sort, it emphasized cooperative efforts between the United States and the private sector and not between NASA and the space administrations of other nations. In the words

---

44 Hoover, ASE, Folder 5, Schweickart letter to Alexei Yeliseyev, September 19, 1983.
45 "U.S. May Boycott Space-Linkup Event," *Washington Post*, May 16, 1985, A21; "Cosmonaut Calls for Weapons-Free Space," *FBIS*, No. 143, July 25, 1985, U1. The U.S. Office of Technology Assessment in October 1984 presented a draft argument against the value of collaborative programs with the Soviets: "The U.S.-U.S.S.R. Intergovernmental Agreement on Cooperative Space Activities: Should it be Renewed?," NASA Headquarters Archive, 10/14/3, Folder 15592. There was widespread opposition within the US government to the Reagan administration's refusal to develop joint missions. See the *Congressional Record—Senate*, February 9, 1984, S 1276–82 for statements in favor of a Congressional Resolution entitled "East-West Cooperation in Space as an Alternative to a Space Arms Race."

of one Republican legislator, in a letter to the White House in September 1983, the Republican Party needed to "use space to break out of the psychological 'Limits of Growth' mentality, and thereby move away from a Liberal Welfare State toward a Conservative Opportunity Society," and that meant shifting the emphasis toward government financing of military space applications and leaving civilian applications to the US free market system.[46] The renewed emphasis on the military implications of space exploration also meant ever tightening controls over technology transfer, driven by fears that even collaborative efforts with friendly Europeans might ultimately (through their contacts with the Soviets) give away supposedly decisive US technological advantages. Such sentiments had a chilling effect on ASE's attempts to build on the precedent of ASTP and build bridges across the Cold War divide. To draw attention away from the politically explosive image of US astronauts making overtures to Soviets without official sanction, the ASE decided to go to Europe with their project and include people who had flown into outer space from both Eastern and Western Europe. Doing so, its founders hoped, would save the ASE from the McCarthyite sentiments of former and active astronauts, many of whom were clearly spooked by the Reagan administration's aggressive Cold War rhetoric and renewed emphasis on the military and national significance of space flight. European participation, it was thought, would prevent the structuring of the event as a bipolar, Cold War project and "avoid the balancing charade of one-of-theirs, one-of-ours."[47] The astronaut Jim Irwin met in Europe "with all of the Euroastros and got a positive response from them in the 'let's all get together' theme." Schweickart also consulted with the French explorer Jacques-Yves Cousteau who recommended that European astronauts be brought into the effort.[48] When the Soviets backed out of a planned astronaut/cosmonaut meeting for May 1984, because of the Soviet boycott of the Los Angeles Olympics and because of the US refusal to remove its Pershing II and Cruise missiles from Europe, the organizers had concluded that only Europe could provide the neutral path they had been seeking. "Joining the Euroastros [...] may indeed be the best way," said Mitchell, in an August 1984 letter to Schweickart. To answer charges that the group would be used by the Soviet side against the US government, organizers made it clear

---

46 Letter from James Muney to the Reagan White House, September 21, 1983, Ronald Reagan Presidential Library and Archive, Outer Space, 170,000–179,999.
47 Hoover, ASE, Folder 4, Minutes of March 3, 1984 meeting at Pepsico headquarters, Purchase, NY.
48 Hoover, ASE, Folder 6, Schweickart letter to Captain Jacques-Yves Cousteau, February 27, 1984.

that non-Soviet participants represented only their own personal views—and not that of the American government or other nonparticipating astronauts.[49]

At first, the organizers contemplated Iceland or the Canary Islands as a meeting place, but later decided to shift to France when they found a private sponsor with a château outside of Paris to host the inaugural "Congress of Planetary Explorers," held from October 2 to 6, 1985. France had long played an important role as intermediary between East and West, as noted throughout this book. Just a year earlier, in October 1984, the French minister of science and technology, Hubert Curien, spoke to the US Congress in favor of an international Mars mission that would use space exploration to break out of the "zero-sum" mentality of superpower politics, as former NASA administrator and ASTP architect Thomas Paine put it on the same panel. Curien told the American audience that his nation had long been accustomed to working with both the Soviet Union and the United States and that it was always France's policy "to establish closer and more open human relationships between scientists, regardless of national barriers. [...] Scientists all over the world long for the free international exchange of ideas."[50] At the height of Reagan's light-saber rattling of Star Wars those words were bound to fall on deaf ears at NASA, but among the ASE advocates they sounded like sweet music.

The October 1985 conference was attended by 25 space travelers, including 8 Soviets, 5 Americans, a Saudi Arabian, Frenchman, Czechoslovakian, Mongolian, Cuban, Romanian, and East German. In addition to lining up the private American corporate sponsor Pepsico, they secured sponsorship from the French engineering firm Constructions Mécaniques de Normandie, whose president owned the chalet where the space travelers planned to meet. Equally important, France was the homeland of Western Europe's first space traveler, Jean-Loup Chrétien, who would play a key role as the French host. Having flown on a Soviet rocket, he was also selected to train for flights on the Space Shuttle. Chrétien was brought into the effort, as Schweickart wrote to him in August 1984, "to minimize the tendency toward political speculation and embroilment in international political issues" and to help function as a "bridge" between the Soviets and the Americans, thus adding a "multi-lateral flavor to the meeting." Removing the effort from US or Soviet soil was especially critical "given the timing of this meeting vis-à-vis the US elections

---

49 Hoover, ASE, Folder 4, Mitchell letter to Schweickart, August 23, 1984; Folder 6, Jack Matlock letter to Schweickart, April 26, 1984; Schweickart letter to Robert McFarlane, April 11, 1984.
50 "Cooperative East-West Ventures," *Congressional Record – Senate*, October 11, 1984, S14022.

and the potential space/strategic weapons talks." Schweickart also reached out to Ulf Merbold, the first West German in space, and to Wubbo Ockels, the Dutchman who was then an astronaut in training.[51] Both "Euroastros" played a potentially useful role as intermediaries who might lessen the politically challenging aspects of ASE at a particularly tense moment in US–Soviet relations. Merbold and Ockels were the first Europeans brought into the Space Shuttle program. They were payload specialists responsible for the European scientific experiments on ESA's Spacelab—given to NASA in exchange for allowing European astronauts to fly on the Shuttle. With a background in science rather than the military, and as representatives of the European Space Agency, they occupied a seemingly neutral and disinterested, nonpolitical space as scientists. Whenever challenged by the military and national imperatives of space flight, advocates of collaboration relied on the Enlightenment notion of science as a supposedly universal and politically neutral endeavor, a role reserved in this instance for the European payload specialists and their scientific experiments.

New Agers and Space Flight in the 1970s

The spirit of détente and of the counterculture of the 1970s, like the aroma of burning incense, hung over the entire enterprise. The Esalen Institute in Big Sur, California, one of the meeting's sponsors and a driving force in the human potential movement, said it wanted to launch CBMs—confidence building measures—rather than ICBMs.[52] It had initiated the first Cosmonaut-Astronaut exchanges through "hot tub diplomacy." Esalen had been started at Big Sur overlooking the Pacific Ocean by two Stanford dropouts. Since the early 1960s, Esalen had searched for ways to link modern life and science to a mystical sense of unity with the cosmos. The spiritual transformations of many astronauts and cosmonauts, including Russell Schweickart and Edgar Mitchell, who had conducted Extrasensory Perception experiments during his Apollo mission, had convinced Esalen in the 1970s that space exploration just might be the key to the kinds of mental transformations needed to save the world from environmental and nuclear destruction.[53] "We thought we

---

51 Hoover, ASE, Folder 5, Schweickart letter to Chrétien, August 29, 1984, Schweickart letter to Edgar Mitchell, September 4, 1984, Schweickart letter to Mitchell, July 27, 1984, Mitchell letter to Schweickart August 23, 1984, Schweickart letter to "Astros," August 15, 1984; Folder 6, Schweickart letter to Ulf Merbold, March 17, 1984; Folder 1, "May 1985 Progress Report."
52 Hoover, ASE, Folder 6, John Edwin Mroz letter to James Hickman, February 13, 1984.
53 Walter Truett Anderson, *The Upstart Spring: Esalen and the American Awakening*, (Reading, MA: Addison-Wesley, 1983), 310.

were astronauts of inner space," said an Esalen Institute executive, "about to break through into new realms of consciousness; we wanted to put man on the psychic moon."[54] Esalen itself had emerged from its founders' frustrations with mainstream science's refusal to consider the potential efficacy of human attitudes and mental power to change politics, culture, and even transform the material world. The goal was to provide a kind of secular religion that would reconcile reason and soul, science and religion, and individual and community.[55]

Esalen's director for Soviet-American exchanges, James Hickman, had traveled to the Soviet Union in the 1970s and discovered many kindred spirits who seemed interested in "physical fitness, emotional health, self-regulation and healing, management of stress, sensory range and acuity, creativity, imaginative problem-solving, worker motivation, initiative, self-reliance, empathy, tolerance of ambiguity, paranormal perception and spiritual understanding."[56] Esalen's Soviet contacts included a number of cosmonauts and Soviet athletes who seemed to endorse the same kind of power of positive thinking, self-awareness, and quest for mental and bodily self-control that Esalen had been promoting, which the Soviets referred to as "*bioinformatika*" (bioinformatics). By the late 1970s Esalen viewed space and computer technology as key to the production of a new human consciousness and to the reconciliation of modern technology and human spirit into a kind of cyborg, a hybrid mechanism just like Syromiatnikov's androgynous docking mechanism. In materials sent to NASA, Esalen noted that

> Like Americans, Soviet citizens are beginning to recognize the power of human consciousness, the unlimited boundaries of "hidden human reserves" (as the Soviets call them.) Like Americans, the Soviets are beginning to yearn for some spiritual dimension that has been missing in their organized, rational lives. It was this common interest in self-improvement and personal growth that led to the creation of Esalen's Soviet-American Exchange Program.[57]

The Esalen program explicitly bypassed official government structures in order to create citizen to citizen exchanges, believing that the transformation of

---

54 "Still on Edge, Esalen Grows Up," *Chicago Tribune*, August 23, 1987, 7.
55 For a general history: Jeffrey Kripal, *Esalen: America and the Religion of No Religion* (Chicago: University of Chicago Press, 2007).
56 "The Esalen Institute Soviet-American Exchange Program," contained in the NASA Library and Resource Center, 10/14/4, 15582.
57 "The Esalen Institute Soviet-American Exchange Program," contained in the NASA Library and Resource Center, 10/14/4, 15582.

minds from below would ultimately transform zero-sum politics above. Esalen in August 1981 had invited Dr. Georgii Skorov, deputy director of the Institute for US and Canadian Studies at the Soviet Academy of Sciences, to receive "instruction in stress management and physical fitness training." Each day of his Esalen retreat was devoted to personal and professional development. Esalen brought Zen masters from San Francisco together with Soviet shamans and faith healers, and attempted to integrate their techniques with modern psychiatry—Hickman's specialty while working earlier at the Menninger Dream Laboratory in Brooklyn in the early 1970s. He called himself "a research psychologist specializing in exceptional human functioning" and was eager to work with Soviet cosmonauts, shamans, academicians, farmers, and athletes to explore "the limits of human psychophysical development." His project of using space exploration to unite humanity—which included direct satellite linkups between the United States and the Soviet Union and bringing together US practitioners of ESP with Soviet advocates of *"ekstrasens"*—made Esalen a key player in the promotion of ASE.[58]

The fusion of technology, spiritualism, and the hot tubs of Esalen resonated with both the Soviet cosmonauts and American astronauts. At one point, when negotiations between cosmonauts and astronauts to form the group seemed to reach an impasse, Edgar Mitchell went to the blackboard and drew a mushroom cloud below a horizontal line, "representing the politics of fear and destruction. On the upper half, he drew an image of the whole Earth, symbolizing the perspective from space of a world without boundaries." By invoking the image of nuclear holocaust, Mitchell highlighted the potential significance of the ASE's deliberations. He wanted to clarify (in response to some criticisms that it was unclear if the ASE wanted to be a "social club or a think tank," and "Elk's Club" for astronauts) that the group was more than just a social gathering of professional space travelers, reminiscing about old times and exchanging stories, though there was plenty of that, too. At stake in their actions was nothing less than the fate of the earth.[59] Indeed, ASE members had a sense of being instruments of historical destiny in which space travel marked an end to the conflicts that arose from national competition. In their own minds, they had become models of the future global citizens, ecologically aware and peace-loving. As ASE founding member Sevastianov put it in a popular Russian-language book translated into English—for both Syromiatnikov and his protégé Sevastianov translating their ideas into English was critical to their projects—the space travelers had "features" that were

---

58 "The Esalen Institute Soviet-American Exchange Program," contained in the NASA Library and Resource Center, 10/14/4, 15582.
59 Vance Brand's letter to Russell Schweickart, March 1984, in Hoover, ASE, Folder 3.

"typical of humanity as a whole in later stages of the Space Age." They would "increasingly differ from the terrestrial average in their individual, moral and even physical qualities," thus giving them a special responsibility as civilization's saviors.[60] Those comments echoed a draft of ASE's mission statement, written by Russell Schweickart and Edgar Mitchell, which claimed that "none [...] but we can speak and act from direct experience of being outside of and looking back on the single home of all the life we know in the universe."[61]

The location for their first meeting had symbolic meaning equal to the grand tasks the founding members had set before themselves. The group thus met in October 1985 "near Paris where Crusaders once passed on their way to Jerusalem." The image of a crusade captured perfectly the group's sense of world-historical mission. The grounds of the private chateau seemed to blend European tradition and modernity, seamlessly integrating bucolic landscapes with visions of new worlds to sow and reap. Two artists among the group—the cosmonaut Aleksei Leonov and the astronaut Alan Bean—brought their works for display at La Geode, a geodesic dome at the New Scientific Museum in Paris. The art was meant to depoliticize the effort, something "cooperative and non-controversial," said Alan Bean. The Swedish computer giant Ericsson sponsored the reception. As if to tone down the harsh rhetoric of the Cold War, "meals were conducted in a leisurely European style," and not in the hurried manner of the Americans. "There was ample time for fishing and boating on the lake," and plenty of vodka for the Soviets.[62] Those unstructured exchanges over food and drink were more than rest and relaxation before the main work of ASE. As with the informal citizen exchanges sponsored by the Esalen Institute more generally, the ASE believed that camaraderie and homosocial bonding among the elite group of space travelers, the fraternity of fliers, were the first critical step toward building alliances across political divides and ultimately to forging new types of consciousness. Emotional satisfaction in human exchanges would point the way to higher, spiritual truths. As one Esalen scholar has noted, "People at Esalen advocated spirituality, emotional disclosure, and men's connection to other men as pathways to a new, better kind of masculinity," one that would be more in tune with the need for

---

60 V. I. Sevastyanov, A. D. Ursul, and Yu. Shkolenko, *The Universe and Civilization*, (Moscow: Progress Publishers, [1979] 1981), 163, 235.
61 Draft of mission statement, in Hoover, ASE, Folder 3.
62 Hoover, ASE, Folder 1, copy of brochure, "1st Planetary Congress, Association of Space Explorers, October 1985, Cernay, France"; folder 3, questionnaire response from Alan Bean to Russell Schweickart.

peace rather than the demands of various military-industrial complexes.[63] It was an echo of the same impulse that had driven ASTP docking engineers—explored in more detail in the next chapter—to find the androgynous docking mechanisms that would help men find a way to relate to each other based on mutual respect and equality rather than seeking a relationship of domination and submission. And it was the kind of spirit that was in too short supply for the Soviet and American lunar cartographers.

While Europe seemed to represent a more relaxed and neutral space than either Moscow or Washington, environmental science provided the ASE with a seemingly nonpolitical theme. Looking for more neutral ground, ASE thus focused in particular on environmental issues—the main theme of the first ASE conference and a topic that participants hoped could unify governments and peoples in Europe regardless of their political or cultural differences. Sigmund Jähn from the German Democratic Republic repeated nearly verbatim Yuri Gagarin's widely published thought after his historic flight about the fragility of the planet and the need to protect it. Wrote Jähn: "Before I flew I was already aware of how small and vulnerable our plant is; but only when I saw it from space, in all its effable beauty and fragility, did I realize that humankind's most urgent task is to cherish and preserve it for future generations." Ulf Merbold of the Federal Republic of Germany was shocked, like his East German counterpart, by the fragility of the planet. "For the first time in my life I saw the horizon as a curved line. It was accentuated by a thin seam of dark blue light—our atmosphere. Obviously this was not the ocean of air I had been told it was so many times in my life. I was terrified by its fragile appearance." His compatriot from the Federal Republic of Germany, Reinhard Furrer, was reminded of his own insignificance by the vastness of space. Space seemed to suggest the limitations of human existence, its finiteness, yet Furrer also experienced a feeling of power and dominion, "like a star that circled the Earth." That combination of power and insignificance, of both limited and limitless possibilities, was a paradox of space consciousness—and a reflection, perhaps, of Europe's own entangled position during the Cold War.[64]

Focusing on environmental topics, the association convinced Jacques Cousteau to give the keynote speech at the first ASE meeting in Paris in October 1985.[65] The intrepid showman and explorer had inspired "Cousteau Societies" throughout Europe and the world, including the Soviet Union and the United States. His invention of the aqualung allowed people to explore

---

63 Marion Goldman, *The American Soul Rush: Esalen and the Rise of Spiritual Privilege* (New York: New York University Press, 2012), 5.
64 Kevin W. Kelley, ed., *The Home Planet* (London: Queen Anne Press, 1988), 140, 158.
65 Hoover, ASE, Folder 6, Schweickart letter to Cousteau, January 10, 1984.

new realms, just as Sergei Korolev's rockets (the chief engineer of the rockets that launched Sputnik, Laika, and Gagarin into space) had allowed humans to go into space. In line with ASE's hopes for space exploration, Cousteau's undersea activities helped to forge a transnational environmental consciousness, opening new worlds yet highlighting the fragility of the only one people inhabited. He was terrified that space exploration "is now almost monopolized by the military." Hunger for knowledge and exploration had inspired the pioneers of space, he claimed. He was struck by the sincerity and friendliness of the sentiments within the fraternity of space travelers. "They all emphasize that our planet is one, that borderlines are artificial, that humankind is one single community on board spaceship Earth. They all insist that this fragile gem is at our mercy and that we must all endeavor to protect it." The exploration of space, in his view, marked the beginning of a new transnational moment in human history, "the birth of a global consciousness that will help build a peaceful future for humankind." He said that space prompted people to contemplate three infinite realms, "the infinitely big, the infinitely small, and the infinitely complex. And from all the beauty they discover while crossing perpetually receding frontiers, they develop for nature and for humankind an infinite love."[66] Citing Teilhard de Chardin, the patron saint of eco-consciousness and inspiration for cosmic thinkers on both sides of the Cold War divide, Cousteau said that space prompted people to contemplate three infinite realms, "the infinitely big, the infinitely small, and the infinitely complex. And from all the beauty they discover while crossing perpetually receding frontiers, they develop for nature and for humankind an infinite love."[67] For the ASE, Cousteau provided a vital link to the past (to the heroic European age of Exploration from which Cousteau emerged) but also to the new environmental and global consciousness of the space age. His ability to connect science and environmental protection to utopian visions of the new kinds of human community made Cousteau an ideal spokesperson for ASE, just as it had also drawn the famous scientist and astronomer Carl Sagan into the organization. Sagan was a television personality with global name recognition, and one whom the ASE founders actively cultivated as an ally.[68] Like Cousteau, he was the epitome of the cosmopolitan scientist, devoting his services to all mankind, rather than to his nation's secret military-industrial complex, and linking his professional identity to a moral agenda of disarmament and environmental protection. Even more, his status as a scientist suggested

---

66 Kelley, *The Home Planet*, unnumbered page in "Foreword," Jacques-Yves Cousteau.
67 Jacques-Yves Cousteau, "Foreword," in Kelley, *Home Planet*, n.p.
68 Schweickart's letter to Chretien, August 29, 1984, in Hoover, ASE, Folder 4.

a moral position that seemed to stand in the rarified space above and beyond the Cold War Imaginary.

Limits

If ASE aimed to transform global consciousness, the Paris meeting was nonetheless a humble beginning. Staging the first meeting in Western Europe, while avoiding the fraught political atmosphere and controversy that would have resulted from a meeting in either the United States or the Soviet Union, also necessarily limited the public relations impact of former cold warriors embracing across ideological and national barriers. The organization also faced a dilemma arising from the contradictory nature of its mission. Organizers scrupulously claimed to be apolitical, but they aimed to create a new politics opposed to the Cold War policies of the superpowers. Schweickart expressed the contradictory apolitical politics of the group: "Clearly it is controversial. [...] But our intent is not political, except in the largest and highest sense of that word." Yet any program advocating the demilitarization of space, in the face of national policies such as Star Wars based on its militarization, had to be political and, in the view of one hostile astronaut, "anti-American." As one newspaper reporter put it, "[the association] sticks strictly to the personal and philosophical, carefully avoiding politics, even though it is world politics that association members would like to see change."[69] The inability to confront the political nature of the entire enterprise was perhaps the greatest limitation encountered by the group.[70] One proposal was to focus on purely technical matters, such as diverting an asteroid from hitting Earth or developing a space rescue capability, yet this assumed that technology and politics were separate realms, a questionable claim. Another approach was to seek out scientists and the idea of scientific investigation as a supposedly neutral territory beyond national interests and political ideology, recruiting European members with scientific expertise as payload specialists and enlisting the aid of highly visible scientists and global popular-culture figures such as Jacques Cousteau and Carl Sagan. But the result of such efforts—as evidenced by the lunar cartography fiasco—was as much to politicize science as to depoliticize space exploration. The Soviet participants—especially in the wake of Reagan's promotion of the Strategic

---

[69] Hoover, ASE, Folder 3, questionnaire response from Harrison Schmitt to Russell Schweickart; Folder 4, Schweickart's letter to Mitchell, August 21, 1984; Folder 4, Schweickart letter to astronauts, January 30, 1984; "Astronauts Compile Book to Support Space Exploration," *Orange County Register*, May 30, 1988, b8.

[70] Hoover, ASE, Folder 4, Schweickart letter to Mitchell, August 20, 1984.

Defense Initiative—seemed to understand far better than their American and European counterparts that pretending things were not fraught with political meaning was political precisely because it promoted the political status quo. During negotiations in 1984 in Cernay to create the group, the Soviet side agreed that "we must preserve the image of oneness for future generations, but we also cannot lose contact with the reality of political struggle"[71] Space technology clearly performed military and political work, enhancing military and strategic objectives even while being presented as part of a peaceful scientific program of unlocking the secrets of the cosmos.[72] Patrick Baudry, the second Frenchman in orbit who flew aboard a NASA Shuttle in 1985, encountered the political and military nature of American Space Shuttle technology. His flight provided a first test of Star Wars technology, reflecting the dirty little secret of the supposedly civilian NASA Shuttle missions that many of the payloads were classified military experiments.[73] Perhaps that was why Baudry, who was recruited to attend the first ASE meeting in Paris in October 1985, ultimately declined the invitation, since NASA had made clear that active astronauts should not participate in ASE if they wanted to fly again on a Space Shuttle mission. That threat put the lie to the idea held by many astronauts—including the ASTP astronaut Vance Brand—that they were free agents, supposedly unlike their Soviet cosmonaut counterparts.[74]

Political differences were not the only barrier space travelers encountered in space. Another limitation was conveying the emotional response that many on both sides of the Cold War had experienced in space. During the first-ever space walk in 1965, Leonov had experienced an intense feeling of oneness with the cosmos as he floated, barely tethered, above the earth below and surrounded everywhere else by the black void of the cosmos. In the early 1970s, some American astronauts claimed that the trip into space "sharpened their religious awareness." A guide to the Houston Space Center in 1973 called this the "astro-effect." Like Mitchell, astronaut James Irwin became interested in finding connections between science and spirituality, setting up an organization called "High Flight Inc.," headquartered in Colorado Springs, to "share a message of scientific exploration and religion."[75] The officially atheist Soviets, of course, did not openly profess faith in Jesus Christ, and probably not in

---

71 Hoover, ASE, Folder 1, "May 1985 Progress Report."
72 Hoover, ASE, Folder 3, questionnaire response from Gerald Carr, Joseph Kerwin, Walter Cunningham to Russell Schweickart.
73 Collins, *Europe in Space*, 131–32.
74 Hoover, ASE, Folder 3, questionnaire response from Gordon Fullerton to Russell Schweickart.
75 "Rebirth Conveyed by 'The Man Who Walked in Space,'" *Evening Bulletin*, May 17, 1965, 1; "Astronauts Find God in Space," *San Diego Union*, May 19, 1973, 9.

private, but they did view their experience through a spiritual lens—preferring the Soviet ideological emphasis on universal brotherhood and a greater awareness of the need to be better stewards of the earth.[76] Oleg Makarov, a psychologist and cosmonaut in the Soviet space program, noted that cosmonauts were often men of few words. But when he listened back to transcripts of conversations between cosmonauts and mission control, "within seconds of attaining Earth orbit, every cosmonaut, without exception, be they a dry, reserved flight engineer or a more emotional pilot, uttered the same sort of confused expression of delight and wonder."[77] Schweickart recalled that "by going up into space and back down, we were able to leapfrog the normal barriers which exist to touch and experience each other directly. This magic must be shared."[78]

But how? The main way was through ASE's 1988 publication the *Home Planet*, which its publisher, Addison-Wesley, said "is a book we really expect to put us on the trade publishing map." The book received 200,000 orders in advance of its publication. ASE members had made its publication a priority since the first ASE meeting in Paris in 1985. They hoped that the high-quality photographs and accompanying comments from space travelers testifying to the consciousness-transforming experience of space flight—150 space photographs and 200 comments—would make believers of its readers, especially given the relatively limited impact of the mere news that ASE had formed and former enemies were now embracing and feasting together. The book was republished simultaneously in 1989 across Europe—in Spain, Italy, Sweden, England, France, and Holland—with quotes in 16 different languages representing space travelers from 18 different countries.[79]

ASE believed the book project would create a vital link between the space enterprise and the international public, thus reenergizing public support for space exploration and rekindling utopian hopes for consciousness-raising that the space travelers had experienced by flying into space. It was the same thought that had inspired Frank White's 1987 *The Overview Effect*, published only a year earlier, whose broad impact on both the scholarly community and wider public has been investigated by the Danish scholar Thore Bjørnvig. Bjørnvig argues that White's thesis—like the tradition of cosmism that predated it by decades—provided an overall philosophy, indeed a religious outlook, that has connected the space venture to transformations in consciousness and world view—perhaps mirroring the

---

76 On atheism, spiritualism, and the cosmos: Victoria Smolkin, *A Sacred Space Is Never Empty: A History of Soviet Atheism* (Princeton, NJ: Princeton University Press, 2018).
77 Kelley, *The Home Planet*, unnumbered page in Oleg Makarov, "Preface."
78 Hoover, ASE, Folder 6, Schweickart letter to James Hickman, June 6, 1983.
79 "Book Notes," *New York Times*, June 3, 1988, C28.

way that the modern nation-state as an imagined community in the late nineteenth and early twentieth centuries became an object of sometimes fanatical worship and faith.[80] As with White, ASE's aim was to make the spiritual and aesthetic qualities of space exploration contagious, and thus politically potent, so that those who had not directly experienced it as space travelers could somehow appreciate it vicariously—and perhaps also be more apt to support funding for space programs.

The Home Planet is a feast for the eyes: the stunning blueness and clouds of the earth against the backdrop of utter blackness, three cosmonauts at sunrise marching toward a launch at the Baikonur cosmodrome, the Shuttle Atlantis lifting off, wispy thin clouds over southern Africa, a massive tropical storm over the Pacific Ocean, brilliant panoramas of deep blue ocean, pictures of astronauts and cosmonauts on space walks, suspended against the blackness over the blueness of the planet below. The book contains images of the moon and the iconic Blue Marble, dramatic multicolored dawns and dusks from space, auroras, and eclipses. Reviewers were thrilled by the dramatic images, calling the book "an entrancing taste of the space experience" and focusing on the emotional and aesthetic, rather than scientific, aspects of space flight.[81] Given the widespread press *The Home Planet* received—and the substantial sales, along with White's book at nearly the same time—the project was certainly a public relations success for the idea that space exploration had enormous implications for the future of human civilization. The more artistically inclined cosmonauts and astronauts, such as Aleksei Leonov and Russell Schweickart, who went on a tour of the United States and Soviet Union to promote the book, believed that paeans to the beauty of the earth could launch people to a place in inner space—the grey matter between their ears—that was beyond their ideological beliefs or national allegiances.[82] They echoed a point that White had made in his 1987 book *The Overview Effect*: "Just as people who had never seen a slave could become adherents of the abolitionist cause, so can those who have never been in space support a vigorous space exploration program." White called these people "Terranauts" and while he realized that "it is not possible to fully replicate the Overview Effect without going into space, similar experiences are available to us all. They can be used as foundations for personal growth and transformation [...] in support of a

---

80 Thore Bjørnvig, "Outer Space Religion and the Overview Effect: A Critical Inquiry into a Classic of the Pro-Space Movement," *Astropolitics: The International Journal of Space Politics & Policy* 11, nos. 1–2 (2013), 4–24.
81 "The View from the Outside," *New Scientist*, October 8, 1988, 57; "Lofty Vision from Outer Space," *Los Angeles Times*, October 28, 1988, 14.
82 "Space Mission on Earth," *USA today*, October 21, 1988, 2.

more peaceful, self-aware, and ecologically careful species."[83] White's view was a common sentiment among the founders of the ASE, not to mention figures in the counterculture ethos of the 1970s that had inspired its creation. It embodied the utopian hope, also a feature of Russian cosmism, that radical estrangement from familiar space would cause a shift in thinking that would make new forms of cooperation and planetary consciousness possible.

But even among the space travelers few became Terranauts; they stubbornly remained Frenchmen, Russians, Germans, Bulgarians, and Poles. The trick, as the Association of Space Explorers put it, was "respecting national interests and international relationships, while rising above their limits."[84] Jean-Loup Chrétien envisioned a unified Europe from space but one that still seemed to privilege its Western and Mediterranean parts. "Around 6 p.m. we were flying north of the Mediterranean, almost right above Marseilles," he wrote, echoing the tendency among space travelers to remark first upon the view of their childhood home. "I know this region well, since I lived there more than twenty years." But then Chretien began to expand his view, taking in all of "France, Corsica, Sardinia, Italy, part of Spain." He also noticed the south—but not north—of England and "part of Germany." He then realized that he could see a good bit of the globe, "all the while distinguishing without difficulty the little details of the place where I was wandering on foot some weeks earlier." To make one of his trips into space more tolerable, Chrétien sponsored a competition among chefs to come up with tastier space food than the drab Soviet fare. "So in a bold gesture aimed partly at improving the cosmonauts' standard of living and partly at giving a little publicity to French cuisine, bids were invited from French food companies in late 1987 to supply cordon bleu meals for the Franco-Soviet flight." The Bulgarian cosmonaut Georgi Ivanov also sought out the comfort of his ancestral homeland when he flew into space. "I remembered my childhood, my hometown of Lovech, the mountains, my relatives, and of course my mother."[85] Not even the experience of space travel was powerful enough to replace national and regional identities with something more universal. Yet the experience of radical estrangement did add another layer of understanding—one that broadened the space traveler's perspective and allowed for an awareness of one's place, not only in a national and local context, but also in the greater cosmos. Ultimately, global and national identities were not necessarily mutually exclusive, just as

---

83 Hoover, ASE, Folder 3, September 6, 1984 draft statement of purpose; Frank White, *The Overview Effect: Space Exploration and Human Evolution* (Boston: Houghton Mifflin, 1987), 68, 70, 72–73.
84 Hoover, ASE, Folder 4, Schweickart letter to astronauts, January 30, 1984.
85 Collins, *Europe in Space*, 138; Kelley, *The Home Planet*, 81, 89.

nation-states have often successfully integrated regional and local identities into the broader nation.

Having traveled to the abstract and spiritual realms of transnational utopia, the next chapter returns to Earth and to the technical designers of the ASTP. It writes the story from the inside out, beginning with engineering design. The focus is on the docking engineers and the main nonhuman protagonist of ASTP: the *Androginno-periferiinyi agregat stykovki*, or, in English, the androgynous peripheral assembly system, known by its acronym APAS. Unlike the lunar mapping project, or the ambitious but unrealized utopias of ASE or Harvest Moon, APAS seemed to succeed as a unifying force precisely because it embodied the idea of collaboration in a mechanical object whose sole, unambiguous purpose was to connect people and things. In so doing it made the goal of peaceful cooperation more tangible as both a sociopolitical and physical reality. Of course, whether that was enough to challenge the Cold War imaginary was another question.

Chapter 3

ANDROGYNOUS COUPLING, TECHNOLOGICAL FIXES, AND THE ENGINEERING OF PEACE

Chapter 1 told the history of ASTP from the perspective of the principal political and diplomatic actors who attempted to use the supposedly neutral sphere of space science and engineering to reset superpower relations. This chapter covers similar terrain but reverses the order of analysis by examining the perspective of the engineers and how they attempted to design a technical solution to the political challenges of détente. Put another way, I discuss the engineering and design of technological fixes to solve the political problem of averting mutual assured destruction (MAD). The goal is to determine how well those fixes functioned politically (as a way to de-escalate tensions between the superpowers) and technically (by enhancing the safety and effectiveness of human habitation in space).

The term "technological fix" was coined in the 1960s by the director of Oakridge National Laboratories, Alvin Weinberg. The basic idea was hardly new. Modern faith in technology had produced a mania for technological fixes, a belief that "solutions founded on technological innovation may be innately superior for addressing issues traditionally defined as social, political, or cultural."[1] The main attraction of the technological fix is that it promises to bypass the cultural and political challenges of changing behaviors and attitudes by shifting the problem to the supposedly objective realm of technical problem-solving, and to the experts and engineers who supposedly have only technical rather than partisan goals. For example, advocates of nuclear power in the 1960s, like solar or wind power today, presented it as a solution to the economic and political dilemmas of fossil-fuel dependence. If it worked as planned, politicians would avoid the hard work of changing deeply entrenched behaviors of energy consumption, providing a cheap way to produce and consume power that would also protect the environment. It was a case of having

---

1 Sean Johnston, "Alvin Weinberg and the Promotion of the Technological Fix," *Technology and Culture* 59, no. 3 (2018), 621.

your cake (energy independence and a cheap power source) and eating it too (blissfully tapping into the electric grid without destroying the environment).

ASTP was a technological fix designed to make superpower relations less dangerous and more secure, and it had the added benefit of advancing the cause of space exploration. Up to that point, with US troops mired in Vietnam and Soviet troops blasting away hopes of reforming communism in Czechoslovakia, little else seemed to be working to mitigate the literally explosive potential of superpower relations. As noted elsewhere in the book, discussions among politicians and managers in the first Nixon presidency had resulted in various memoranda of agreement for collaboration with Brezhnev, which prepared the handoff (or perhaps a Hail Mary, to continue the American football analogy) of the political challenge of détente into the open arms of aerospace engineers. The technical problem of collaboration was hashed out among Soviet and American engineers in the 1970 discussions, who now occupied ground zero in the techno-politics of détente.

Negotiations focused first on a linkup between the Soviets and the nascent Skylab project at NASA (which would be launched in 1973 and 1974). But due to the existing designs of docking systems for both sides, the Soviets quickly rejected this idea as requiring joint construction of not just the docking mechanisms but of all other aspects of launch and capsule systems to permit the docking. This was because existing docking systems, as conceived by Soviet and American engineers, involved one spaceship (the male) penetrating the other (the female), and neither side had the will, time, or money to figure out who was going to penetrate and who was going to be penetrated, much less how to redesign existing systems to accommodate the penetrating/penetration (they were all men). As is often the case in technological fixes, the fix itself creates a whole new set of problems that make the "fix" seem more like a new problem in need of additional fixing. Such a redesign, from the Soviet point of view, would have meant supplying sensitive information about the design of their systems that might not be reciprocated by the American side (the same fears that doomed the joint lunar mapping project discussed in the previous chapter). Moreover, the Soviet task seemed primarily to provide support services for the star attraction, that is, the new technology of the American Skylab. Besides, Brezhnev and Nixon both wanted a quick fix as well as a technological one, and linking up with Skylab was neither quick nor technologically simple. While the discussions were at first tense and marked by mutual suspicion, the more engineers and managers from both sides talked, the more relaxed the atmosphere became. As with the political principals and managers, the Soviet engineers appreciated the informality and openness of the American partners, as well as their hard working, hard partying spirit, and this facilitated an atmosphere of trust that encouraged the search for a design principle that would maintain parity and mutual respect.²

Still, the technical challenges were daunting, and bound to be made even more challenging because of the political demand for parity. "To realize a docking by means of identical mechanisms [...] was impossible," noted the Soviet flight director Eliseev, because that meant designing and building everything from scratch. The only solution was to find a universal docking mechanism that would connect peripherally to the two existing systems (Apollo and Soyuz), and thus allow both sides to meet each other in space on their own terms and in their own space systems. It would take more than two years from 1970 to work out the design for the mechanism, during which the quest for parity would be challenged by the different nature of both systems. For example, the United States used pure oxygen in space, while the Soviets used a mixture that was closer to air on Earth as a blend of oxygen and nitrogen. This meant that the different internal environments would mix during docking, depending on which crew was the visitor and which the host. The visitors would therefore have to enter the docking module and adapt to the air of the host. So if a neutral space between the two could be created it could provide for the transfer of one crew to the other system as the transferring crew adopted to the breathing system of the other. As the mission continued, each system would take turns adapting to the needs of the other, practicing survival in a foreign but friendly environment.³ The engineering challenge thus dovetailed with the sociopolitical challenge of providing an interface between two fundamentally different systems without one system dominating the other and imposing its will on the other. The end result was that everyone survived. The outcome not only of the mission but also of détente would hinge on the ability to maintain the appearance, if not reality, of technical parity, thereby placing engineering into the forefront of finding a way back from the brink of nuclear holocaust that aerospace engineers, of course, had also helped to design.

The Buddha of Docking

Vladimir Syromiatnikov, the lead docking engineer for the Soviet side, enthusiastically embraced the challenge of finding a politically and technically functional docking design. He is a remarkable and underappreciated figure in space history who garnered all the Soviet, Russian, and international accolades that an aerospace engineer could receive: the Lenin Prize in 1975, the NASA Distinguished Public Service Medal, the prize in his name with the

---

2 A. S. Eliseev, *Zhizn': Kaplia v more* (Moscow: Aviatsiia i kosmonavtika, 1998), 100–102.
3 Eliseev, *Zhizn'*, 103; on the engineering idea for this system for equalizing air systems from October 1973: ARAN, F. 1678, op. 1, ll. 67–68.

International Association for the Advancement of Safety, and many others. He taught himself English and then French, which he quickly mastered through collaborations with both NASA and the French space program.[4] Until his death in 2006 from leukemia he continued to teach new generations of engineers in a number of institutes. He was an enthusiastic advocate of computer systems and technology, which made perfect sense, since the utopian ideas often associated with the early days of computer connectivity dovetailed with his notions about the deep importance, symbolically and physically, of the very act of docking, whether on Earth or in space. His mission was therefore far broader than ASTP and involved nothing less than creating a "school of docking," as the famous Soviet space engineer Boris Chertok noted, with disciples who would carry on his socio-technical vision of a global space network that would link "the space systems of Russia, America and Europe" and, in so doing, provide bridges across cultures, languages, and ideologies.[5]

Born in 1933 in Archangel, Syromiatnikov was one year older than Yuri Gagarin. Like the first cohort of cosmonauts, he was a child of the horrors of World War II, experiencing the humiliation, suffering, and extreme privations of the Nazi invasion. His father was a vice-provost at the Archangel Forest Institute who had narrowly avoided arrest during Stalin's Great Terror for associating with supposed enemies of the people. His mother and father moved to Leningrad and the young Vladimir went with his sister to Moscow to live with relatives, later joining his parents in Leningrad just as the Nazis invaded. During the war the family was evacuated from Leningrad, undergoing the infamous 900 Day Siege by surrounding Nazi forces, and moved to Gorky Oblast', and then in August 1945 to the city of Stroitel' in the Moscow Oblast'. The younger Syromiatnikov went to primary school in the Moscow Oblast' city of Kaliningrad (now named after the rocket engineer and his future patron Korolev), which was a center for military–industrial production, and in the late 1940s emerged as the hub of strategic rocket and space programs. The experiences of the war, combined with the romance of space exploration, drew him to aerospace engineering in the late Stalin years. After finishing school, where he excelled in both his studies as well as sports and chess, he studied engineering at the famous Bauman Higher Technical Institute and then, in 1956, joined OKB-1 NII-88, the center for the space

---

4 When working with American counterparts he refused the services of translators and insisted on speaking English. He would double-check and correct all official NASA translations of his conversations into English, which often held up the official acceptance of meeting minutes. Interview with Caldwell Johnson, May 12, 1998, League City Texas, NASA Johnson Space Center Oral History Project, 54–55.
5 Syromiatnikov, *100 rasskazov Chast' 1*, 6.

and missile industry run by the father of Soviet rocketry, or Chief Engineer as he was known publicly until his death in 1966, Sergei Korolev. The young engineer worked in the strategically vital area of developing missile guidance systems and the development and deployment of payloads—satellites, dogs, and people—into orbit.[6]

Syromiatnikov's early inspiration in the Soviet military–industrial complex, according to Chertok, was to achieve the strategic parity with the United States and thus prevent a repeat of the horrors of invasion and mass death at the hands of the Nazis.[7] It was common for those who came of age and studied in the immediate postwar period to devote themselves to technical fields—rocketry, telemetry, radar, nuclear technology, telecommunications, and computers. This was their way of capturing some of the glory of their elders who fought against Nazis. Too young to fight on the front lines of the war, and thus to enjoy the prestige and honor that came from active military service during the war, Syromiatnikov's generation compensated by developing strategically important technologies to fight the next battle in what soon would be called the Cold War.

With the dropping of the bombs on Hiroshima and Nagasaki, and the fresh memories of the horrors of war, Syromiatnikov's generation needed little motivation to excel in their studies, which they ultimately hoped would contribute to making the Soviet Union the economic, military, and technological equal of the United States. A testament to his talents and personality, Syromiatnikov began working almost immediately after Sputnik as a senior engineer in charge of producing durable objects for use in the vacuum of space. He was enthusiastic, curious, and optimistic. He continued his studies as a graduate student in the mechanical engineering department at Moscow State University in 1962, where he also worked with other professors and students to design and construct objects for the various missions of the Soviet space program. The dramatic successes of Sputnik and then of Gagarin's flight were a confirmation of the success of the collective efforts of thousands of engineers and a promise of even greater things to come. In 1968 he defended his doctoral dissertation on the gauges that he had designed for long duration in space. Like many of his colleagues, he retained close links between theoretical and academic work and translating those ideas into reality. He thus forged close ties to the academic world until the end of his life, working in the classroom as an engineering and computer science professor (professor of

---

6 Vladimir Syromiatnikov, biografiia i deiatel'nost', http://yubik.net.ru/publ/59-1-0-10329?fbclid=IwAR1g55eDTnQMgxoKhA-Lmf_TWxqZPAJ_DvXaG1RJvEvO UrMHzbTv1_pVNls.

7 Syromiatnikov,*100 rasskazov Chast'1*, 6.

technical cybernetics at Moscow State University), in addition to a manager and designer in the Soviet and Russian space programs. In 1979 he became a doctor of technical sciences and in 1989 achieved the highest academic title in the Soviet Union of "Professor."[8]

He was well liked, curious, good-natured, hardworking, creative, and constantly aware of the connections between the technological and human worlds. He often carried a notepad in which he could sketch out design ideas wherever they might appear in his mind's eye. His American colleagues affectionately called him "Big Cheese" ("Syr" in Russian means cheese).[9] Many have an enduring image of him riding the public trolley, intensely devouring some book, either technical or literary. He attempted to bridge what C. P. Snow in the West called the "Two Cultures" of humanities and sciences and what Soviets referred to as the divide between the lyricists and the engineers. As such, he hardly fit the profile advanced by some historians of the narrowly educated Soviet engineer unable to see the broader connections between technology and society.[10] His favorite artist was the poet, actor, and singer Vladimir Vysotskii, whose lyrics and songs he knew by heart (he honored the legendary singer, actor, and songwriter at his gravestone in 1980, along with the cosmonaut Georgii Grechko). He developed a long list of colleagues and friends in the secret and open worlds of Soviet engineering and academia, and then internationally (becoming the first Russian citizen in 1995 to become an acting member of the American Institute of Aeronautics and Astronautics as well as the International Academy of Astronautics). A personal talent for connecting with people was reflected in his professional engineering interest in designing mechanisms to link objects in space. Those objects, in turn, would join different cultures and political systems into heterogenous networks that would unite people to different political systems, and to the technological devices and artifacts that modern industrial civilization had produced. To use the term of the French philosopher and historian of technology Bruno Latour, the new society that he enabled through docking would be "technology made durable": an amalgam of human and nonhuman actors crossing the Cold War divide between the United States and Soviet

---

8 Syromiatnikov, biografiia i deiatel'nost', http://yubik.net.ru/publ/59-1-0-10329?fbclid=IwAR1g55eDTnQMgxoKhA-Lmf_TWxqZPAJ_DvXaG1RJvEvOUrMHzbTv1_pVNls.

9 Patricia Sullivan, "Vladimir Syromiatnikov Designed Docking System for Space Capsules," *Washington Post*, October 1, 2006, https://www.washingtonpost.com/wp-dyn/content/article/2006/09/30/AR2006093001038.html.

10 For the argument that the Soviet system produced narrowly educated engineers: Loren Graham, *The Ghost of the Executed Engineer: Technology and the Fall of the Soviet Union* (Cambridge, MA: Harvard University Press, 1993).

Union.[11] Syromiatnikov later imagined himself as a Soviet Hermes, the divine trickster of ancient Greek mythology who was a protector of roads and travelers. Hermes could move freely between the divine and human worlds and cross boundaries and barriers, just like the androgynous docking mechanisms he designed.[12]

Engineering for Safety

For Syromiatnikov, docking, whether at sea or in space, is always a moment of heightened importance. As a technical accomplishment it requires a carefully planned, precise and choreographed maneuvering of immense objects. Getting it wrong can have disastrous and deadly consequences, but especially in space, with capsules the size of tractor trailers moving at 25,000 miles per hour. In some ways the act of docking was similar to a mating ritual, and it certainly has invited such imagery. But the parallel breaks down if one considers the careful planning required for a successful docking. It lacks spontaneity and uses mechanical steering and guidance systems far removed from the points of contact. Syromiatnikov also enjoyed docking as a test of his ability to calculate the trajectory of objects traveling thousands of miles an hour through various atmospheric layers and into the vacuum of space, and under the complex gravitational pulls of multiple celestial objects. Once completed, the act of docking connected humans across physical spaces, allowing for the exchange of much-needed supplies and human company. With the completion of the technical phases of docking that linked one physical system with another, docking then became cultural, linguistic, political, and social, as people from far away, and often living in isolation for long periods of time, suddenly were able to step across the threshold of their ship and into a different world.

For Syromiatnikov the creative challenge of uniting two very different space systems, designed and built in completely different social and political contexts, was an almost religious experience of witnessing universal connectedness. The feeling was similar to the "overview effect" experienced by cosmonauts and astronauts viewing the earth from space and discussed in the previous chapter. Making these connections physically possible transformed

---

11 Bruno Latour, "Technology Is Society Made Durable," *Sociological Review* 38, no. 1 (1990), 103–31. Latour developed the concept of Actor Network Theory: Michel Callon, "Society in the Making: The Study of Technology as a Tool for Sociological Analysis," in Wiebe E. Bijker, Thomas P. Hughes, and Trevor Pinch, eds., *The Social Construction of Technological Systems: New Directions in the Sociology and History of Technology* (Cambridge, MA: MIT Press, 1987), 83–103.

12 Vladimir Syromiatnikov, *100 rasskazov o stykovke i o drugikh prikliucheniakh v kosmose i na zemle, Chast' 2, 20 let spustia* (Moscow: Logos, 2010), 212.

the docking engineer and planner into a potentially powerful agent of change. No wonder Syromiatnikov thought of himself as a modern-day Hermes. At one point he described his role as a theater director. "Cosmonautics became a specific art under the dome of the universe with millions of people as its audience." He frequently referred to his docking technologies, and the new kinds of worlds their connections created, as instruments of "destiny."[13] He noted that individual space ships, like human beings, had limited utility; they had to be connected with each other to engage in meaningful work, a task he and his Soviet associates began to pursue with the success of the first Vostok missions.[14] The moment of docking was pregnant with transformative possibility, marked by intense emotions, feelings of danger, hope, and the anticipation of new things to come. It made perfect sense, therefore, that political leaders in the original Nixon–Kosygin accords immediately identified docking as the logical starting point for the policy of détente. "Docking, by definition" as Syromiatnikov was fond of saying, "is already a form of cooperation."[15] In one of his many philosophical moments, Syromiatnikov connected his engineering to a grander vision of a new kind of world:

> During time of the ancient Greeks the gods did not live so high above people on Mt. Olympus, less than 3000 meters above sea level. The more civilization developed, the higher the gods rose, and the further away they went from people. We did not meet them in our orbits around Earth or to the Moon. The more deeply and broader we learned about the surrounding space, the more mysterious the forces in the sky became. It was just as the first space-rocket scientist K. Tsiolkovskii imagined: the more we penetrate the universe, the more mysterious and inexplicable the world becomes, governed by some unclear first organizing principle. Tsiolkovskii operated with terrestrial and heavenly categories, trying to connect them with the help of his multi-stage rockets. He deified humanity, its origin and intellect. He believed in humanity, in the ability of people to colonize the universe, starting with its own cradle—Earth. In order to continue this journey it was necessary to divorce ourselves of short-term motives and profit, to move away from politics, to transcend the borders that divide people on earth. Perhaps then Hermes would again move closer to people and fulfill his mission: to be a protector of shepherds and travelers, rocket engineers and cosmonauts, and also

---

13 Vladimir Syromiatnikov, *100 Stories about Docking and Other Adventures in Space and on Earth* (Moscow: Universitetskaia kniga, 2005), 14, 18.
14 Syromiatnikov, *100 Stories*, 134–35.
15 Ibid., 13, 391.

trade and profit. He will facilitate mutually advantageous international cooperation, to put it into stilted language.[16]

If docking had great potential cultural and political significance for Syromiatnikov it also reflected an aspect of engineering that had been conspicuously ignored in the early years of the space race and Cold War, that is, safety. The Cold War in the late 1940s had greatly increased the tolerance for risk-taking in politics and technology, dramatically raising the stakes of victory or defeat as both sides began to develop large arsenals of weapons of mass destruction. As scholars have noted, ideas about risks and safety were couched in the language of scientific objectivity but were themselves socially constructed, often in accordance with the desires of powerful economic and political interests.[17] A high tolerance for risk-taking and dangerous technology had produced the doctrine of MAD and transformed strategic superpower parity into a game of chicken with weapons of mass destruction aimed at each other. The appetite for risk-taking, however, was not limitless and together with high-profile disasters and technological failures it could produce new regimes focused on risk reduction and safety, as reflected in the new move toward arms control and limiting the testing of nuclear weapons after the Cuban Missile Crisis. An increasing awareness of the negative consequences of excessive risk, including the possibility of destroying the earth, the damage to the environment highlighted by Rachel Carson, the use of Agent Orange in Vietnam, the accidents that led to deaths in both the US and Soviet space programs—all these things and more helped to generate a new focus on safety in the 1960s and 1970s.

ASTP emerged from a nascent global culture of safety in the 1960s. It marked a transition from a politics based on risk-taking to a politics focused on global and individual security. The "test" of the Apollo-Soyuz Test Project (ASTP), for example, was to save lives in space in the event of a catastrophic failure of a crewed ship or station in orbit, and speaking more broadly, the saving of lives by preventing nuclear war between the United States and the Soviet Union. Syromiatnikov claimed that his American colleagues, in part, had been inspired by the 1969 Hollywood movie, *Marooned*, featuring a blockbuster cast of Gene Hackman, Gregory Peck, and James Franciscus. It hit theaters as both sides were launching into negotiations in 1970 for the docking project that was to anchor

---

16 Syromiatnikov, *100 rasskazov, Chast' 2*, 216.
17 On the social construction of risk: Scott Sagan, *The Limits of Safety: Organizations, Accidents and Nuclear Weapons* (Princeton, NJ: Princeton University Press, 1993); Diane Vaughn, *The Challenger Launch Decision: Risky Technology, Culture and Deviance at NASA* (Chicago: Chicago University Press, 1996).

détente.¹⁸ In the film a Soviet spacecraft comes to the rescue of a disabled American spacecraft in orbit. One astronaut has already died and the other two were drifting into unconsciousness. But the Soviet spacecraft was too small to accommodate the two astronauts and lacked oxygen for them. Fatally, it also lacked compatible mechanisms for docking with the American spacecraft. An American rescue vehicle finally arrived and the Soviet cosmonaut helped to rescue the two surviving astronauts. The movie highlighted the central problem of crewed space flight, namely, the extreme risk associated with having no backup safety and rescue system. Flipping the script of the movie and preventing death in space would require a universal docking mechanism that spaceships of any design could use to facilitate the rescue. To borrow from Syromiatnikov's interest in Greek mythology, the spirit of Ares, the God of War, had inspired the Cold War and its appetite for risk-taking. Hermes (who in Greek mythology also rescued Ares from imprisonment) would bring the world back to peace and safety. As Syromiatnikov once remarked, modern space technology was the "inheritor of ancient Greek mythology," embodying all its contradictions but also meanings and lessons.¹⁹

ASTP was thus an important test case in the creation of both technical and political regimes of safety during the Cold War. In the interests of safety, both sides had to learn to adapt to the systems of command and control of the other. The Soviet flight director noted that neither side had the right to take measures that would put the other side's crew at risk. This guiding principle was central to the larger policies of détente, which were based on the notion that the actions taken by one side could put all lives at risk. Creating ever more elaborate regimes of mutual dependence would in turn heighten a mutual appreciation of safety and security.²⁰

Syromiatnikov was a new breed of engineer valued for his ability to make the Cold War, and space travel more generally, safer for its participants. He had the added advantage, unlike his American colleagues, of witnessing the horrors and insecurities of World War II, which had inspired the risky quest for parity in nuclear weaponry and rocketry, but paradoxically had also made the world a much more dangerous place in the process. From his privileged vantage point deep within the Soviet military–industrial complex, he had turned space engineering from a weapon of war and into an instrument of peace activism. Of course, the very act of docking was itself a risky procedure. "Docking is never a routine event!" he once wrote.²¹ But just as defense intellectuals could

---

18 Syromiatnikov, *100 Stories*, 378–79.
19 Syromiatnikov, *100 rasskazov, Chast' 2*, 220.
20 Eliseev, *Zhizn'*, 104–5.
21 Syromiatnikov, *100 Stories*, 375.

imagine that weapons of mass destruction could be "peacekeepers" and prevent war, the risks associated with docking could pay dividends—if the docking worked—by improving the chances that the superpowers could survive the disastrous consequences of their own ideological and military divisions.

Moscow to Houston: We Have a Docking Problem

Even before ASTP, both sides were separately working on a docking system that the ASTP would dub the "APAS" (*Androginno-periferiinyi agregat stykovki*, or androgynous peripheral assembly system for the American side). Its roots go back to the mid-1960s, when the Soviet engineers, led by Korolev and Syromiatnikov were attempting to develop a new docking mechanism between different Soviet capsules. Prior to ASTP, the Soviets were using a "mama and papa" docking technology (the colloquial reference among Soviet engineers for the "shtyr'-konus") that was obviously gendered and involved a passive and active partner. The Americans had used a similar design referred to more formally by NASA engineers (also all male) as "male–female." These types of docking systems required the penetration of one capsule by the other, which would cause one side (given the male-dominated and macho engineering cultures on both sides) "to feel their position of humiliation," in addition to the added burden of having to design both capsules to accommodate penetration.[22]

The design idea for the mama–papa system, said Syromiatnikov, came from "the age-old principle of mating on Earth mastered by Mother Nature [...] two free-flying spacecraft, similar to buses in size and mass, would get coupled and then structurally engaged, and then would fly in this mode until separation." Similar to their counterparts in the world of defense intellectuals in the United States, the Soviet engineers often imagined their work in sexual terms.[23] Mating thus became a convenient shorthand for complex engineering couplings. Through the mid-1960s docking simulations were popular events among space managers, engineers, and politicians in the OKB-1 NII-88 facility, a kind of mechanical peep show. "Docking became a popular performance, something like an erotic show of a space character," remembered

---

22 Natalya Serkova, World Wide Gold, *e-flux*, no. 93, 2018, https://www.e-flux.com/journal/93/213267/world-wide-gold/; Viktor Khokhlov, "Kuda khodiat mechty: razmyshleniia v godovshchinu kosmicheskogo iubileia," *Gefter*, March 23, 2015, http://gefter.ru/archive/14617.
23 For the sexual images and language of strategic defense in the Pentagon: Caron Cohn, "Sex and Death in the Rational World of Defense Intellectuals," *Signs* 12, no. 4, (1987), 687–71.

Syromiatnikov. "Hold the stallion," said one engineer, positioning the probe at the entrance of the cone.[24]

But even before the planned docking with the Americans, the chief engineer Korolev had been frustrated by the technical limitations of the mama–papa docking systems. The Soviets in the early 1960s were moving from merely launching capsules into space to actually joining them together, like Lego pieces, for projects involving longer-term habitation and space colonization. He pushed Syromiatnikov to design a new kind of docking system, fundamentally different from the mama–papa system, that would create a pressurized tunnel between the two docked spaceships and not require the reengineering of both ships to accommodate the "mama–papa" penetration (one as the penetrator and the other as the receiver). Syromiatnikov had continued to work on that system even after Korolev died in 1966 and Gagarin's death in 1968. "The docking system we designed and developed in 1968–70 had androgynous docking rings with a set of structural latches," wrote Syromiatnikov, though they had not yet coined the term "androgynous" to describe that system. Those latches were designed to attach to both docking ships and produce a pressurized transfer tunnel once the capsules had connected to each other externally.[25]

While both sides appeared to have been in various stages of producing docking systems based on the androgynous concept, the first meetings in 1970 between American and Soviet engineers on October 24 and 26 in Moscow (referred to later as "Great October Revolution in the relationship between cosmonautics and astronautics") initially contemplated using the more conventional docking systems. The Americans thus first proposed "an Apollo-type receiving cone to be installed into the Soviet transfer tunnel," which the American engineer Caldwell Johnson illustrated with slides of a Gemini capsule docking in which "the active part is placed on the nosecone. […] This is the classic conception of the male and female part." The proposal, however, was a nonstarter as the Soviets had no intention of being the passive partner. Said Syromiatnikov: "Our goal was to have a full-fledged and equal partnership on a joint project with such activities as engineering and design, followed by the development and testing of the new concept with actual docking in space, namely—APAS."[26] Truth be told, the Americans were also dissatisfied with the design, and like the Soviets they had also been contemplating a new

---

24 Syromiatnikov, *100 Stories*, 164, 168–69, 177.
25 Ibid., 339–40, 379, 395.
26 Syromiatnikov, *100 Stories*, 339–40, 379, 395. Caldwell Johnson's presentation in Moscow is contained in: Caldwell Johnson Presentation, Moscow, October 26, 1970, ARAN, f. 1678, o. 1, d. 108shch, ll. 43–53.

docking system. Caldwell Johnson, Syromiatnikov's NASA counterpart, explained that their male–female system meant that the docking mechanism

> occupies the very passageway that you want to open [...] and it should not be that way, because all kinds of things can go wrong. If you can't get it out of there properly, then it's no use to even have docked it [...] it's like having everything in the doorway. Even after you connect, you can't open the doors because you've got all this stuff in the way.

The Americans therefore came into the negotiations prepared to consider a new design approach after their male–female proposal clearly fell flat with the Soviet engineers.[27] It was an instance where the technical and political requirements of the design seemed to coincide. The "mama–papa" system was unacceptable because of the patriarchal attitudes that shaped Cold War politics (that neither side wanted to be the submissive, penetrated partner) but also because it would have been technically problematic, as well as prohibitively expensive, to redesign the capsules of both sides to accommodate the penetration of one by the other.

Johnson thus sketched out the desired attributes of a future system, which just so happened to reflect the new docking system that Syromiatnikov had already been designing for linkups between Soyuz and Salyut capsules in the Soviet space fleet for the past two years. "First," said Johnson at the meeting, "the mechanism should be androgynous, that is, it could be grabbed onto from either side and would not have a male and female part." During the docking either side could play the role of active or passive partner, meaning that one would agree to be active and initiate docking maneuvers, and the other would agree to be passive and stay still, so that both sides could then grab each other. Either side could also be the active or passive partner in disengaging.[28] Years later Johnson recalled, "We had lucked out and had prepared ourselves for the very thing that they wanted to talk about when they got to it." If the Soviets immediately understood the design principle that Johnson was proposing, precisely because they had already been working on it and would propose the same concept at the October meeting right after Johnson, they were a bit perplexed by the word "androgynous," which appears misspelled in the Russian translation of the meeting transcription in the Academy of Sciences archive as "endogennyi" instead of

---

27 Interview with Caldwell Johnson, April 1, 1998, League City Texas, NASA Johnson Space Center Oral History Project, 22–23.
28 Caldwell Johnson Presentation, Moscow, October 26, 1970, ARAN, f. 1678, o. 1, d. 108shch, ll. 43–53.

"androginnyi."[29] The Soviet translator apparently did not understand the meaning of the word "androgynous" that Johnson had used. Syromiatnikov admitted as much, noting that Johnson right after the meeting "enlightened" him on the subject. As Johnson explained it in 1998, the idea of an "androgynous" mechanism had been bantered about in NASA conversations even before the meeting with Syromiatnikov.

> We used the term "androgynous," that is, no sex, no male, no female type of thing, which, see, the old probe and drogue was. So you couldn't have two male spacecraft or two female spacecraft docked. So we wanted something that was neuter, either one. And so we devised this thing—it's a hole with things around it that would get together this way instead of something going this way. We worked that thing.

The American side, like the Soviet side, was "stunned" by the convergence of design, politics, and engineering. Johnson recalled he "had no idea this thing would move so fast. [...] And I almost dropped my teeth, you know."[30] The technological fix for superpower relations was in.

The simple idea, then, of an androgynous docking system was that two distinct systems could be docked without one having to be penetrated by the other. The "APAS" would have grabbing mechanisms attached to both objects to be docked, with a passageway created between them when they interlocked. The engineering and design of either object would not depend on the engineering and design of the object to which it would attach. Depending on the circumstance, one side could be the active partner (initiating the grabbing) and the other the passive partner in the docking (waiting for the embrace), but the roles could also be reversed. It was a hug in space. The design itself was both a clever solution to avoiding reengineering the capsules of both sides so that they could dock, and an attempt to disarm the idea of sexual domination in the Cold War implied by previous "mama–papa" docking designs. In this way the basic docking system design for ASTP had been agreed upon, along with a description that distinguished it from the previous generation of "mama–papa" docking technologies both sides had used. By mid-1971 the

---

29 Interview with Caldwell Johnson, April 1, 1998, League City Texas, NASA Johnson Space Center Oral History Project, 24; Caldwell Johnson Presentation, Moscow, October 26, 1970, ARAN, f. 1678, o. 1, d. 108shch, ll. 43–53. Syromiatnikov's presentation that followed Johnson proposed the same concept as Johnson, though he did not yet call it "androgynous." ARAN, F. 1678, o. 1, d. 108shch, ll. 54–62.

30 Interview with Caldwell Johnson, April 1, 1998, League City Texas, NASA Johnson Space Center Oral History Project, 24–25; April 27, 1999, 58.

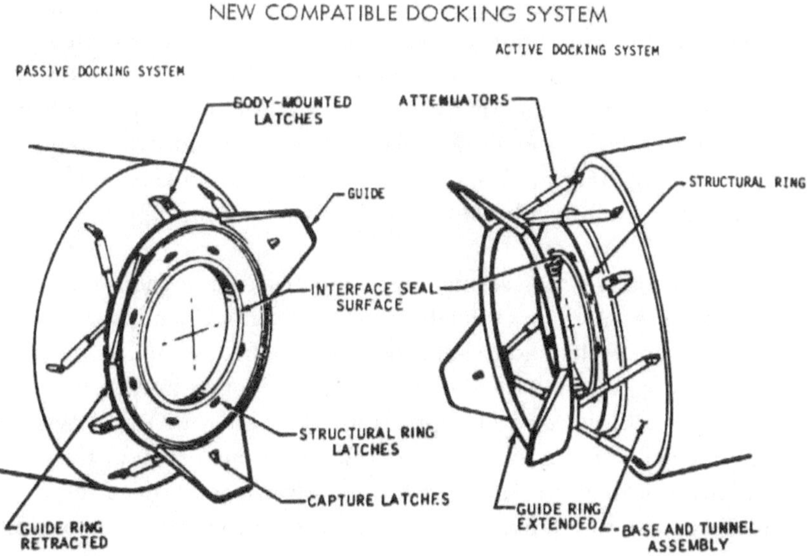

Figure 3.1 A drawing of the APAS design
Source: NASA

mechanism was officially dubbed "androgynous," derived from the "androgyne" of Greek mythology. It was both functionally superior to the mama–papa design and also met the political demands of détente—a seamless blend, seemingly, of technology and politics.[31] Syromiatnikov would spend the next four years working with his American colleagues to develop the new system and translate it into a physical reality that ultimately became a universal interface and docking mechanism for space linkups all the way to the present day.

Syromiatnikov did admit that the "mating of identical parts, such as fire hose flanges or railway couplers," was not entirely novel. The design itself was a simple solution to a complex problem, like so many successful designs for functional objects and mechanisms. What made the approach unique was to apply it to the immensely more complex task of docking superpower rivals in space. "We were to connect two identical docking rings with a complex configuration, comprised of many different elements."[32] Syromiatnikov himself became obsessed with the idea of androgyneity, having just learned it from his American colleague in the October 1970 meeting. He named his dog "Apasik" and after the Soviet Union collapsed produced a line of vodka

---

31 Syromiatnikov, *100 Stories*, 418.
32 Syromiatnikov, *100 Stories*, 340.

called Apasnaya, a play on the Russian word for dangerous "opasnaia," and trademarked the term "Androgynovka" for his vodka line. He incorporated androgyneity into his daily conversation after the "October Revolution" meeting, regaling two poor American women at a Houston party after a day of working on APAS "about androgynous creatures and structures that, according to the myths of ancient Greece, were miracle workers."[33] In his memoirs he described his thoughts after the October 1970 meeting:

> The first meeting gave a strong impetus to new androgynous ideas. [...] One way or another, my thoughts were preoccupied with androgynous configurations. Why had the androgynous configuration become so attractive? [...] Why had these ideas obsessed designers and pushed them to create a fully androgynous apparatus? Why, after the ASTP, were we still attached to these ideas, did we maintain our belief in them and even advance them to a new level? All these are good questions, as the Americans like to say. Surely, along with the subjective fancy attraction, there were good reasons for such persistence, especially since it wasn't that easy to realize the androgynous concept in practice. APAS turned out to be a hard nut to crack for us, its "parents." Indeed, there had to be good reasons, or again, as the Americans like to say, one had to feel strongly enough to take this kind of a long and difficult road. Even more so, since in both countries well-developed docking mechanisms had already been built and tested in space by that time. Later [Caldwell] Johnson used to joke, suggesting absolutely different reasons for the unwillingness of engineers to use probe-and-cone, or male-female, configurations: none of the countries wanted to play a female role in space before the eyes of the world. Who knows, maybe there was something to this. Later continuing with the joke, we started saying that with androgens, both partners are on top.[34]

These were ways of looking at engineering and its broader meaning that perhaps only a patriarchal culture could produce. (On the Soviet side all the engineers except one were male, which was true also of the American side.) As part of this patriarchal culture Syromiatnikov and his American colleagues expressed a fear of being the female dominated by the male. The fear was exacerbated by broader homophobic attitudes in which the act of penetration could be immediately interpreted as an all-male act in which the homosexual top

---

33 Ibid., 400, 475.
34 Syromiatnikov, *100 Stories*, 395.

would feminize the passive male bottom.³⁵ The key was to avoid "assemblages," in the words of one queer studies scholar, that would threaten the heterosexual vitality of the nation, and docking was potentially one of these homo-national assemblages.³⁶ In addition, vertical orientations during the Cold War were important in expressing dominance, and the aerospace age had produced many new ways to display domination over others from above: through spying cameras, rockets, satellites, lunar rovers, national flags, and Lenin bas-reliefs on the moon. The goal of getting higher than the other side had fueled the space race and the quest for lunar bragging rights. The United States seemed to win that battle for vertical superiority with the Apollo moon landings, but the Soviets countered with the successful Soviet lunar missions beginning in September 1970. Not coincidentally, the Soviets were willing to work out a joint design for a docking project in October 1970, right after a successful uncrewed mission to the moon, since they now felt they had achieved the same vertical position over the earth as the Americans. The Soviets were also aware that their successes came just as the United States was scaling back its ambitions in space, even as the United States faced the humiliations of Vietnam and the energy crisis.³⁷ Meanwhile, the Soviets countered with a lunar lander in January 1973 that carried a Lenin bas-relief and Soviet coat of arms to the lunar surface.

If the Cold War was fueled by the quest for vertical supremacy, having both sides join horizontally at the same altitude above Earth could just possibly end it, or so the engineers and politicians hoped. In the case of the ASTP, the two sides thus approached each other from the same altitude, replicating the meeting on the Elbe in World War II between Soviet and American allies and thereby establishing parity and reducing the focus on submission and domination. The horizontal coupling also marked the chronological dividing line between the earlier space race and the new era of space cooperation. This point was to be made explicitly in the 1973 Paris Air Show with a mock-up of the androgynous coupling. The plan for the joint exhibit—held outside of the country exhibits of the United States and Soviet Union in a spot exactly equidistant between the American and Soviet pavilions—was explicit that two capsules would be "situated horizontally in a docked position."³⁸ APAS was thus a way to engineer parity and to reduce the quest for domination in the

---

35 Syromiatnikov, *100 Stories*, 421–22.
36 Jasbir K. Puar, *Terrorist Assemblages: Homonationalism in Queer Times* (Durham, NC: Duke University Press, 2017).
37 Interkosmos report assessing scaled-back US ambitions in space and across the globe: ARAN, f. 1678, op. 1, d. 287, ll. 77–78.
38 ARAN, f. 1678, op. 1, d. 294, ll. 25, 112.

US–USSR relationship, although with one important caveat that threatened to reignite Cold War competitive instincts.

Since the Soviets would often claim that the original idea for APAS was theirs, the American endorsement of the Soviet design suggested to some that the Soviet Union had imposed its will on the American side. Johnson, Syromiatnikov's American docking colleague, supported the Soviet claim of priority for the design even though he was aware that he would be criticized for "caving in" to the Soviets back in Houston. He justified the decision as purely technical but understood the political subtext. "Even many years later," noted Syromiatnikov about Johnson, "he often referred to this decision and tried to explain the reasons for making it." It didn't help that Syromiatnikov began comparing himself—he was left-handed—to the Russian "Levsha" (which means lefty in Russian and someone adept at the most finely skilled craftsmanship). The Levsha was a mythical figure in the time of Tsar Nicholas I who could make a horseshoe for a flea and in doing so proved that Russian engineers were superior to their European counterparts. He said he used the term to make a boring story more interesting, and that he did not mean to imply that he was superior to his foreign colleague and good friend, though he admitted he had, "added a witty design decision to optimize the future mechanism that eventually ensured the real international interface." Syromiatnikov also remembered that when his Soviet team came to Houston in the fall of 1973 to work on APAS, hordes of American contractors and NASA engineers came visiting to view his docking design, "as if it was a Russian miracle." It was an echo of the docking simulations/shows back at OKB-1 NII-88 in the 1960s. Later, at a press conference after the docking on July 17, 1975, Boris Petrov, head of the Soviet Interkosmos, responded to a Western reporter's question about who invented the design. He answered that the design was primarily Soviet and mostly the idea of Syromiatnikov, who would be available at the next press conference to provide more details. When that conference occurred the next day, Syromiatnikov attempted to fudge his answer, but in a way that still made clear that he was the inventor: "I don't want to have another sleepless night, and therefore I will not say who personally designed the mechanism." Petrov immediately added: "The docking mechanism is the combined effort of specialists of two countries. It is an international child. And as an international child the child is androgynous." Caldwell's willingness to let the Soviets claim priority for the androgynous design, despite the risks he took in doing so of making the Americans appear less clever than the Soviets, pleasantly surprised the Soviet side and helped to establish a friendly working environment, within a broader political context of détente, that was now tilting horizontally rather than vertically.[39]

One point of dispute in particular set the tone for further collaboration after the docking agreement was made: the issue of whether or not the androgynous clasping rings would have three or four "fingers" to grab each other. The Americans proposed four and the Soviets three. Johnson said the Soviets were suspicious of the American side and believed that the Americans would never give in to the Soviet three-finger design, but he surprised the Soviets. As Johnson remembered it, the Soviet side came into the meeting to discuss the number of fingers issue and immediately said to the Americans: "We've decided it's a good idea for you to do it our way." Everyone then laughed and Johnson then did something completely unexpected: He agreed. "It is very interesting, to have somebody ask you to do something, and you say okay, then they don't know what the hell to do. They wanted to fight, I guess." He felt the Soviet side thought it was a trick, "And it wasn't any trick! [...] But we got along fine. It was a very cooperative group of people."[40] Johnson's common sense, his willingness to take heat from some American colleagues and bosses, and his ability to leave his ego out of the collaboration played no small role in pushing the project forward. "You son of a bitch," he remembered some American colleagues saying after he gave in to Soviet demands. "You gave away. What did you give in to those bastards for?" But Johnson responded that "we want to get on with the program; we don't give a damn which way it is," to which he recalled this response: "Yeah, but, goddamn it, you give in to those son of a bitches." It helped that both the Soviet and American engineers who worked together had immense respect for each other's technical capabilities. "The Russian team was first rate," remembered Johnson, who was mightily impressed by their engineering. "They were crackerjack engineers" and Syromiatnikov in particular was "brilliant."[41]

Johnson's respect for the Soviet engineers was only reinforced when he saw the impoverished conditions in which the Soviet space program

---

39 Syromiatnikov, *100 Stories*, 426–27, 454, 474; Transcript of ASTP mission communications, Part 5 (SR 61/2–SR 83/1), Part 6 (SR 83/2–SR 95/2), https://history.nasa.gov/astp/gallery.html. For Johnson's claim that the United States first came up with the androgynous design: Interview with Caldwell Johnson, April 1, 1998, League City Texas, NASA Johnson Space Center Oral History Project, p. 25. In fact, as with many invention disputes, both sides seem to have come up with the design at more or less the same time as they headed into discussion for a joint docking project in October 1970.
40 Interview with Caldwell Johnson, April 1, 1998, League City Texas, NASA Johnson Space Center Oral History Project, 26–27.
41 Interview with Caldwell Johnson, April 1, 1998, League City Texas, NASA Johnson Space Center Oral History Project, 26–27; April 27, 1999, 59–61.

operated. "Everywhere you went, you could see that they made do with things that we wouldn't make do with," noted Johnson, marveling at the Soviet accomplishments.

> Their labs had wooden oil floors. The plaster was cracked on the walls. There were light bulbs hanging down on a cord that you reached up and turned the switch. You know, all their equipment was kind of crummy, crummy stuff. Now they made up for it with industry. They worked hard and [were] very conscientious people. [...] They didn't spare themselves, you know. They were really dedicated.

He remembered that the NASA teams brought gifts of IBM Selectric typewriters to replace "these old mechanical clunkers" that the Soviet secretaries used. "And they just—they just marveled at it." When the Soviet teams in the United States first saw a Xerox machine, they were amazed. "Anybody just walks up and makes a copy?" they asked, and one wondered why they didn't just start copying dollar bills. "They were a great bunch, though."[42]

Interfaces and Rehearsals

It is perhaps no accident that the Soviet side embraced the idea of APAS as an ideal techno-political design. The docking mechanism was a mechanical mirror of the idea of peaceful coexistence embraced by Khrushchev and Brezhnev in which the Soviets believed both sides could live in peace and interact with each other while still retaining their different socioeconomic and political systems. APAS, in other words, was a technological manifestation of Soviet foreign policy, an example of "society made durable," to use the terminology of Bruno Latour (just as the intercontinental ballistic missile was a mechanical expression of the doctrine of MAD and its social expression in Cold War culture). That was very different from the American conception of containment or the increasingly popular conception of "convergence" in some intellectual circles in both the West and the Soviet Union of the 1960s and 1970s. Convergence connoted the blending of systemic attributes to create something fundamentally new. Androgynous coupling, meanwhile, created a hybrid system that preserved the unique attributes of the separate systems while connecting them to each other and making them mutually accessible. The spirit of hybridity, as embodied by APAS, also explicitly rejected the guiding US policy of containment, designed by the US State Department

---

42 Interview with Caldwell Johnson, April 27, 1999, League City Texas, NASA Johnson Space Center Oral History Project, 62–63.

Russia expert George Kennan, who envisioned Soviet capitulation and assimilation to the American system through a policy of pressuring the Soviets economically and politically, thereby exposing the weaknesses of the Soviet system and forcing them to relinquish their own supposedly dysfunctional ideology in favor of capitalist democracy. Clearly distinct from the ideas of convergence and containment, the docking mechanism of APAS thus embraced the spirit of "peaceful coexistence" (*mirnoe sosushchestvovanie*).[43]

Détente, like APAS, created interfaces (economic, technological, political, and cultural) that made both systems accessible to each other. Both sides recognized that to make this scheme work they needed to build a relationship of trust so that they would put aside the fear that mutual accessibility would lead to efforts by one side to sabotage the other side (through spying activities, theft of intellectual property or other forms of political subterfuge). Central to the program of training leading up to the mission in July 1975 was thus a series of confidence-building measures. Engineering working groups from both sides arranged joint meetings in both the Soviet Union and the United States. The technocratic spirit of problem-solving allowed both sides to meet in the supposedly neutral and nonideological space of engineering. Feelings of mutual trust were to emerge from the progressive and joint solution of common problems. The fact that the focus of collaboration was on the interconnection, and that there was minimal need to work together on fundamental capsule design issues, made it possible for each country to produce its docking units on its own, "ensured by standardizing a minimal number of interfacing units," allowing both sides "the freedom [...] to use their own methods, concepts, and components." The experience of meeting to discuss progress, then retreating home to continue the docking system, and then returning again to report on progress, and finally docking, was immensely gratifying for the Soviet engineers. This was precisely the idea of détente as well—that neither side would impose its system on the other and both sides would recognize that there were multiple ways to approach the creation of a political and social system. The Soviet engineers developed a new vocabulary from their meetings with their American colleagues, starting with the very term "androgynous" that they used to name their docking design. The Soviets, wrote Syromiatnikov grew fond of the American word "interface [...] denoting inner, facing each other surfaces and other borders of two mediums." Like the word docking, interfacing became an almost higher calling in the context of ASTP that meant making incompatible things—objects, people, ideologies and systems—suddenly compatible. The

---

43 Brezhnev's letter to Nixon, presented by the Soviet US ambassador Anatolyi Dobrynin, August 5, 1971, Nixon Library and Archives, National Security Files, Henry A. Kissinger Office Files, NSC HAK, Country Files-Europe-USSR, Box 66.

Soviets began to see interfaces everywhere. The Soviet Academy of Sciences, for example, had little to do with the development of Soviet space technology, yet it was designated as the primary interface with NASA because the Soviet space industry existed within the secret world of the Soviet military–industrial complex. The Academy of Sciences thus became the docking mechanism that permitted NASA to connect with the Soviet space industry. The Paris Air Show in 1973 became a public interface to the previously secret Soviet space industry, as the Soviets displayed a mock-up of the APAS to the world. The Soviets also constructed a new testing site for ASTP, outside of the normal testing sites deep within the secret Soviet military–industrial complex, that they viewed as a simple solution—a "neutral zone" just like APAS—to the problem of connecting secret worlds to open ones (the site later became the center for all testing of Soviet international missions and thus went from being a temporary interface for ASTP to the formerly secret Soviet space industry to a permanent one—once again, an illustration of Latour's idea of technology as "society made durable").[44]

Socializing before and especially after meetings was critical to trust-building, as Soviet engineers were taken to Disneyland—their interface with American culture—during visits to design the docking interface at Rockwell facilities in Downey, California. Similarly, during their social interfaces on Soviet territory, American engineers were treated to the Russian traditions of hospitality, which involved icebreakers with usually substantial quantities of food, drink, and merriment. Cosmonauts were assigned the job of entertaining their colleagues: Leonov, for example, was charged with taking the American crew hunting, while Vladimir Dzhanibekov, of the backup crew, was to host a party at his apartment.[45] At one banquet with his American colleagues, Syromiatnikov made a toast to APAS and their mission, playfully quoting Balzac: "Love begins with a touch."[46] The parties sometimes had a homoerotic quality. At a bash at the hotel Rossiya in the fall of 1973, for Caldwell Johnson's 50th birthday, the Soviets filled a three-liter Samovar with vodka. They took vodka in teacups and took pictures of each other holding long sausages and grinning broadly and suggestively. "Our party was loud and completely male," wrote Syromiatnikov. Soon after, the Soviet engineers—without their female secretaries, who were not allowed to travel abroad—went to Houston for more testing and drinking to rejoin, as Syromiatnikov put it, "his androgynous brothers." There was a big party in Houston to honor the October Revolution in 1973 that included the American astronauts, as

---

44 Syromiatnikov, *100 Stories*, 429–30, 460–61, 532.
45 ARAN, f. 1678, op. 1, l. 14.
46 Syromiatnikov, *100 Stories*, 440.

everyone drank from plastic cups and sang revolutionary songs. The one Soviet female engineer, who designed the seal for the docking mechanism, was not allowed to travel to the United States with her male colleagues, just as the female secretaries of the Soviet engineers were forced to stay in the Soviet Union. At a dinner later that evening, looking out over the Pacific Ocean, Syromiatnikov made a toast in which he mentioned his trip five years earlier to the Pacific Ocean in the Soviet Far East and proposed a toast to "pacifists." He had quite a bit of California wine and the best steak he had ever eaten, and before returning to the Soviet Union the Soviet engineers managed to squeeze in a trip to Las Vegas. Those experiences were among the personal benefits of interfacing with his American colleagues, along with the superior American toilet paper, which the Soviet engineers brought back in large quantities to the Soviet Union in their suitcases. They also asked their American colleagues to bring them US toilet paper (another kind of interface with American culture) for their visits to Soviet space facilities. The Soviets had to give the Americans their due: they did make better toilet paper.[47]

Administrators from both programs, and especially cosmonauts and astronauts, frequently visited each other's facilities for training and technical meetings and each other's homes and families for socializing. These pre-flight social and business exchanges provided opportunities for confidence-building and a kind of dry run for the exchanges during the flight that in turn were crucial for the success of détente by proving that mutual accessibility would not pose a security threat to either side. By all accounts, the business and social meetings proved successful in achieving this goal, though there was some concern on the American side about succumbing to the seductive pleasures of Russian hospitality. In order to build trust and to avoid the impression that one side might owe something to the other side, the visiting side always paid for its travel expenses, something that conflicted with the Soviet cultural tradition of taking responsibility as a host for the needs of the guest. The American side feared that accepting Soviet hospitality expenses would potentially compromise their independence from the Soviet system, illustrating yet again the porous boundaries between politics and social and technical engineering.

Lights, Camera, Action

Right before the launch of Apollo on July 15, 1975, President Gerald Ford broadcast a message to both mission controls and crews. His message was careful to maintain parity by noting the feats of Yuri Gagarin and John Glenn, of both Goddard and Tsiolkovskii as the fathers of modern rocketry, and of

---

47 Syromiatnikov, *100 Stories*, 479, 481, 484, 515.

Apollo 11 and the Soviet lunar missions as great advances in lunar science and human exploration.[48] Mutual and peaceful accessibility to each other's geographical and political space was central to the carefully choreographed program of activities for the nearly two days of docking. Over the course of the docking four exchanges were planned, beginning with a first visit by American crew members to the Soviet capsule, and then three other exchanges, with the Soviets getting the all-important first visit. During these interactions, a crew member from the capsule's country would always be present in both capsules. The construction of the itinerary was a complex affair that shared much in common with the construction and performance of a screenplay, though with limited opportunities for rehearsal and the technical challenges of broadcasting the performance to a global audience. To make matters even more complex, the show's primary actors, the cosmonauts and astronauts, were also responsible for maintaining the lighting systems and cameras during the show.

Parity was to be achieved linguistically by having the crews speak in the native language of the people they were speaking to. The Soviet crew thus spoke English to the American crew, and the American crew spoke Russian to the Soviet crew (and both jokingly used the portmanteau "Rouston," for Russia and Houston). In this way the burden was on the native listener rather than the non-native talker to interpret words and act upon them. For example, the American commander Thomas Stafford in his thick Texas accent would use the Russian expression, "Kak po maslu," (like cutting through butter) to Leonov as an acknowledgment, and Leonov would respond: "OK" in English.[49] The point of the language protocols was to minimize the extent to which misinterpretation by the listener, leading to mission failure, might threaten the political goals of détente, not to mention the lives of both crew members. Listening rather than talking was thus put into a position of primary importance. In addition, the language training made each side aware of its vulnerability and mutual dependence by forcing the non-native speaker to confront—in halting, thickly accented, and grammatically imperfect words—the humbling challenge of communicating to a native speaker. Built into the program was an abort plan, or to put it in sexual terms, a withdrawal of consent for mating, should either system be endangered by the technical difficulties of the androgynous coupling.

While the docking was a formidable technological triumph, the act of docking also performed symbolic political work. The docking was thus to occur

---

48 Transcript of ASTP mission communications, Part 2 (MC 17/1–MC 38/3), https://history.nasa.gov/astp/gallery.html.
49 Syromiatnikov, *100 Stories*, 564; "'Soyuz-Apollon': nad El'boi," *Vesti.ru*, July 15, 2010, http://www.vesti.ru/article/2088534.

at the point in which the two capsules were flying over the two Germanys, whose division had itself been a byproduct of the Cold War and the inability of two former allies to determine the exact conditions of peace for postwar Europe. The linkup provided a kind of fresh start or redo, a turning back of the clock to a time before the Cold War was even imagined as an outcome of World War II. The Soviets referred to the handshake in the capsule as the "Elbe in space," in reference to the handshake between US and Soviet forces on April 24, 1945, on the Elbe River near Torgau, Germany.[50] Seen from the perspective of that moment, when the Cold War had not happened, ASTP represented a return to a temporal and geographical space in which an open-ended future existed and Germany itself had not been divided and a wall built to separate East Germany from West Germany. In actual fact, the docking did not take place over the Elbe but apparently over Spain, though the Soviets noted that it was somewhere between Spain and the Soviet Union in the first post-meeting press conference and that it was hard to say exactly since the docked craft continued to move rapidly during the docking procedure at a speed of eight kilometers per second. When the question about the location of the docking was repeated by a reporter, and then a variant asked about where the handshake took place after docking, the Soviet public relations person, Boris Petrov, simply said it was somewhere perhaps near Amsterdam, but that the question had already been answered. Ultimately, the myth of the Elbe fly-over for the docking was so compelling that the facts about where the docking actually occurred got sucked into the black hole of historical amnesia. In an interview on the 35th anniversary of ASTP, Leonov continued to insist that the docking occurred over the Elbe, adding for dramatic effect: "Thirty years before [the docking] our fathers and grandfathers shook hands on the Elbe and thirty years later we shook hands over the Elbe!" The newspaper editors took their cue from Leonov and titled the article: "Soyuz-Apollo: over the Elbe."[51]

The Objects of Peace and the Exchange of Gifts

Both sides used the transport of commemorative items into space to express the goals of political equalization. The list itself of items, hashed out through agreements and conversations between the two sides over a number of years,

---

50 Viktor Khokhlov, "Kuda khodiat mechty: razmyshleniia v godovshchinu kosmicheskogo iubileia," *Gefter*, March 23, 2015, http://gefter.ru/archive/14617.
51 Transcript of ASTP mission communications, Part 5 (SR 61/2–SR 83/1), Part 6 (SR 83/2–SR 95/2) https://history.nasa.gov/astp/gallery.html; "'Soyuz-Apollon': nad El'boi," *Vesti.ru*, July 15, 2010, http://www.vesti.ru/article/2088534.

was designed to produce a hybrid inventory of symbols and ceremonial objects. Especially important was the symbolic space occupied by national flags. Ever since the placement of the US flag on the moon, the nationalization of space had been a key way for the United States to express its imperial ambitions. That approach nonetheless offended many, as evidenced by the many letters sent to Nixon declaring that the planting of the flag was a violation of the spirit of internationalism and peace that should govern space exploration. In this instance, space was imagined as a process of double but equal colonization by the United States and the Soviet Union. The crews would thus exchange five flags with each other, including five small US flags (8" × 12", measured in the US system of inches) to be exchanged for five small USSR flags (205 mm × 410 mm, measured in the Soviet metric system). The flags "symbolized the contribution made by a great many people from all over the United States and the Soviet Union. Such contributions were essential to the first major joint venture by these two spacefaring countries."[52]

While celebrating the flight as a process of managed competitive colonialism—perhaps similar in some ways to the 1885 Berlin agreement between European powers that attempted to set ground rules for European imperialist takeovers of Africa—the two sides also imagined the docking as the expression of a transnational project devoted to the advance of all humanity, in line with the increasing view of space exploration as a transnational enterprise. The Soviets would thus carry into space a United Nations Flag (3' × 5', and the biggest of the flags), that would then descend back to Earth on the Apollo capsule, "symbolizing our common goal of peacefully exploring space for the benefit of people all over the world and in recognition of the contribution to this and other cooperative space projects made by people from many nations." An additional set of flags went into space but would not be exchanged in order "to symbolize [the role of each nation] in the first international flight."[53]

The two sides also carried separate pieces of commemorative plaques to be assembled jointly in space. The plaques, representing "two permanent symbols of the first international human spaceflight," formed two individual medallions with crossed flags and docked spacecraft. While the commemorative plaques celebrated the spirit of international cooperation, other objects expressed the related spirit of ecological consciousness, which was itself a result, in large part, of the view from space. The United States offered white spruce seeds to the Soviets, who returned the favor with seeds of native trees, so as

---

52 https://history.nasa.gov/astp/documents/Objects%20Exchanged.pdf.
53 One large US flag, 3' × 5', and five small US flags, 8" × 12"," and one large USSR flag, 3' × 6', and five small USSR flags, 205 mm × 410 mm. https://history.nasa.gov/astp/documents/Objects%20Exchanged.pdf.

to create a "living and growing monument to the first cooperative human spaceflight." The seeds celebrated the new space-age environmentalism, "the product of new scientific developments in forestry" that would "call attention to the new awareness of Earth brought by spaceflight. Perception of the planet from space heightens humankind's appreciation of Earth's natural beauty and our understanding that we all share responsibility for its preservation." The principle of parity was maintained by selecting seeds from trees in Rhinelander in the state of Wisconsin, which was determined to be most similar to the climate of Moscow.[54]

There were more silver medallions presented to individual crew members and a certificate of docking from the International Aeronautical Federation (Federation Aeronautique International, FAI), which had certified aeronautical

Figure 3.2 The cosmonauts and astronauts assemble the commemorative plaque in orbit

Source: NASA

---

54 https://history.nasa.gov/astp/documents/Objects%20Exchanged.pdf; Transcript of ASTP mission communications, Part 10 (MC 148/2–MC 166/1) https://history.nasa.gov/astp/gallery.html.

achievements since its formation in 1905. The flight also paid homage to the politics of détente for which the entire project had been a test. There were six copies of the May 1972 Nixon–Kosygin Agreement,

> concerning cooperation in the exploration and use of outer space for peaceful purposes (three in English and three in Russian), by which both nations made a commitment to conduct not only the Apollo-Soyuz Test Project, but also a wide range of continuing cooperative activities in such fields as space meteorology, the study of the natural environment from space, the exploration of near-Earth space, the Moon, the planets, and space biology and medicine.[55]

While the idea of androgynous docking mechanism set the tone for a project that aimed to treat both sides in the same manner and to preserve the distinctiveness of both cultures and systems, there was one aspect of the symbolic program that pointed toward a joining together that would be not one or the other, but an amalgam of the two into something new. This was the test to produce a lead-gold alloy (three samples) in the electric furnace of the docking module. The project was a Soviet idea that originated with visions of space as an arena for industrial activity. Kubasov, Leonov's Soviet ASTP crewmate, had gone down in space record books on October 11, 1969, as the first human to weld in space. The notion of building upon this feat and creating a blast furnace in space seemed somehow logical to the Soviet side, and the Americans indulged their crewmates, as all happy couples often do with the strange obsessions of their partners. Said the joint planning documents: "The uniform mixing of unlike materials in space created a new substance that symbolized the success people and nations found in putting aside their differences to work together in space. *The unusual environment of space acts as a catalyst through which both men and materials may combine to yield useful applications for the benefit of all.*"[56] As one Russian scholar has noted, the docking mechanism of ASTP was like the androgyne figure of the alchemical traditions of early and medieval Christianity. It involved, "the union of irreconcilable elements, the merging of opposites," which "not only gives birth to the sought-after philosopher's stone, but also helps to achieve universal wisdom and eternal intellectual enlightenment."[57] Kubasov described the meaning of the welding experiment to global television audiences during the mission:

---

55 https://history.nasa.gov/astp/documents/Objects%20Exchanged.pdf.
56 https://history.nasa.gov/astp/documents/Objects%20Exchanged.pdf.
57 Natalya Serkova, "World Wide Gold," *e-flux*, no. 93, 2018, https://www.e-flux.com/journal/93/213267/world-wide-gold/.

I think that this area has a great future. It seems to me that some time will pass, and mankind will have many new metals, many new alloys, with new qualities—we'll be obtaining these materials in conditions which could never be created on the Earth, but which could be available only in space. And it seems to me, that the time will come when space will have whole plants, factories, for the production of new materials and new substances with new qualities, which could be obtained or made only in space.[58]

The Return to Zero-Sum Back on Earth

Despite the goal of equalizing power relations between the two sides, the game of one-upmanship continued through the years of contacts and joint development. These incidents, the subject of the chapter's final section, provide important reminders about the limitations of technological fixes. The attitudes that produced the Cold War, it turns out, were unusually resistant to the amalgamating forces of blast furnaces in space.

There were many such incidents over critical but also seemingly trivial issues that represented, on the part of both sides, an instinctual and at times conscious resistance to the goal of escaping from the zero-sum politics of the Cold War. For example, both sides accused the other of having more dangerous and less secure technology. The Soviets noted the dangers associated with the American reliance on pure oxygen, which had already resulted in the incineration of the Apollo 1 crew in 1967. Meanwhile, the Soviet mission control director Yuri Mozzhorin took umbrage at American arrogance: "In the Apollo-Soyuz program the Americans openly expressed their lack of confidence and safety in the functioning of our space technology and systems and expressed the fear that this represented a serious threat to their astronauts during docking and the joint flight of the capsules. That opinion was widely disseminated in their press."[59] Their pride wounded by American disdain, the Soviets redoubled efforts to update their mission control and to prove to the American side that their technology was every bit as good as the American technology, perhaps even better. "In general, our mission control made a good impression on the Americans," wrote the Soviet mission control director,

---

58 Transcript of ASTP mission communications, Part 18 (MC 272/1–MC 285/2), https://history.nasa.gov/astp/gallery.ht.
59 N. A. Anfimov, ed., *Tak eto bylo…: Memuary Iu. A. Mozzhorina: Mozzhorin v vospominaniiakh sovremennikov* (Moscow: OAO 'Mezhdunarodnaia programma obrazovaniia, 2000). http://epizodsspace.airbase.ru/bibl/mozjorin/tak/06.html, this is chapter 6, downloaded June 12, 2018.

Mozzhorin, in his memoirs. "Yours is as good as ours," said NASA's James Fletcher, as quoted by Mozzhorin, in defense against the claim among many Americans that the Soviet technology was inferior.[60] The Soviet flight director Eliseev went further, bragging that, "functionally our mission control was no worse than the American mission control, and in terms of comfort exceeded it," including a better buffet, rest areas, and accommodations for guests. The Soviet leadership spared no expense in keeping the buffet well stocked with the best food, realizing that national pride and the traditions of Russian hospitality were at stake. "It might seem strange now," Eliseev wrote many years later, "but otherwise we would have been ashamed before the Americans."[61]

Sometimes, the advantage of one side was equalized by the advantage of another. So while the Soviets were superior to the Americans in terms of ground control of the orbiting capsules, the Americans allowed their astronauts more manual control. Mozzhorin recalled another episode that illustrated the challenges of equalizing power relations between the two sides. To accommodate NASA observers, the Soviets built a three-story hotel next to their new mission control center for the flight where NASA observers could work during the mission. The rooms were outfitted "with nice imported furniture," purchased with the precious black gold of petro-dollars created by the Siberian oil fields. Mozzhorin had been charged with ensuring the Americans received all the information they required and in the most comfortable circumstances. And then Mozzhorin was contacted by the KGB and the Soviet Foreign Ministry, who informed him that "there was an order to observe the principle of parity" and that the Soviets had violated that order, not by failing to create living conditions for Americans equal to what the Americans provided the Soviet side, but because the Soviet arrangements for the Americans were far superior to those the Americans had provided to Soviet observers in Houston mission control. In Houston NASA had provided "Spartan conditions" for the Soviet observers and engineers; there was no place for them to lie down in mission control and getting access to decent hotel rooms and food was difficult. The Americans had failed to match the Soviet provision of hospitality and so the Soviets closed the hotel for American observers (it was later turned into offices for Soviet space officials and engineers) and set

---

60 "Istoriia TsUPa: Trud, radosti, mytarstva," *Nauka i zhizn'*, No. 8, 2005, http://epizodsspace.airbase.ru/bibl/n_i_j/2005/7/istoria-tsupa.html, downloaded June 11, 2018. Syromiatnikov, disliked NASA's administrator Fletcher because of his disdain for Soviet technology and thought George Low, who respected Soviet technology, was far more qualified. Syromiatnikov, *100 Stories*, 558.

61 "Istoriia TsUPa: Trud, radosti, mytarstva," *Nauka i zhizn'*, No. 8, 2005, http://epizodsspace.airbase.ru/bibl/n_i_j/2005/7/istoria-tsupa.html, downloaded June 11, 2018.

out "domestically manufactured" Soviet chairs and couches for the American observers.[62]

The question for parity could often take a comical turn. Caldwell Johnson remembered that during one visit to Leningrad, which was notorious for having Giardia bacteria that causes severe intestinal infection, the American engineers suffered debilitating diarrhea. When they complained, their Soviet hosts said: "Nonsense. Nothing wrong with the water in Leningrad. You brought this [problem] with you." Parity was achieved when Soviet engineers came to the United States and stayed in a motel. The Soviets, remembered the docking engineer Johnson, "were walking around barefoot and taking showers in the stalls, and they all came down with absolutely the worst cases of athlete's foot you've ever seen. We've got a whole bunch of little viruses that the Russians don't have any protection against." When the Soviets complained, the Americans told them: "Nonsense. You brought it with you." The NASA doctors did take pity on them and gave them a powerful ointment that "just smelled awful, and you could tell these guys a mile away."[63]

The stakes in maintaining parity rose considerably for the all-important and much-anticipated meeting of the two crews. As Eliseev remembered it, the Soviets constructed a joint plan of the mission that would make the first meeting between the two crews take place in the Soviet capsule. He considered getting the first meeting a coup. The American side had apparently not been paying close enough attention, and by the time they objected to the arrangement it was already too late to change the sequence of crew activities. As the fateful moment of the first crew exchange approached, Eliseev was called into a meeting with the political and military leader Dmitrii Ustinov and informed that Brezhnev had typed out a note that was to be read verbatim to the joint crews at the moment of the handshake (something that had not been on the itinerary).

> I smiled in response and felt disgust inside. Why hadn't they told us earlier? We could have prepared for it. Now what were we to do? The note was not included in the itinerary. The greeting had to be conveyed at precisely the time that the crews would be embracing each other. And we were supposed to interrupt the natural flow of events. The greeting would be read out as the cosmonauts and astronauts were floating freely in the cabin. Everyone would have to face the screen, faces toward the

---

62 "Istoriia TsUPa: Trud, radosti, mytarstva," *Nauka i zhizn'*, No. 8, 2005, http://epizodssp ace.airbase.ru/bibl/n_i_j/2005/7/istoria-tsupa.html, downloaded June 11, 2018.
63 Interview with Caldwell Johnson, April 1, 1998, League City Texas, NASA Johnson Space Center Oral History Project, 27–28.

viewers, and pretend like they were listening attentively. We could not request of our cosmonauts that they immediately should arrange the Americans after the meeting and turn their view toward the camera.

Eliseev told Defense Minister Ustinov that he would prefer that a professional television announcer read the greeting, and the television announcer was immediately sent to mission control and told to read it word for word. But the announcer, after looking at the words he was supposed to read, turned pale and answered in a panicked voice that he could not read the message, because it was signed "L. Brezhnev," and it would not be proper for him to read "L. Brezhnev" out loud to the world. Yet he also said he did not have the authority to take the liberty to say "Leonid Brezhnev" or "Leonid Il'ich Brezhnev," because it was not in the General Secretary's original note. With only minutes to go before the meeting in space and delivery of the message Eliseev explained the announcer's conundrum to Ustinov, who pretended that he had not heard what he was told. "I understood that he did not want to take responsibility for this seemingly trivial decision." Eliseev then noted the urgency and said. "I recommend [saying] 'Leonid' Brezhnev." Ustinov remained stone-faced and silent, until finally two others chimed in: "I propose that we agree to this," to which the other said: "That sounds normal to me." Ustinov made a slight nod, in the manner of a kind of Russian Godfather, to indicate his agreement and Eliseev hurried to the announcer with no time to spare and told him: "Read 'Leonid.'" Eliseev then had to inform the Soviet crew, just before the meeting with the astronauts, of their new mission to assemble the American guests to listen to the reading of Brezhnev's greeting. The moment then arrived as the Soviet ship awaited its American guests. "Everyone had the feeling as if right before our eyes there was occurring a transition from dangerous confrontation to friendly collaboration." Eliseev recalled that the embraces, joy, and sheer excitement of the moment overshadowed the reading of the comments completely, and that what remained was the memory of the exchange of flags and other commemorative items. It was only later, upon reviewing the video of the scene, that he noticed something he had not first seen: When the hatch opened, the American crew held back from entering the Soviet capsule and instead insisted on inviting the Soviet crew into the area of the docking module, thus attempting to change the plan from a meeting in Soviet territory to the neutral territory of the APAS module between the two capsules. "The cosmonauts did not take the bait. Their patriotic feelings were no less developed than those of the Americans."[64]

---

64 Eliseev, *Zhizn'*, 107–8.

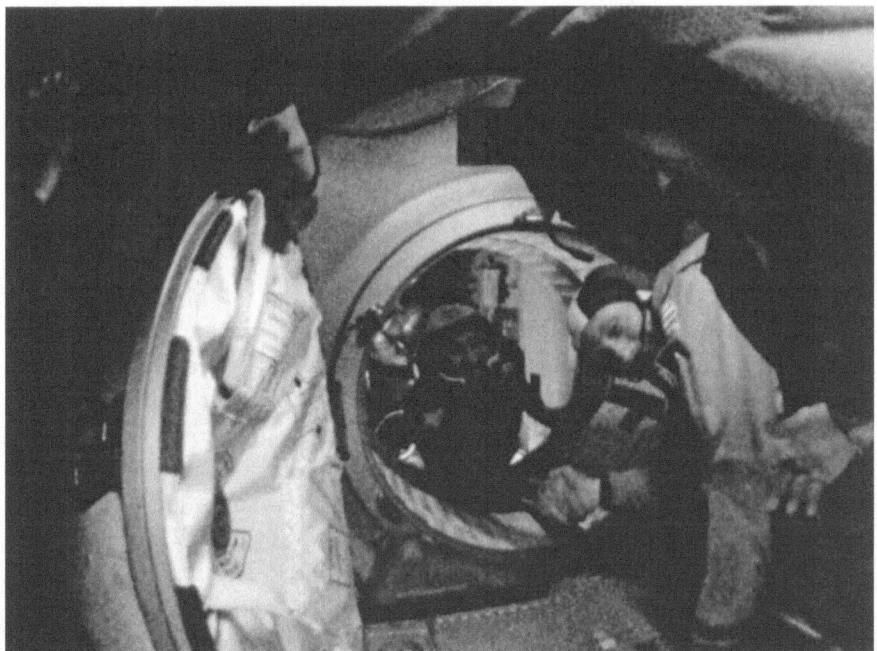

Figure 3.3 The ASTP handshake in space
Source: NASA

The confusion of that moment is reflected also in the mission transcripts. Deke Slayton and Stafford were clearly hesitating to enter the Soyuz capsule. A mission control operator then told them: "You're supposed to go into the Soyuz." Leonov reiterated after this: "Come in here and shake hands. Our viewers are here. Come here please." It appears from the one grainy photo of the event— it is curious that a ceremony that had been so hotly anticipated was so poorly documented visually—that Stafford stayed in the module, thus refusing Leonov's entreaties. In this photograph Leonov seems to have made sure that the handshake could not take place across the threshold of the Soyuz capsule entrance and thus thrust his arm and hand into the docking module where Stafford grabbed it and the picture was taken (shaking hands across a threshold of a door is strictly forbidden in Russian culture and a harbinger of very bad luck). Stafford then apparently entered the Soviet capsule, having maintained the handshake on the neutral territory of the APAS docking module. Just to make things even more confusing, the Soviets later claimed the handshake had taken place in their capsule. At any rate, the impression from the transcripts of that meeting is that confusion reigned despite all the planning and scripting, and that there was plenty of room to spin the events after the fact.⁶⁵ Leonov, a notorious story teller, embellished even more years later. He claimed that the meeting had actually occurred while the Soviet crew was out of communication with mission control, and when they got back into communication with mission control in Moscow, the operators on the ground instructed them to open the hatch and let the Americans in, to which Leonov said: "Why? They're already here sitting with us!" A long and awkward moment of silence followed, according to Leonov, and finally mission control asked how the meeting went, and then everyone broke out in applause.⁶⁶

While details of the handshake "over the Elbe" remain contested, one thing is clear: Both capsules were a mess, as the American crew noted when the hatch to the Soviet capsule opened up. Stafford said it looked like there were "snakes" in there, a reference to the crazy tangle of cables floating everywhere. Leonov could not find an extension cord for the camera he was supposed to use (it was not in the bag where it was supposed to be) so he had to use the shorter plug on the camera. The Soviets, in fact, had constant challenges in handling their end of the video transmissions, though ultimately they made it work. Leonov also could not locate a power supply unit and adapter, which were not where they were supposed to be and nowhere else in the capsule, as far as he could tell. "And how about the power supply cable, the adapter?," he asked Soviet mission control, which responded a few minutes later: "Don't look for it any more. It's not there," suggesting that they had a "doh" moment upon realizing that someone forgot to pack it.⁶⁷ The excitement of the moment and the technical challenges of maintaining communication and visual links across so many different systems (including cameras inside the capsule that were upside down), combined with clumsy attempts to manipulate the encounter to the benefit of the American or Soviet side and objects for camera equipment floating everywhere, gave the encounter an air of spontaneity and comic relief. Brezhnev, as noted earlier, had attempted to hijack the crew encounter in space with the first greeting before anyone had a chance to proceed with the many other planned activities. The interlude was even odder given the emptiness and clichéd nature of Brezhnev's words, which also mentioned that the age of space cooperation had begun with Sputnik and the first man in space, but ignored the Apollo

---

65 Transcript of ASTP mission communications, Part 5 (SR 61/2–SR 83/1), https://history.nasa.gov/astp/gallery.html.
66 "'Soyuz-Apollon': nad El'boi," *Vesti.ru*, July 15, 2010, http://www.vesti.ru/article/2088534.
67 Transcript of ASTP mission communications, Part 5 (SR 61/2–SR 83/1), https://history.nasa.gov/astp/gallery.html.

moon landing (in contrast to Ford, who maintained strict parity in mentioning the achievements on both sides in his earlier pre-launch comments). The Soviet announcer did sign off with a touch of spontaneity unbeknownst to all but Eliseev and the announcer, as agreed upon back in a panicked Soviet mission control room that had only minutes earlier learned of Brezhnev's note to be read to the crews: "Leonid Brezhnev," he intoned as he finished reading the General Secretary's hackneyed note, and not "L. Brezhnev," as Brezhnev had written. Curiously, the Soviet English translation of the transcript inserted "Applause" after Brezhnev's comments—though that was missing in the American transcript of the same reading. Who applauded is not clear, and it is the only part of the transcript for the entire mission of communications—tens of thousands of words—where the word "Applause" followed a statement.[68] Perhaps the applause related to Leonov's story about the Americans greeting the Soviets in their capsule while Soviet mission control was out of contact with the capsules? At any rate, Brezhnev's interventions had a surreal quality and were disarmingly ridiculous.

Ford also had the opportunity to speak again right after Brezhnev. He engaged in a long chat, asking each member of both crews questions about their training, meals, and impressions. The whole scene, as conveyed through the transcripts, seems to have been confusing for the crews greeting each other; but it did provide a clear contrast between the affable and chatty Ford and the formal words of Brezhnev, inserted unannounced into the proceedings like a front-page party proclamation in the newspaper *Pravda*. Unintentionally, Brezhnev had put himself into a position of inferiority relative to Ford and the Americans and undermined the assiduous Soviet efforts to maintain parity with his clumsy attempt to upstage Ford and be first. The Soviets sensed as much, at least based on the press conference that followed. In response to John Dancy of NBC News about why Brezhnev had not personally delivered remarks, unlike President Ford, the Interkosmos chief Boris Petrov had this to say:

> Leonid Brezhnev's message was read in a strong, resonant voice which was meant to cover all communications—possible communication defects, and this was done in order that there be no misunderstandings by the cosmonauts of his message [...] I know that not only in the control room but also in many people's houses the voice sounded very resonant, loud and clear. I am certain that even if Leonid Brezhnev spoke himself, the message would have been just as clear and resonant. I can only ask, for instance, what's the

---

68 Transcript of ASTP mission communications, Part 5 (SR 61/2–SR 83/1), https://history.nasa.gov/astp/gallery.html.

difference? May I ask the correspondent the opposite question? Leonid Brezhnev had his message read out and general—President Ford read his message himself. Why was that? Why wasn't it the other way around?[69]

As to a question at the next press conference about whether Brezhnev, like Ford, would directly address the crews at some point in the mission, Petrov abruptly closed the press conference. Truth be told, it often did not matter what the cosmonauts or leaders said to television audiences, because, as reporters at the press conferences noted, the audio quality was so poor that audiences often could not really understand what was being said.[70]

The confusion continued as the two crews exchanged the gifts—awkward laughter, cameras in the wrong position, noise clicks from unknown sources of interference, dropped audio and video. And then they proceeded to eat the tubed and pouched dishes from both countries that included borscht, steak, turkey and cranberries, dark Russian bread, and many other items. For the first breaking of bread between the crews, Leonov brought out tubes for his American colleagues with labels from Soviet vodka brands that read "Stolichnaia," "Russkaia Vodka," and "Staraia Vodka," and then said they had to drink before eating. "It is a very big Russian tradition," he added, claiming that for a moment the Americans actually believed he was serious. The tubes contained borscht soup.[71]

The second day was filled with exchanges and meals in both capsules, as well as television events in which the cosmonauts and astronauts would make comments on each other's space food, and then conduct of a variety of experiments and more ceremonies. Over the course of the mission live television broadcasts from the docked capsules concentrated on the crews describing their meals and the view of their territories below them to global audiences. After the second day the crews seemed to warm to the idea of sharing each other's space and relaxing in each other's company. Viewers witnessed men at work and play engaged in homosocial bonding and declaring how much they really liked being around each other. One of the most striking features of this socio-technical imaginary of global peace was the complete absence of women. It was an all-male world, designed and operated almost exclusively by men, with a supporting cast of women as secretaries unseen in the

---

69 Transcript of ASTP mission communications, Part 5 (SR 61/2–SR 83/1), https://history.nasa.gov/astp/gallery.html.
70 Transcript of ASTP mission communications, Part 5 (SR 61/2–SR 83/1) Part 6 (SR 83/2–SR 95/2), https://history.nasa.gov/astp/gallery.html.
71 "'Soyuz-Apollon': nad El'boi," *Vesti.ru*, July 15, 2010, http://www.vesti.ru/article/2088534.

Figure 3.4 The American astronauts eat borscht soup from tubes with Soviet vodka labels

Source: NASA

background, mediated by a mechanical androgyne.[72] Perhaps the Americans and the Soviets had achieved parity relative to each other, but they also joined together over the rest of the world in a position of vertical dominance, commenting upon and gazing down upon all the other nations who had not achieved their superior vantage point. Linked together by global relay stations, both the Soyuz and Apollo capsules traveled over the entire globe in just hours, tracking weather and transmissions and commenting upon the geographical domains over which they now flew—over and over again, armed with the vertical gaze as masters of the earth. Perhaps, in the end, they could come together more like equals precisely because they shared a feeling of superiority over everyone else.

Parity was also difficult to maintain because of the technological and physical differences between the two capsules and space systems. "In the course of the whole project Apollo was the favorite," remembered Syromiatnikov. "It was bigger, heavier, and 'smarter' than its partner was, since at that time

---

72 Transcript of ASTP mission communications, Part 14 (MC 208/4–MC 224/1), Part 15 (MC 225/1–MC 244/2), https://history.nasa.gov/astp/gallery.html.

we were not able to provide the Soyuz with an onboard computer. During the flight, when performing joint operations, Apollo had to be much more active."[73] The Apollo capsule had a crew of three, as opposed to the crew of two for the Soyuz.[74] The mere fact that one word had to come before another in describing the mission automatically also violated the quest for parity. The Americans thus called the mission "Apollo-Soyuz" while the Soviets called it "Soyuz-Apollon." The emblem attempted to overcome this problem by putting the words Soyuz and Apollo on the edge of a circular patch.

The act of docking, despite the androgynous mechanism, also had to be choreographed to preserve equal relations. During the mission there were actually two docking procedures, a plan that was designed to maintain the all-important focus on parity. Among the planned events was the initial docking, followed by the exchanges of crews, and a later decoupling and re-docking before the ending of the mission. For the first docking the Americans had played the active role of maneuvering the ship to join the coupling mechanism to the Soviet capsule, which played the passive role (though their capsule, as noted earlier, got to host the first crew exchange). In anthropomorphic terms, the Americans initiated the hug. Who would be the passive or active partner, as one might expect, became a matter of some dispute in the initial discussions. As Syromiatnikov noted, "The bigger the prestige factor, the less room there is for reason."[75] In the second coupling the roles were reversed as the Soviet capsule played the active role—the hugger initiator—and the Apollo the passive role. The docking at first went according to plan as the Soviet capsule maneuvered its way to connect with the Apollo capsule. But then the Soviet side felt two forceful jolts from the American capsule, and it had become clear, to use Stafford's favorite term, that the docking was not going "kak po maslu." A moment of panic ensued, since the force of the impact could have been enough to cause a catastrophic failure, though the Soviet flight engineer noted that "the strength of [Soviet] construction saved the mission." The Soviets realized that during the docking the American side had gone from being passive to active by incorrectly turning on side jet thrusters, a maneuver that was strictly forbidden in the instruction manual. After the flight the two sides discussed the incident and at first the American side categorically denied that its thrusters had been turned on, but an examination of the telemetry indicated that they had been turned on by mistake. "We left this incident on the conscience of the American side," said the Soviet flight engineer Eliseev, although Syromiatnikov later remembered that the Soviet

---

73 Syromiatnikov, *100 Stories*, 394.
74 Ibid., 417.
75 Ibid., 547.

side was not entirely blameless. The incident itself impressed the Soviets, not only because of the possibly tragic consequences of the mistake, but also because it seemed to represent a blatant American violation of the principle of parity, planned or by mistake. The Americans had gone into active mode without Soviet permission.[76] It was a reminder that the engineering of parity, like the goal of eliminating zero-sum politics from Soviet-American relations, could suffer catastrophic failure in a moment's notice. The transcripts of the mission communications do not reveal any verbal reactions to the event, but the press did learn of a "hard docking" and asked a question the following day at a press conference about its cause and whether or not the cosmonauts had any reaction and were fearful or anxious at the time. The answer was no, and the reporters were told that Syromiatnikov would be getting together with his American colleagues later to discuss what had happened. More information would be made public as soon as it became available. And that was it.[77] Ultimately, both sides agreed to divert attention away from the incident in the interests of diminishing chances for postflight controversies, and the unpermitted American pelvic thrust was forgotten.

The Message Gets Lost in Translation

Try as they might, both sides were often unable to communicate the central idea of parity that the mission was designed to convey, especially in the United States, where the mediascape showed its technical ignorance. In the US context, the dominant narrative was one of being "screwed"—quite literally—by the Soviets. That story line began with the lead-up to ASTP and in the years that followed, but was perhaps best illustrated in the December 1975 issue of the pornographic magazine *Playboy*. The magazine ran a story with accompanying images that expressed in graphic and explicit terms a common zero-sum view of American-Soviet relations that ultimately hastened the demise of détente. The article was part of a special section presented in the style of *National Geographic* magazine called *National Pornographic* (the "journal of the National Pornographic Society"). The ASTP image is across from one page with an article titled, "Mysterious Insects Battle for Survival," which shows a number of insects mounted on other insects during mating. The ASTP article is titled: "Historic Emission in Space." It contains two distinct images: one of a mock-up of the capsules which is not even remotely close to the actual appearance of the Apollo and Soyuz capsules. The

---

76 Eliseev, *Zhizn'*, 110; Syromiatnikov, *100 Stories*, 575, 582.
77 Transcript of ASTP mission communications, Part 11 (SR 147/1–SR 156/2), https://history.nasa.gov/astp/gallery.html.

caption of their docking reads: "US crew sends message to Soviet craft: 'Is it in yet?'" The other shows a naked man mounting a naked woman from behind and on top. The man is the Soviet Union, while the woman is the United States. The caption reads: "East meets West in the vast, weightless reaches of outer space. Soviet cosmonaut radios, 'My bird has landed!' while pretty U.S. astronaut muses aloud: 'I wonder why this reminds me of the U.S. Soviet grain deal.'"[78]

Of course, the article and associated images were intended to amuse, but they also reflected an increasingly anti-Soviet position that fueled opposition to détente and give rise to a renewed Cold War under Presidents Jimmy Carter and Ronald Reagan. If Syromiatnikov had worked painstakingly to engineer the flight in a way that would remove the implication that one side, the male, was dominating the other, the female, that message was completely lost on much of the American public. In the *Playboy* issue, and in a good portion of the anti-Soviet press in the United States, ASTP was interpreted as a dangerous give-away of American technological superiority that also had put the United States into a vulnerable position: in this case, the feminized United States had literally been taken from behind by the male Soviets. The reference to the grain deal—a controversial taxpayer subsidized sale of US grain to the Soviets as part of détente that was widely panned as a US-taxpayer give-away to the communist enemy—reinforced the connection between the flight and American humiliation. It was a stark reminder of the difficulty of changing political culture from a zero-sum mentality in the Cold War to a win-win proposition. Even more, the purposeful design of androgynous docking latches that would obviate the need for a "mama–papa" docking was completely ignored in favor of the narrative of domination and subordination—exactly the opposite of the intent and one that the homophobically inclined culture could only interpret as the United States being the bottom. The *Playboy* article noted, deploying sophomoric sexual innuendo appropriate for the magazine's audience:

> The first coupling in outer space was a fitting climax to the joint venture undertaken by the United States and Red Russia. Commie space technicians successfully completed docking maneuvers by inserting their vehicle into the opening of the American module, although NASA officials had insisted that the Bolshevik vehicle be provided with a heat-resistant sheath (painted bright red, of course)—for the prevention of disease only. Inside the U. S. capsule, cosmonaut and astronaut joined in a historic embrace that will be remembered as one giant *shtup* for mankind.[79]

---

78 "Historic Emission in Space," *Playboy*, December 22, 1975, 209.
79 "Historic Emission in Space," *Playboy*, December 22, 1975, 209.

The article diverged not at all from the standard conceptions in American culture of communism as invasive and aggressive in its violation of American space, first with the penetration of the vehicle and then of the sex act, which takes place in the feminized American capsule and requires the Soviet side to wear a condom to prevent the spread of the communist disease to the American body politic. The increasingly bellicose American attitudes were definitely noticed by Syromiatnikov toward the end of his ASTP collaboration when he visited the United States in 1974. He remarked upon the virulent anti-Soviet and anti-détente attitudes during his last visit to the United States, which surprised and saddened him, especially in light of the popularity of détente back in the Soviet Union and how much the hostility contrasted to the much more welcoming atmosphere of 1972 and 1973. Reflecting the contrast in attitudes, one of the most popular magazine images of ASTP was in the Soviet satirical journal *Krokodil*.[80] Its July 1975 issue had a cover which showed the two capsules meeting together over Earth. As the androgynous docking latches come together over Earth, they squeezed the mid-section and groin of a Trojan Warrior, who is forced to drop his sword. The warrior is labeled "Cold War." The representations of the capsules clearly convey the androgynous docking mechanism in which neither side penetrates the other and in which the end result of the non-penetrating docking is peace. The contrast between the *Krokodil* and *Playboy* images says much about the very different public attitudes that framed the Cold War and echoes points made in the following chapter about the bellicose and aggressive posture of the United States in comparison to the Soviet Union.

While Watergate had emboldened the anti-Nixon and anti-détente forces within the Democratic Party, those attitudes were also reinforced by the increasingly prominent Soviet dissident community in the United States and the way it increasingly seemed to shape American attitudes toward the Soviet Union. The Soviet ASTP engineers, on one of their business trips to the United States, encountered immigrants from the Soviet Union who accosted them in New York City at the UN mission, yelling out obscenities. "They must have read too much Solzhenitsyn," quipped Syromiatnikov noting that politics and engineering did not mix well (despite the obvious political mission of ASTP!). He preferred to put his energy into docking, repeating his mantra: "Docking is cooperation!" adding that he rarely ran into dissidents among Soviet engineers, who were oriented toward solving problems rather than creating them. "There were no dissidents among us," he proclaimed, and if there were, they, "never became good managers, engineers, or any other type of real professionals."[81]

---

80 Syromiatnikov, *100 Stories*, 515; Cover of *Krokodil*, July 21, 1975.
81 Syromiatnikov, *100 Stories*, 463, 489.

The termination of détente was completed in space through Reagan's 1983 Strategic Defense Initiative. While Nixon started his presidency with the idea of space collaboration, Reagan began his with remilitarizing space and a renewed attempt to achieve vertical superiority in American-Soviet relations. Gaining a position above your enemy, with a laser shield, would produce a kind of erectile dysfunction in the Soviet Union's arsenal. The engineering of androgyneity could not transcend the patriarchal ideas that drove international relations. Cold War politics in the United States seemed to be broken in a way that technology was unable to fix.

The next and final chapter takes up the problem of collaboration in space from a more explicitly comparative perspective. The focus will be on using the story of ASTP to compare US and Soviet approaches to collaboration, and in the process to test certain assumptions about the differences between the US and Soviet systems in the late Cold War, namely, that the Soviet Union was supposedly bellicose and secretive and the United States friendly and open to the world.

Chapter 4

SECURITIZATION AND SECRECY IN THE COLD WAR: THE VIEW FROM SPACE

Thomas O. Paine, the scientist, General Electric (GE) executive, and former NASA administrator in the Nixon administration, traveled to Moscow in October 1987 to attend the "International Space Future Forum." He was shocked by the attitudes he encountered. US officials were "evasive about space goals, and suspicious of dealing with foreigners," while the Soviets pursued projects of "cooperation with European and Japanese space capabilities." He was struck by the "openness of Soviet scientists compared to the uncertainty, aimlessness, and […] xenophobia of Washington space officials."[1] Paine's observations highlight a surprising turn of events: While the US space program was hostile to international collaboration, the Soviet Union was opening its space programs on numerous fronts—with France in 1966, with the United States through the Apollo-Soyuz Test Project (ASTP) in the first half of the 1970s, and with other communist and noncommunist nations. This chapter evaluates Cold War regimes of information management and secrecy through the prism of ASTP and its aftermath. Its goal is to explain the surprising end point of the Cold War in which the Soviet Union, and not the United States, had stepped into the role of defending more open information exchanges against the global forces of militarization and classification, led by the United States. The move toward greater openness in the Soviet Union originated in the late 1960s, suggesting that the Soviet system of the Brezhnev era was anything but stagnant as it developed orbital stations and extensive programs of scientific and technological collaboration with friendly and formerly hostile foreign powers in the 1970s and 1980s. Those programs, and

---

1 NASA Historical Reference Collection, "Observations on a Trip to Moscow to Attend the International Space Future Forum Celebrating the 30th Anniversary of Sputnik," LEK, Row 14, D. 4, Folder 15582; Reagan Presidential Library Archive, Outer Space, OS 388000–539999, Box 4, October 16, 1986, letter from John McLucas to Ronald Reagan.

science and technology exchanges more generally, gave the Soviets a seemingly neutral and technocratic sphere that transcended the binary ideological oppositions of the Cold War, ultimately making détente and Soviet outreach to the noncommunist world possible. As a result, the Soviets began to dismantle the elaborate system of secrecy for which it was notorious, anticipating, at least in part, Gorbachev's policies of new political thinking (*novoe politicheskoe myshlenie*) and *glasnost'* in the late 1980s.[2]

Regimes of Secrecy across the Ideological Divide

During and after World War II, the United States and the Soviet Union viewed science and technology as instruments of national power.[3] Both countries, for example, devoted more funding to big science and technology projects, creating a closed model of scientific and technological research tied to national security. That Cold War model of secret science and technology, encouraged by the spectacular success of the US Manhattan Project and driven by the seeming ideological imperatives of the Cold War, often challenged Enlightenment conceptions of science as a transnational republic of learned scholars, whose commitment to knowledge supposedly transcended ideological and national differences. Both models of science and technology operated side by side during the Cold War, entangled at the actual level of individuals—who often worked as engineers, space travelers and scientists in both the open and closed worlds—and at the level of rhetoric and ideology.[4] As the *New York Times* noted in 1985: "In principle, science is international. Its borders are not meant to coincide with those of nations." Yet such ideals

---

2 On challenges to the idea of Brezhnivite stagnation, which do not include discussions of Soviet space exploration and collaboration: Dina Fainberg and Artemy M. Kalinovsky, eds., *Reconsidering Stagnation in the Brezhnev Era: Ideology and Exchange* (Lanham, MD: Lexington Books, 2016); Edwin Bacon and Mark Sandle, eds., *Brezhnev Reconsidered* (New York: Palgrave Macmillan, 2002); Susanne Schattenberg, *Brezhnev: The Making of a Statesman* (London: I. B. Tauris-Bloomsbury, 2021).
3 Naomi Oreskes and John Krige, eds, *Science and Technology in the Global Cold War* (Cambridge, MA: MIT Press, 2014).
4 See Marsha Siefert, "Meeting at a Far Meridian: US-Soviet Cultural Diplomacy on Film in the Early Cold War," in Patryk Babiracki and Kenyon Zimmer, eds., *Cold War Crossings: International Travel and Exchange across the Soviet Bloc, 1940s–1960s* (College Station: Texas A&M University Press, 2014), 166–209. The article discusses the 1961 novel *Meeting at a Far Meridian* by the American physicist-turned-novelist Mitchell Wilson. It told the story of an American and Soviet physicist, both involved in secret military nuclear programs, who attempted to breach the Cold War model of classified science in which they were both implicated.

were quickly abandoned, "when governments believe security risks outweigh scientific benefits."[5]

The United States, for example, often claimed to be a bastion of free information exchange, supposedly directing its expertise toward the benefit of all humanity, as the US Space Act of 1958 had mandated. The United States televised Shuttle missions live and described various international experiments and payloads in reporter press packets. Missing from those press releases, however, were the many secret Shuttle payloads devoted to the Strategic Defense Initiative (SDI) program. In 1985, the Pentagon, which funded 70 percent of all federal scientific research, began requiring security clearances for many scientists who attended international conferences.[6] Classification, meanwhile, almost always trumped openness, as Casper Weinberger noted in a National Security Council memorandum in August 1986: "Our military space program is healthy and impressive, but this is not something we can go public with. If anything, our devotion to military space works against us abroad and with large segments of our own population."[7]

The urge to restrict information flow was driven by a number of factors. For the Soviets, the government perceived secrecy, like science and technology, as an instrument of power. Yet there was no obvious ideological imperative to keep secrets, beyond the general proposition of enhancing national security. The Soviet goal, however, wasn't simply to prevent foreigners from gaining knowledge of Soviet science and technology. Lacking confidence in their own science and technology, Soviet leaders feared that openness would reveal a weakness that might invite invasion and degrade the Soviet strategic and military position in the eyes of the rest of the world. The concealing of a position of perceived weakness thus motivated the Soviet system of classification as much as a desire to protect a scientific or technological advantage.[8]

If feelings of insecurity played a role in erecting the elaborate system of classification in the Soviet Union, just how and why is less clear. As Chapter 1 on the Cold War imaginary noted, conceptions of security are influenced as much by ideological biases and cultural practices—the culturally constructed perception of the other as friend or foe—as by concrete acts by the other of

---

5 "Space Arms Projects Ignite Debate on U.S.-Soviet Science Exchanges," *New York Times*, July 1, 1985, A1.
6 Ibid.
7 Ronald Reagan Presidential Library and Archive, Outer Space, 388000–539999, Box 1.
8 NASA Historical Reference Collection, LEK 10/14/2, "The Soviet Union and the United States in Space: Memorandum on the Seminars of March 23–April 20, 1965," 9. On the fear of appearing inferior before the United States: A. S. Eliseev, *Zhizn': Kaplia v more* (Moscow: Aviatsiia i kosmonavtika, 1998), 101, 103.

either friendship or hostility.⁹ The transfer of scientific and technological information thus became "securitized" by the Soviets during the early phases of the Cold War, driven by the perception of an existential threat "which calls for extraordinary measures beyond the routines and norms of everyday politics."¹⁰ Soviet tendencies to construct the capitalist other as an existential threat were driven by Marxist-Leninist ideology but even more by the profound trauma caused by the mass destruction of the Nazi invasion and occupation. Feelings of vulnerability fed an inferiority complex relative to the United States, which was perceived to have economic and technological advantages that the Soviets lacked, thereby encouraging efforts to secure and classify information. To take just one example of this inferiority complex, after the successful launch of an American orbital launch vehicle on April 4, 1968, the rocket engineer Boris Chertok and his colleagues—who received privileged access to television reports on Apollo from the West—commented on the "enormous presence" of computer technology in pictures from Houston's mission control center. The images of US computer technology reminded them of their own inferior position and of the distance they had to travel to catch up with a technologically advanced competitor.¹¹

In contrast to the United States, at least at the level of rhetoric, the Soviet Union had no strong ideological or legal commitment to open-access that those in favor of more open transfers of information might use to counter systems of classification. Moreover, the Soviet space industry was managed by the Soviet missile command and lacked the mandate of openness and collaboration contained within the enabling legislation of NASA in 1958.¹² These factors—along with the well-known Stalinist legacy of conspiratorial politics and secrecy—facilitated the securitization of Soviet science and technology, making the Soviet willingness to desecuritize its space program, as will be illustrated shortly, all the more striking.

---

9 On the culture of secrecy within the Soviet space industry and the way it clashed with the increasingly public nature of Soviet space exploration: Asif A. Siddiqi, "Cosmic Contradictions: Popular Enthusiasm and Secrecy in the Soviet Space Program," in James T. Andrews and Asif A. Siddiqi, eds., *Into the Cosmos: Space Exploration and Soviet Culture* (Pittsburgh: University of Pittsburgh Press, 2011), 47–76.
10 Michael C. Williams, "Words, Images, Enemies: Securitization and International Politics," *International Studies Quarterly* 47, no. 4 (2003), 514.
11 Boris Chertok, *Rockets and People. Volume IV. The Moon Race* (Washington, DC: NASA History Series, 2012), 155.
12 Soviet space engineers often resented their inability to connect Soviet space successes with their own labors, prompting a voluminous memoir literature from engineers after the Soviet collapse: Asif. A. Siddiqi, "Privatising Memory: The Soviet Space Programme Through Museums and Memoirs," in Martin Collins and Douglas Millard, eds., *Showcasing Space* (London: London Science Museum, 2005), 98–115.

In comparison to the Soviet Union, the United States was driven by what might be termed a superiority complex. US engineers and politicians believed that mastery of technology had provided the decisive advantage that allowed the United States to emerge victorious from World War II, constituting, in the words of the Pentagon's R&D director in 1975, "one of the few assets we have left with which to barter on a worldwide basis."[13] Typical of that confidence, which often trespassed into the realm of arrogance, was this comment from US senator William Proxmire, a determined opponent of space collaboration, in August 1975: "Our communications were more advanced, our astronauts better trained than their cosmonauts, and our ground crews more proficient." Collaboration with the Soviets had only produced, "a flow of our superior technology from this country to the Soviet Union."[14] The historian Michael Sherry has analyzed the emergence in the United States of a culture of technological arrogance and fanaticism, which relied on technological fixes rather than negotiation and political solutions to resolve international conflict. The reliance on air power, computers, radar, and nuclear bombs to defeat Germany and Japan carried over from World War II and into the Cold War, producing government-funded "Big Science" with perceived public and national security benefits.[15] Soviet successes in space, at least initially, were a threat to this belief in technological superiority and they provided a powerful argument for the securitization of technology transfers. They also helped to forge a view of space exploration as a competitive venture linked to national security—a "space race"—rather than a collaborative enterprise devoted to all humanity.

Feelings of technological superiority had a paradoxical effect on US regimes of secrecy. On the one hand, US faith in technological mastery meant that it would be possible to be open about plans for space conquest without an excessive fear of being embarrassed by failure (the "can-do" American spirit). That approach dovetailed with US rhetoric about the fundamentally open nature of the US political system and culture (in reality, the classification of information grew dramatically in the post-War period in the United States, even with the passage of the Freedom of Information Act in 1966). While belief in technological and scientific superiority inspired the confidence needed

---

13 "Currie Urges Restraint on Technology Exchange," *Defense Space Business Daily*, May 13, 1975, 8F.
14 "Was a Handshake in Space Worth $225 Million?," *National Enquirer*, August 19, 1975, 20.
15 Michael Sherry, *The Rise of American Air Power: The Creation of Armageddon* (Yale University Press, 1987), 219–300; Peter Galison and Bruce William Hevly, *Big Science: The Growth of Large-Scale Research* (Palo Alto, CA: Stanford University Press, 1992).

to be open about space plans, paradoxically it also emboldened those who argued for the securitization and the classification of information. Secrecy advocates believed that superior technological capabilities had provided the United States with its principal advantage in the international military and economic arena, and consequently open transfers of information were believed to pose a threat to US hegemony.[16] The response to this threat was the restriction of technological transfer and the creation of a complex licensing system involving the Department of State, Department of Defense (DoD), and the Treasury Department. The securitization of technology thus became a key strategy in the ideological struggle with the Soviet Union in the 1970s and 1980s, transforming classification into a fundamental aspect of American political culture and diplomacy and challenging broader assumptions about the open nature of the American system.[17]

Meanwhile, the Soviets, despite their traditions of secrecy and the absence of an ideological justification or legislative mandate for openness, could be compelled to collaborate in part to gain access to foreign technology—or at least to get some sense of just how far behind they might be, and to determine if the risks of exposing their own weaknesses might be worth the benefits of getting a closer peek at foreign technology. Moreover, as will become apparent below, in the process of collaborating the Soviets often discovered that their fears of technological backwardness had been unwarranted, and that they could therefore desecuritize what had previously been securitized, moving aspects of their space program, "off the 'security' agenda and back into the realm of public political discourse and 'normal' political dispute and accommodation."[18] Finally, traditions of Soviet internationalism, though not legislatively mandated as with NASA, nonetheless encouraged the Soviets in the 1970s and 1980s to open up their space industry to collaboration and to overcome the argument for the securitization of their space program.[19]

---

16 L. M. Gray, "A Case Study on the Transfer of Technology," August 1, 1975, Defense Advanced Research Projects Agency, in NASA Historical Reference Collection, ASTP Technology Transfer, LEK 7/6/3.

17 Peter Galison, "Removing Knowledge," *Critical Inquiry* 31, no. 1 (2004), 229–43. For an examination of the culture of fear that imperiled democracy and openness in the United States in the 1980s: Elaine Tyler May, *Fortress America: How We Embraced Fear and Abandoned Democracy* (New York: Basic Books, 2017).

18 Eliseev, *Zhizn'*, 102; Williams, "Words, Images, Enemies," 523.

19 Christine Evans has explored the collaborative impulses in the Soviet satellite communications arena, which also set precedents that contributed to ASTP: "Dividing the Cosmos? INTELSAT, Intersputnik, and the development of transnational satellite communications infrastructures during the Cold War," in Mari Pajala and Alice Lovejoy, eds. *Remapping Cold War Media: Institutions, Infrastructures, Networks, Exchanges* (Bloomington: Indiana University Press, forthcoming 2022).

This involved, for the Soviets, the partial dismantling of their elaborate regime of secrecy and a reconceptualization of space exploration as a collaborative, international project which would also help to realize the long-standing policy of "peaceful co-existence" initiated by Khrushchev and continued by Brezhnev. The Soviet goal was to reduce tensions with the United States, to advance its own alliances within and beyond the Soviet bloc countries, and to use space science and technology as part of what became known as "the scientific-technological revolution" (*nauchno-tekhnicheskaia revoliutsiia* or *NTR*), in which space technology represented the third and final phase of human mastery over nature ("the *kosmizatsiia* of human activity [...] of the relationship between human beings and nature [...] and of human consciousness"), following the revolutions of electrification and chemistry.[20]

The Soviets thus created Interkosmos in the 1960s to coordinate the collaborative deployment of space resources within and beyond the Soviet bloc.[21] As Brezhnev remarked in 1980, "in space affairs socialism is true to its core principles. Here socialism emphasizes collaboration, mutual aid, and internationalism." Those words were more than rhetoric—though the rhetoric was critical in deconstructing conceptions of national security as something requiring securitization—and they were supported by Soviet funding of scientific and communications satellites for its allies and for human spaceflights with socialist and nonsocialist partners.[22]

All of these complex and contradictory attitudes framed the encounter between the Soviet and US space industries in Apollo-Soyuz and afterward. Those encounters challenged many preconceived notions on both sides about secrecy and openness and helped to place space exploration in the Soviet case outside the realm of emergency politics that had justified regimes of secrecy under Stalin and Khrushchev. The end result, in the Soviet case, was to create the political will in the 1970s to desecuritize rather than restrict flows of

---

20 V. I. Sevastyanov and A. D. Ursul, *Era kosmosa: obshchestvo i priroda* (Moscow: Znanie, 1972), 40–51; K. D. Bushuev, *Soyuz i Apollon: rasskazyvaiut sovetskie uchenyi, inzhenery, y kosmonavty—uchastniki sovmestnykh rabot s amerikanskimi spetsialistami* (Moscow: Izd. Politicheskoi literatury, 1976), 5–6, 249. On Soviet environmentalism and attitudes toward mastering nature: Douglas R. Weiner, *A Little Corner of Freedom: Russian Nature Protection from Stalin to Gorbachev* (Berkeley: University of California Press, 1999).
21 On the creation of Interkosmos to solidify Soviet relations with socialist and nonsocialist countries: Arkhiv Rossiiskoi akademii nauk (ARAN), f. 1678, op. 1, d. 1, and fond 1678, op. 1, more generally. Christine Evans has been researching the history of satellite communications and thus is providing an important piece to the emerging story of space collaboration.
22 V. I. Kozyrev, S. A. Nikitin, *Polety po programme "Interkosmos"* (Moscow: Znanie, 1980), 3, 64; Eliseev, *Zhizn'*, 115–20.

scientific and technological information. The United States, meanwhile, had by the mid-1980s reinforced the habits of secrecy, securitization, and evasion that US leaders, ever fearful of the communist bogeyman, reflexively attributed to their ideological enemy.

France and the Desecuritization of Soviet Science and Technology

As in so many other areas already noted in this book, France played a key role not only in encouraging the United States and Soviet Union to embark on détente but also in the desecuritization of the Soviet space industry. French planners, according to US policy analysts, "tended to view scientific and technical cooperation [...] as a means of broadening relations with the USSR [and] offsetting political tensions in other areas."[23] Encouraged by the French eagerness to share information and driven by its own policies of peaceful coexistence, the Soviets thus pursued closer scientific ties with France since the mid-1960s.[24] A Soviet scientific delegation went to Paris in October 1965 and proposed sending French payloads on Soviet rockets.[25] That deal was then formalized, along with a broad program of scientific and technological exchange, during de Gaulle's visit to Moscow in 1966. The visit produced a joint declaration that introduced the idea of détente into the political vocabulary of the Cold War, and most importantly for this chapter's purposes set a precedent of desecuritizing science and technology that the Soviet Union would later follow in the ASTP.[26] Subsequently, France was the first noncommunist nation with which the Soviets collaborated in space exploration, and also the first to send high-level science ministry officials—including those involved in nuclear weapons and power—to visit formerly closed Soviet space facilities.[27]

---

23 NASA Historical Reference Collection, 10/14/3, Folder 15592, "Draft Study: The U.S.–U.S.S.R. Intergovernmental Agreement on Cooperative Space Activities: Should it be Renewed?," September 13, 1984, 13.
24 ARAN, F. 1678, op. 1, d. 108m, ll. 14, 80.
25 *Pravda*, April 3, 1966, Speech by the president of the USSR Academy of Sciences M. V. Keldysh. On technocratic trends in the post–World War II Soviet Union: Slava Gerovitch, *From Newspeak to Cyberspeak: A History of Soviet Cybernetics* (Cambridge, MA: MIT Press, 2012); on technocratic trends in post–World War II France: Gabrielle Hecht, *The Radiance of France: Nuclear Power ASTPand National Identity* (Cambridge, MA: MIT Press, 1998).
26 "Excerpts from the French," *NYT*, December 10, 1966, 1.
27 "De Gaulle Invites Soviet Science Tie," *NYT*, June 23, 1966, 1; "France in Space: Collaboration with Both U.S. and U.S.S.R.," *Science*, December 24, 1965, 700; "Soviet-French Co-operation in Space," *New Times*, October 1972, 15; ARAN, f. 1678, op. 1, d. 307, l. 10.

Following Brezhnev's visit to France in October of 1971, collaborative efforts expanded to a yearly conference of nearly two hundred French and Soviet space scientists and included television broadcasts between the two countries using the Soviet Molniia satellite system (in opposition to the US-dominated Intelsat consortium).[28] By the early 1980s, 10 percent of France's overall budget for cooperative ventures was devoted to Soviet projects and 60 percent of its space science budget.[29] Those contacts with France had initiated an important moment of scientific and technological collaboration that began to lift the national security veil from the Soviet scientific establishment. For both the Soviets and the French, science and technology provided a seemingly neutral sphere that could help to forge economic and political ties across ideological boundaries and to ease Cold War divisions in Europe. In short, thanks to France, Soviet leaders became far more open to the possibility of declassifying at least some of their scientific and technological infrastructures.[30]

Beginning in the late 1950s, the United States had also proposed scientific cooperation with the Soviets. The goal was to ease tensions and to promote the image and popularity of American democracy to the rest of the world. The 1958 Lacy-Zarubin Agreement was the first of many scientific and technological exchanges that, in part, paved the way later for proposals by John F. Kennedy to collaborate with the Soviets on space missions, though just how serious Kennedy and later Johnson were about these overtures is unclear. Some US officials seem to have counted on a Soviet rejection of offers of collaboration to highlight the closed nature of the Soviet system and to underscore the supposed openness of the US system. At any rate, following Gagarin's historic flight in 1961, Kennedy largely abandoned cooperative efforts and focused instead on beating the Soviets to the moon.[31] The escalation of the Vietnam War under Johnson created additional barriers to collaboration, as did the intensification of the sense of being in a "space race" to the

---

28 On Soviet-French collaboration on color television satellite broadcasts: ARAN, F. 1678, op. 1, d. 108d, ll. 117–22.
29 NASA Historical Reference Collection, 10/14/3, Folder 15592, "Draft Study: The U.S.-U.S.S.R. Intergovernmental Agreement on Cooperative Space Activities: Should it be Renewed?," October 9, 1984, 9.
30 ARAN, f. 1678, op. 1, has numerous files, totaling thousands of pages, devoted to French-Soviet collaboration in a broad range of scientific and technological fields and these files suggest contacts at an earlier date, in 1965, that were more extensive than cooperative efforts with fellow socialist countries.
31 John Logsdon, *John F. Kennedy and the Race to the Moon* (New York: Palgrave Macmillan, 2010).

moon, with the outcome of the Cold War seemingly hinging on victory or defeat.[32]

But it was the election of Richard Nixon as president, as noted earlier, that reinforced the US commitment toward space collaboration in both word and deed. Collaboration and openness might just counter the emotions of fear and insecurity that had encouraged the securitization of space technology on both sides.[33] Those ideas dovetailed with increasingly popular Soviet conceptions of collaborative space exploration as a panacea that would lead humanity down the path toward a more perfect global community.[34] While Nixon seems to have taken such rhetoric seriously,[35] as did Brezhnev,[36] he also saw scientific collaboration as a way to advance US interests and to promote a US-style policy of détente, in imitation of the French example, that would help get the United States out of Vietnam and enjoy the economic benefits that Western Europeans gained from their own growing connections with the Soviet Union. Frank Borman's 1969 visit to the Star City training center—the French had already visited the site as well as the secret Baikonur launch facility—was a significant breach of the Soviet system of information control and secrecy; Borman was the first US citizen to visit the secret launch center. Borman's laying of a wreath at Lenin's tomb elicited howls of outrage from US anti-communist politicians. Borman's enthusiastic and friendly reception in the Soviet Union was a revelation for the Nixon administration, and it convinced Nixon and Kissinger that desecuritizing Soviet space technology could be a boon for US diplomacy and also help to transform the Soviet Union into a more open and friendlier place with which to do business.[37]

A notable feature of US sources documenting these first encounters between US and Soviet space officials and cosmonauts and astronauts is that they all expressed surprise at the Soviet eagerness for contact and collaboration. That

---

32 Dodd L. Harvey and Linda C. Ciccoritti, *U.S.-Soviet Cooperation in Space* (Miami, FL: Center for Advanced International Studies, University of Miami, 1974), 172–3.
33 Frank White, *The Overview Effect: Space Exploration and Human Evolution* (Boston: Houghton Mifflin, 1987).
34 V. I. Sevastyanov and A. D. Ursul, "Space Age: New Relationship between Society and Nature," *Space World*, no. 1 (1972), 31–39.
35 Frank Borman, in an interview conducted by The Nixon Archive and Libraries, said that Nixon had "an almost boyish enthusiasm" for Apollo 11 and was genuinely touched and inspired by the moon landing.
36 See Donald J. Raleigh, "'Soviet Man of Peace': Leonid Il'ich Brezhnev and His Diaries," *Kritika: Explorations in Russian and Eurasian History* 17, no. 4 (2016), 837–68.
37 NASA Historical Reference Collection, 1/3/1, "Borman, Frank NASA Post-Apollo 8"; Nixon Presidential Library Research Files, Nixon Presidential Materials Project, White House General Files, Subject Files, Outer Space, OS 3 Box 1, August 5, 1969, Borman letter to Henry Kissinger; "Borman Sees Siberian Technical Show," *New York Times*, July 9, 1969, 1.

eagerness contrasted with assumptions in US national security memoranda that the Soviets would never tolerate the kind of information exchanges needed for genuine collaboration.[38] To the great surprise of the US government, the Soviets allowed a NASA film on Apollo 11 to be shown to audiences in the Soviet Union in October 1969. The director of the Sternberg State Astronomical Society in Moscow screened the film eight times and presented 11 lectures on its content—each time to packed venues. "The film had audiences of 1,000 each at the Moscow and Odessa planetaria and a group of 400 honor high school students in mathematics and science at Moscow." NASA scrambled to get a Russian script for the film and another copy and also began taking seriously the possibility of real collaboration.[39] The head of MGM studios, with Nixon's enthusiastic support, also managed to get his film *2001: A Space Odyssey* shown to select audiences in the Soviet Union in July 1969 at the Moscow Film Festival. Nixon had arranged the film's showing to prepare the way for US-Soviet collaboration, since contact between Soviet and American space scientists was central to the plot of the film. In effect, he treated a Hollywood film screened for Soviet audiences as something akin to an act of declassification, which in many ways it was: peeling back the obsessive systems of information control and censorship that the Soviets directed toward their own citizens. Nixon told Soviet filmgoers that the film dealt, "with the broad range of man's technical and spiritual development. It is my hope that this cinematic look into man's past and his future at this festival will help to bring a better understanding of our world and perhaps offer that intellectual stimulation so necessary if we are to solve our problems in the spirit of international brotherhood."[40]

If Nixon showed a growing faith in collaborative space technology and science as a key to world peace and changing Soviet behaviors, it was also becoming clear that the main barriers to collaboration originated mostly from the US side—a point that the official Soviet history of the flight noted repeatedly and with good justification.[41] NASA's director Paine wondered if NASA's

---

38 Nixon Presidential Library Research Files, National Security Study Memorandums, NSSM 70 to NSSM 76, Box H-162, "Cooperation between the US and USSR in Space Activities, Prospect and Opportunities," April 8, 1970.
39 NASA Historical Reference Collection, 10/14/4, 15590.
40 Nixon Presidential Library Research Files, Nixon Presidential Materials Project, White House General Files, Subject Files, Outer Space, OS 3 Box 1, August 7, 1969, Nixon letter to MGM Studios head Louis F. Polk Jr.; CO 158, Box 70, July 11, 1969, Nixon letter to the Moscow Film Festival.
41 Nixon Presidential Library Research Files, Nixon Presidential Materials Project, White House General Files, Subject Files, Outer Space, OS 3 Box 1, November 24, 1969, letter to Peter Flanigan; Bushuev, *Soyuz i Apollon: rasskazyvaiut sovetskie uchenyi, inzhenery, y kosmonavty*, 6, 27.

Cold War culture could tolerate the kind of openness that the new relationship with the Soviets would require. In April 1969 he expressed concerns in a memo about the closed nature of NASA culture and its ability to conduct itself more openly and collaboratively.[42] In September 1970, before resigning to take over GE, Paine wrote that cooperation with the Soviets would require "courageous and innovative steps by our own government." The United States would need to be "both generous and confident; it must also recognize that international cooperation necessarily implies international interdependence. As you well know, it will be necessary to remind many of our own people constantly that we cannot have significant international cooperation without some real dependency, each side upon the other."[43] One particularly vexing challenge was to convince the Pentagon that desecuritization, even with friendly Western Europeans, would involve a level of openness and technology transfer that would not jeopardize national security.[44] Doctor heal thyself.

Perceptions of US insincerity had also eroded trust in the previous decade. The policy of shaming the Soviets, by publicly exposing their penchant for secrecy and stonewalling, had become a key component of NASA's relationship with its Soviet space counterparts. NASA had offered invitations to Soviets to attend launches since the early 1960s, and the Soviets always refused, recognizing that should they accept they would be bound by the principle of reciprocity to allow Westerners to attend their launches. Soviet rejections of the invitation in the 1960s had become so common that within NASA and the US intelligence world no one believed that the Soviets were capable of cooperating.[45] Robert Gilruth, the head of NASA human spaceflight, recalled that his Pentagon and CIA briefers, prior to his visits to the Soviet Union in the early 1970s to negotiate cooperative projects, told him that "the Soviets would break our hearts when we get over there. We would talk, and they would talk, but there would be few positive results. They would not cooperate."[46] In short, by the early 1970s, the national security bureaucracy was convinced that the Soviets were incapable of collaborating with the United States because, as a

---

42 LOC, Thomas Paine Papers, Box 23, Folder 3.
43 LOC, Thomas Paine Papers, Box 23, Folder 4.
44 Nixon Presidential Library Research Files, Nixon Presidential Materials Project, White House General Files, Subject Files, Outer Space, OS 3 Box 1, October 27, 1970, National Security Decision Memorandum 72; OS Outer Space 1/1/71 [1971–72] [1 of 3], January 8, 1971, April 23, 1971, NSC Memoranda to Henry Kissinger.
45 Nixon Presidential Library Research Files, Nixon Presidential Materials Project, White House General Files, Subject Files, Outer Space, OS 3 Box 1, December 2, 1969, Borman letter to Peter Flanigan.
46 NASA Historical Reference Collection, "Gilruth, Robert K. (Bio)," 1/6/2, March 25, 1975, interview by E. C. Ezell.

confidential White House study in April 1970 put it, of "the suspiciousness and antagonisms generated by the conflicting nature of our two systems and the Soviet obsession with secrecy as such."[47]

It was therefore all the more surprising when the Soviets responded positively to Western overtures, giving the go ahead for a July 1970 agreement to expand scientific and technological collaboration (though many American officials, observed the Soviet participant Vladimir Syromiatnikov, remained visibly skeptical of Soviet intentions).[48] The Soviet shift in attitudes, as noted in Chapter 1, was a result of efforts by Academy president Keldysh to open up Soviet science and technology as well as Brezhnev's own commitment to collaboration—the latter a continuation of the Khrushchev policy of peaceful coexistence that had inspired the first scientific and cultural exchanges in the late 1950s. The future ASTP flight director Aleksei Eliseev recalled that the July 1970 agreement had "opened the door for normal working contacts between specialists."[49] Deputy NASA administrator George Low, in October 1970, reported back to Kissinger following a trip to Moscow to gauge Soviet interest in working together. "Our people have just returned from Moscow, after a most successful discussion with representatives of the Soviet Academy of Sciences concerning joint efforts to develop compatible space rendezvous and docking arrangements. [...] In marked contrast to our experience of the past decade, the Soviet side appeared to be entirely direct and open, clearly intent upon reaching a positive result." The delegation received "full access to the Soviet human spacecraft space craft simulator. [...] All systems were explained and all questions answered." There was none of the expected "hesitation or fencing," he added, and in every respect the Soviets met NASA's standard of open communication necessary for such a joint engineering mission. Soviet engineers later referred to that October 1970 meeting as the launching point for a new international phase in their professional lives and in the Soviet space program.[50]

Meanwhile, the previous and ongoing collaboration with France helped to assuage Soviet fears. Exchanges and contacts were bolstered at the very highest levels by a series of friendly letters between Nixon and Brezhnev—critical, in the case of Nixon, in convincing him to confront the considerable

---

47 Nixon Presidential Library Research Files, National Security Study Memorandums, NSSM 70 to NSSM 76, Box H-162, "Cooperation between the US and USSR in Space Activities, Prospects and Opportunities," April 8, 1970.
48 Vladimir Syromiatnikov, *100 Stories about Docking and Other Adventures in Space, Vol. 1* (Moscow: Universitetskaia kniga, 2005), 390.
49 Eliseev, *Zhizn'*, 100–101.
50 NASA Historical Reference Collection, 10/14/4, 15590. Syromiatnikov, *100 Stories*, 379.

resistance to collaboration and openness within the Pentagon and NASA itself. In a letter to Nixon on August 5, 1971, Brezhnev—the "man of peace" in Donald Raleigh's interpretation—said he did not want to allow "the course of events [to] push mankind toward new disasters, immeasurably more terrible than anything that we have lived through so far? [...] We firmly proceed from the belief that settlement of world problems should not be sought by crossing swords." He reiterated his desire to "develop Soviet-American relations. We are certain that, given a mutual desire, those relations could become an important factor in strengthening peace and ensuring greater security for all states." While acknowledging ideological differences, Brezhnev—who considered Nixon "a man he can deal with forthrightly," according to Kissinger—wanted to find supposedly neutral areas where there could be mutual cooperation, especially in "trade and cooperation in the fields of outer space research, studies of the World oceans, preservation of the environment, and public health. These spheres of human activity are of growing importance in the life of the people [and] more dependable ways should be sought to solve the problems of disarmament, including the question of the prohibition of nuclear weapons." Their general course was "peaceful coexistence. When we declare this principle in the highest forums in our country and on the world arena, we do it in earnest." The Soviets, Brezhnev added, were not engaging in disarmament talks to gain some sort of "tactical advantage," a claim that also dovetailed with Nixon's own attempts to convince the world of his sincere desire for peace.[51]

The exchange of letters was crucial in building trust and in convincing both sides in May 1972 to sign a wide-ranging agreement for scientific and technological exchanges in eleven different areas, with space exploration and ASTP as the first major test of the new political line of desecuritization by both sides.

The Experience of Collaboration

Nixon administration officials hoped that ASTP would open up the Soviet space program—including allowing Western journalists, scientists, engineers, and politicians to attend Soviet launches and visit Soviet training and rocket construction facilities—or at the very least shame the Soviets, as had been the practice in the 1960s, by revealing their unwillingness to do those things. As it turned out, ASTP accelerated the desecuritization of the Soviet space industry already under way as a result of collaborative projects with the French.

---

51 Nixon Presidential Library Research Files, National Security Council Files, Henry A. Kissinger Office Files—NSC HAK, Box 66, August 5, 1971, Brezhnev letter to Nixon; Box 68, May 11, 1973, memorandum from Kissinger to Nixon.

At a May 14, 1975, news conference, just following a first-ever visit of ASTP astronauts to the Tiura-Tam launch site, the US ASTP crew described in great detail, and with humor and astonishment, the details of their visit: the huge dimensions of the launch site, the kinds of things located on the grounds, the flora and fauna, their impressions compared to Cape Canaveral, accommodations and food, and the fact that the site was not in fact located in Baikonur but in a place called Tiura-Tam.[52] Surprisingly, the joint project also exposed the growing strength of the secrecy regime in the American system, challenging the claim, as one NASA public relations official put it, that Americans always reported their affairs, "openly, candidly, and promptly (in real time)."[53] For example, it was the Americans, rather than the Soviets, who refused to participate in a joint film project on ASTP, fearing that a 90-minute feature documentary film would limit NASA's ability to control the narrative (the Soviets, it will be recalled, had little problem allowing an uncensored NASA film on Apollo 11 to be screened with Soviet audiences in 1969). George Low, deputy NASA administrator, said he gave "serious consideration to the advantages and disadvantages of a joint film on ASTP"—in fact NASA had in principle agreed to it—before deciding against it. "Our own shorter films will be much less expensive and much more useful to television and educational programming," he noted. The shorter NASA-produced films, plus the TV coverage, "will convey the joint mission accurately and effectively to the entire world."[54]

Meanwhile, the Soviet engineer who designed the docking module for ASTP, Vladimir Syromiatnikov, remembered a seemingly Soviet ritual of secrecy when he was working in Rockwell facilities in Downey, California. He encountered what the Russians called a "regime establishment," including US security officials who followed him everywhere, even to the bathroom. He looked down at the desktop he was using and noticed a loose-leaf calendar left by his American predecessor. The pages of each month contained "advice on how to keep classified information," reminding the desk's occupant that "a potential enemy was spying and eavesdropping and doing other things that we, even quite experienced in these matters, did not know about yet [...] I got the idea that such precepts could be useful at home" and requested from his NASA colleagues that he receive one such calendar as a souvenir to show his Soviet colleagues that the Soviet Union was not the only paranoid superpower.

---

52 NASA Historical Reference Collection, LEK 8/2/6, Stafford, Thomas P. (1976–79), "ASTP Crew Press Conference, Johnson Space Center, Houston, Texas, May 14, 1975"; "Astronauts Tell of Huge Soviet Spaceport," *Washington Post*, May 15, 1975, A3.
53 NASA Historical Reference Collection, "Public Affairs Operations Plan: Apollo Soyuz Test Project, July 1975," "ASTP Guest Lists/Press," 7/6/3, May 23, 1975.
54 NASA Historical Reference Collection, LEK 2/3/2, Tatitscheff, Alex, Interpreter, ASTP.

132 COLLABORATION IN SPACE AND THE SEARCH FOR PEACE

Figure 4.1 The ASTP news center for the world's press
Source: NASA

The NASA hosts gave the Soviet engineers nicely wrapped calendars when they left. Upon returning, the Soviets opened their gifts and found normal calendars without the recommendations on how to protect classified information. The calendars, it turned out, were for American eyes only.[55]

The Americans, meanwhile, had second thoughts about allowing the Soviets any control over the representation of events to US live television audiences. Joint access in real time to the other's television programming was one feature of the press coverage agreement between the two sides.[56] In the months leading up to the launch of ASTP, the NASA public relations office feared that a possible Soviet broadcast from space to America in July 1975—a description of a flyover of Leningrad, for example—might be filled with "propaganda" about "the razing of Leningrad, relocation of people, rebuilding, etc. This

---

55 Syromiatnikov, *100 Stories*, 523.
56 ARAN, f. 1678, o. 1, d. 392, l. 72.

in itself may not be too bad, but information I have received concerning the recent training session in Moscow indicates that even more 'propaganda' has been added with references such as 'Revolution,' Great Patriotic War, etc." The letter from the NASA ASTP program director to the NASA public affairs office, based on a review of a Soviet script for the eventual flyover, suggested that unless they could review beforehand what the Soviet commentators planned to say, "we should eliminate the TV tours of Florida and the USSR as a joint activity," since the Soviet side would likely try to project its view of the world onto its commentary for American viewers. The NASA program director added at the end, perhaps aware that his letter was violating the spirit of open and uncontrolled communications for which the United States was supposedly known: "[This] is not intended to be censorship, but rather a review of the propriety of the activity in the context of a joint activity."[57] The NASA manager's position hardly supported the claim of one American journalist regarding the relaxed style of the Americans, as compared to the supposedly uptight Soviets: "Under the influence of the free-and-easy people [of NASA], the Soviets relaxed."[58] Caldwell Johnson, the NASA docking engineer, later recalled his Soviet visits: "The only difficulty that I ran across was with our people, with our embassy people and people like that which was horrible. You know, they acted like we were in a shooting war or something and we ought not to even talk to one another." He remembered being briefed by the CIA and FBI before his visits and warned not to "'drink a vodka with them. Don't even wink at one of the women. Don't walk around the streets by yourself,' and all this kind of stuff. That was a bunch of crap. Nothing like that went on. It was all fine."[59]

Yet despite these largely hidden conflicts, ASTP ultimately forged new communication channels between the two countries, surprising both sides with the degree to which it was possible to desecuritize one of the Cold War's highest profile Big Science projects. The project's successful conclusion on July 15, 1975, the famous handshake in space between the US and Soviet crews that docked their separate spaceships, established a precedent that emboldened advocates of peaceful collaboration in both governments, prompting the United States to consider putting July 15 on the ceremonial calendar as "International Cooperation Day."[60] Eroding the Soviet system of secrecy was also critical in

---

57 NASA Historical Reference Collection, May 12, 1974, letter from NASA ASTP Program director to assistant administrator for public affairs.
58 June 22, 1975, *Chicago Tribune*, 1.
59 Interview with Caldwell Johnson, April 1, 1998, League City Texas, NASA Johnson Space Center Oral History Project, 27.
60 NASA Historical Reference Collection, "ASTP 1974," 7/6/1, October 16, 1974, Memorandum.

raising trust between the two nations and in convincing some Americans that perhaps their technology was not so superior after all. The 1972 agreement had produced numerous working groups in which American and Soviet engineers and scientists met every year, visiting each other's countries and often developing close friendships that defied stereotypes.

While secrecy promoted suspicion and tension, and tended to justify more classification, openness facilitated trust and collaboration, providing a powerful rationale for more openness and declassification, especially for the Soviets. Eliseev recalled being surprised that the "Americans, by their character, are in many ways similar to us. [...] They love jokes, they were good hosts, and they were open in the relationships with friends. We really liked this." The Soviets gained confidence from their encounters that as "professional specialists we were not inferior to the Americans, and if one speaks of the broadness of interests and general erudition, I think we were better. At any rate, one way or another we immediately developed completely friendly relations." The Soviets especially appreciated the respectful attitude of US engineers toward Soviet space technology, which gave Soviet officials confidence in their ability to work in an open and collaborative international environment.[61] ASTP American director Glynn Lunney in July 1975 called the ASTP mission a "breakthrough" that worked out far better than he had anticipated with the signing of the agreement in 1972. "Not a breakthrough in the sense of any new engineering system but in the larger sense of how people from two countries can work together on a common project, how teams from two countries can be brought together to solve problems."[62] American astronauts visited Soviet sites that did "not appear on maps" and that were never "before open to us." The Soviets broadcast their 1975 ASTP launch and landing live—another first—and provided real-time air-to-ground communications to the Americans. The Soviet willingness to provide live coverage to their own population reflected a certain level of confidence in their own technology but also a new commitment to open information exchange as more useful politically than secrecy and obfuscation—a change that one US space journalist called "dramatic."[63] When the astronauts and cosmonauts shook hands in the Soviet capsule, the handshake itself marked the transition away from securitization

---

61 Eliseev, *Zhizn'*, 102; Bushuev, *Soyuz i Apollon: rasskazyvaiut sovetskie uchenyi, inzhenery, y kosmonavty*, 164.

62 July 21, 1975, *NYT*, 4.

63 Nixon Presidential Library Research Files, Nixon Presidential Materials Project, White House General Files, Subject Files, Outer Space, OS 3 Box 9, Folder 2, October 31, 1973, letter from NASA administrator James Fletcher to Richard Nixon; October 12, 1974, *NYT*, 2; "Apollo-Soyuz Mission Signals New Era in Space," June 18, 1975, *Philadelphia Inquirer*, 4; "U.S. Newsmen Visit Soviet Space Center," May 13, 1985, *NYT*, 8.

for both sides. The mood in Soviet mission control "was such that before our very eyes we passed from confrontation to friendly collaboration."[64]

Detailed agreements between both sides provided unprecedented access to reporters to Soviet facilities and committed both sides to the maximum possible publicity, "as fully, widely, and promptly as possible." Contrary to US expectations, NASA received from the Soviets "complete and detailed technical information in response to all questions concerning the Apollo Soyuz Test Project and support facilities."[65] Aleksei Leonov, to the surprise of NASA officials, provided a briefing in July 1973 to US engineers and officials—"very frank and descriptive"—regarding the various landing challenges that the Soviets faced in previous human spaceflight missions, something that the Soviets had never discussed in public, including the tragic death of three cosmonauts during the descent of Soyuz 11 on June 30, 1971, whose official cause and investigation had previously been classified.[66] Yuri Mozzhorin, the Soviet manager of flight control, remembered that the Americans constantly questioned the safety and reliability of Soviet technology; those queries wounded the pride of the Soviet side but also compelled Soviet engineers to provide the greatest possible detail about their systems to assuage these concerns and to prove that their technological capabilities were equal to those of the Americans.[67] The Soviets opened up their new spaceflight control center outside Moscow to the Americans, overcoming resistance from the KGB, which wanted to create a fake flight control center where Americans could sit to view the launch and track its progress. Brezhnev, at the insistence of the defense minister Ustinov, instructed Andropov to permit this significant dismantling of the Soviet system of secrecy, which the advocates of openness, such as Mozzhorin, considered a pivotal moment in the desecuritization of the Soviet space program, despite the concerns of the KGB head Andropov.[68] When the Americans and journalists arrived, one of the managers of the center remembered that all the Soviet workers in the control room were "in shock." "In the 'holy of holies' they had let in not even citizens of 'the countries of

---

64 Eliseev, *Zhizn'*, 109.
65 NASA Historical Reference Collection, "ASTP, July 1975," 7/6/2, July 31, 1975, letter from NASA director of public services to Thomas J. Fleck; ARAN, f. 1678, op. 1, d. 392, ll. 71–88 (drafts of the press agreements between the two sides).
66 NASA Historical Reference Collection, "US/USSR July Working Group Meeting," July 20, 1973, "ASTP-73," 7/14/1.
67 Bushuev, *Soyuz i Apollon: rasskazyvaiut sovetskie uchenyi, inzhenery, y kosmonavty*, 27.
68 N. A. Anfimov, ed., *Tak eto bylo...: Memuary Iu. A. Mozzhorina: Mozzhorin v vospominaniiakh sovremennikov* (Moscow: OAO 'Mezhdunarodnaia programma obrazovaniia, 2000). Cited from the online version, chapter 6, downloaded June 12, 2018: http://epizodssp ace.airbase.ru/bibl/mozjorin/tak/06.html.

people's democracy,'" but the very "powerful enemy—the Americans from which we had done everything to hide our facilities," he remembered. "There were some curious things that happened. When the column of vehicles left Moscow by the Yaroslav highway, the Americans got worried. They thought the flight control center was in Star City. According to their intelligence from satellite photos there was a big construction site there." The Moscow flight control center acted in collaboration with its Houston counterpart and each also provided critical backup for the other in the event of some technical failure. The two superpowers now had each other's backs, and direct, unimpeded, uncensored, real-time access by phone and video to all of the other side's communications, with the presence of reporters from both countries given full entry to the other side's mission control. Mozzhorin was proud that the American press frequently complimented him on the timely, accurate, and complete information, which "was not characteristic of us previously," that he provided to the press corps of both the United States and the Soviet Union.[69] In a letter to the Soviet Academy of Sciences, the ASTP flight commander Thomas Stafford thanked the Soviets for allowing American television stations and crews to enter previously closed areas.[70]

The Soviet willingness to desecuritize its space program impressed the Congressional Research Service: "The sharing of engineering skills and opening up of previously 'sensitive' Soviet materials and 'restricted' areas to the United States can only be regarded as a positive step toward cooperation. [...] The Soviet space program has existed within a seemingly impenetrable wall of secrecy, which led to negative attitudes on both sides."[71] Nixon in early 1974 met personally with Soviet engineers at NASA facilities and impressed the visiting Soviets by offering some words in Russian. ASTP commander Thomas Stafford, in a letter to Nixon on April 24, 1974, wrote: "For all of us at NASA it was an honor to have you. [...] The Russian engineers with whom you stopped and chatted commented that it was one of the highlights of their entire lives. The words you spoke in Russian certainly made a great hit with them." They were making great progress,

> and we have worked out the majority of difficulties in putting together a most difficult and diverse technical mission. We all feel that this mission will

---

69 "Istoriia TsUPa: Trud, radosti, mytarstva," *Nauka i zhizn'*, No. 8, 2005, http://epizodsspace.airbase.ru/bibl/n_i_j/2005/7/istoria-tsupa.html, downloaded June 11, 2018; *Tak eto bylo*, cited from the online version, chapter 6, downloaded June 12, 2018: http://epizodsspace.airbase.ru/bibl/mozjorin/tak/06.html.

70 ARAN, f. 1678, o. 1, d. 391, l. 27.

71 NASA Historical Reference Collection, "Background and Policy Issues in the Apollo-Soyuz Test Project," Congressional Research Service, January 31, 1975, 39.

be a great symbol in indicating to both the Russian and American people and the rest of the world that, if our two countries can cooperate on such a difficult task, there is not any problem that we cannot solve if we work together in good faith and mutual understanding."[72]

Indeed, the biggest benefit of ASTP was not the actual technology of docking, but the comraderie between ideological foes that facilitated the flow of information between both sides. Feelings of comraderie constructed a reality for its participants—a willingness to collaborate grounded in a technocratic commitment to problem solving and open information exchanges—that ultimately challenged the Cold War feelings of fear and mutual distrust. From the Soviet and American crews and down through the engineers and program managers in the flight control centers in Houston and outside Moscow, Soviet sources remembered the working relationship with the Americans, without exception, as excellent and friendly.[73] Said one American diplomat: "It's not a question of who gets the most out of it. This is helping us get along in a dangerous world, and everybody benefits from that."[74] That openness made believers out of many previously skeptical Americans in the US government and NASA, providing confidence in the possibility of collaboration, enhancing feelings of trust, and reducing the feelings of fear and insecurity that had justified regimes of secrecy and information control. Even before ASTP's successful conclusion, Soviets were already eager to expand collaborative efforts, according to Chester Lee, an ASTP program director, who was sure of the genuine Soviet commitment to information exchange and who remarked on the "frankness, confidence, and personal working relationship" between Soviet and US technical directors, and between the hundreds of engineers and managers on both sides.[75] From the Soviet perspective, at least, the joint commitment to solving complex

---

72 Nixon Presidential Library Research Files, Nixon Presidential Materials Project, White House General Files, Subject Files, Outer Space, OS 3 Box 9, Folder 2, April 24, 1974, letter from Thomas Stafford to Richard Nixon.
73 Syromiatnikov, *100 Stories*, 373; Eliseev, *Zhizn'*, 104; "Istoriia TsUPa: Trud, radosti, mytarstva," *Nauka i zhizn'*, No. 8, 2005, http://epizodsspace.airbase.ru/bibl/n_i_j/2005/7/istoria-tsupa.html, downloaded June 11, 2018.
74 Istoriia TsUPa: Trud, radosti, mytarstva," *Nauka i zhizn'*, No. 8, 2005, http://epizodssp ace.airbase.ru/bibl/n_i_j/2005/7/istoria-tsupa.html, downloaded June 11, 2018.; NASA Historical Reference Collection, "ASTP, 1974," 7/6/1, September 13, 1974, Memorandum.
75 NASA Historical Reference Collection, "US/USSR July Working Group Meeting," July 20, 1973, "ASTP-73," 7/14/1; on the friendship between Leonov and American cosmonauts: *Pravda*, July 4, 1975, 1; on vodka parties, Syromiatnikov, *100 Stories*, 479–81.

engineering problems in an atmosphere of openness and more transparency was the best way to transcend ideological hostilities, prevent war, and advance human progress.⁷⁶

Harbinger of *Glasnost'*

Seen in the broader context of the history of secrecy, the late 1960s and 1970s reversed the seemingly unstoppable trend toward classification during the Cold War. The Soviet space program, in the climate of détente between the Soviet Union and France and later the United States, set a precedent of more open exchanges that in some ways anticipated the official policy of *glasnost'* under Gorbachev (albeit in a far more restricted way that was limited primarily to scientific and technical elites). Just as Nixon attempted to extract himself from Vietnam as a peacemaker and to transcend ideological divides in constructing a new foreign policy, Brezhnev had imagined himself to be a man of peace who based his foreign policy, in part, on preventing the Soviet Union from reliving the horrors of World War II and on the idea of peaceful coexistence that had originated with his predecessor Khrushchev. As Kissinger remarked to Nixon, the war remained for Brezhnev "an earthshaking experience. [...] He knows something of the human disaster of war—one should credit him with abhorrence of it, though, of course, he uses fear of war in others to obtain political ends."⁷⁷ Both Nixon and Brezhnev were inspired by global visions of Earth and of themselves as stewards of humanity; both viewed science and technology as a neutral ground that would allow for a reset of the US–Soviet relationship on pragmatic and technical rather than ideological terms; the commitment of both to collaboration made it possible to desecuritize the Soviet space industry, at least partially. Economic motivations also played a role, as both Nixon and Brezhnev were seeking to defray the exorbitant costs of space exploration by pooling resources and technologies. For the Soviets, this shift marked the important realization, so far as regimes of information exchange are concerned, that openness might be more useful politically and economically than secretiveness.⁷⁸ Mozzhorin, the ASTP flight director, noted that Soviet space industry officials decided it made more sense, given the fact

---

76 Bushuev, *Soyuz i Apollon: rasskazyvaiut sovetskie uchenyi, inzhenery, y kosmonavty*, 53–60, and on a detailed Soviet description and praise of the American engineers with whom the Soviet engineers worked, 141–45.
77 Nixon Presidential Library Research Files, National Security Council Files, President's Trip Files, President's Moscow Trip Jan-Apr [Part 1], Kissinger Memorandum to Nixon, "The Soviet Leaders."
78 "U.S. Space Team at Soviet Center: First Foreigners to Visit the Mission Control Area," *NYT*, October 19, 1974, 1.

that they were collaborating, to be open about their technical capabilities rather than to sow suspicion with obfuscating cover stories that would force the Americans, "to glean information as previously from newspapers and resident spies." The Soviet engineers, moreover, had lost the fear that exposing their technological capabilities to the Americans would make them appear inferior. Growing pride in their technological prowess made them eager to show off their accomplishments, knowing that their new flight control center, remembered Mozzhorin, "had made a big impression on NASA officials."[79] The Soviet docking engineer Syromiatnikov echoed these thoughts in his own memoir, noting that ASTP "contributed to further changes, to *perestroika*. I do not know where Gorbachev acquired his *novoe myshlenie* (new mentality), but for sure, we got it from the first Soviet-American space project." The precedent of publicizing the formerly secret Soviet space industry could not be overturned, he added, transforming engineers into public figures and making space exploration and docking a public spectacle in Soviet society. Star City and other formerly secret sites remained "semi-open […] foreigners could get access to those places, primarily because Americans had worked there during ASTP. Employees […] were no longer obliged to invent 'legends' or look for academic 'covers and roofs' to conceal their essence from 'foreign spies." The secret Soviet engineering world, in short, had gained "a little window (*fortochka*)" into other systems with different ideologies and cultures.[80]

As for the claim that the United States would be giving up a technological advantage by working with the Soviets—a recurring challenge for the Nixon administration and later for Ford and Carter—those with expertise in engineering and science noted that the Soviet Union and United States approached spaceflight and docking from very different positions that mostly precluded larger technological and information transfers in either direction.[81] Moreover, the Soviets could have easily learned about US space engineering from open, published sources, making US regimes of secrecy seem irrational and politically damaging. A US Office of Technology Assessment (OTA) report noted: "Because Soviet scientific publications are not as complete and detailed, because translations are not always readily available, and because few American scientists have learned Russian, those scientists found that personal contact with their Soviet counterparts was the most useful means of

---

79 *Tak eto bylo*, cited from the online version, chapter 6, downloaded June 12, 2018: http://epizodsspace.airbase.ru/bibl/mozjorin/tak/06.html.
80 Syromiatnikov, *100 Stories*, 382, 609, 612–13.
81 Edward Clinton Ezell and Linda Neuman Ezell, *The Partnership: A History of the Apollo-Soyuz Test Project* (Washington, DC: NASA History Series, 1978), 355; Bushuev, *Soyuz i Apollon: rasskazyvaiut sovetskie uchenyi, inzhenery, y kosmonavty*, 20–21, 50.

exchange." Most informed sources agree that the most important thing the Soviets gained from ASTP was not any particular technology—indeed, in some ways Soviet technology for docking was superior—but the US system of project and contractor management, including the documentation, tracking, and systematization of management and engineering systems (a method dubbed total quality management and originally created in Japan after World War II and borrowed by US corporations under the direction of the consultant guru William Edwards Deming).[82] Many US scientists, meanwhile, concluded that they were net beneficiaries of the collaborative efforts by the late 1970s.[83]

The world of 1975 thus seemed to be one that promised less secrecy and classification and more information exchange, cooperation, and friendship. The Cold War model of secret science and technology seemed to be waning. Following ASTP, the Soviets eagerly anticipated a host of collaborative projects with the United States, France, and its own communist allies, boldly predicting that international space missions would involve "more and more" people and constitute a key moment in human progress toward a more perfect and peaceful world.[84] To accommodate the anticipated internationalization of human space exploration, Soviet cosmonauts tapped into their experiences with US comrades during ASTP to study the challenges of "crew interrelationships in international space flights," requiring English-language proficiency as part of the professional preparation of Soviet explorers of the cosmos.[85] According to the ASTP flight director Eliseev, the joint collaboration helped to desecuritize space exploration and transform it from a secretive endeavor to one that was far more public and open. The preparation for joint flights, as well as the launches and news coverage from the new Soviet flight control center outside Moscow—designed in part to replicate the more open mission control center in Houston—constituted a way of conducting human space exploration that had rejected the conventions of secrecy that had been standard

---

82 NASA Historical Reference Collection, "Trip Report: Observation of Working Group No. 3 at Academy of Sciences Moscow USSR," "ASTP—Aerospace Advisory Panel," 7/6/3, November 27, 1974; also on the Soviet borrowing of American systems of documentation: Bushuev, *Soyuz i Apollon: rasskazyvaiut sovetskie uchenyi, inzhenery, y kosmonavty*, 65–66; Syromiatnikov, *100 Stories*, 493–94.
83 "Draft Study: The US–U.S.S.R. Intergovernmental Agreement on Cooperative Space Activities: Should it be Renewed?," October 9, 1984, 5–6, NASA Historical Reference Collection, 10/14/3, Folder 15592.
84 Bushuev, *Soyuz i Apollon: rasskazyvaiut sovetskie uchenyi, inzhenery, y kosmonavty*, 17.
85 A. A. Leonov, B. F. Lomov, and V. I. Lebedev, "K probleme obshcheniia v internatsional'nykh kosmicheskikh poletakh," *Voprosy filosofii*, no. 1 (1976), 56–69; A. A. Leonov, V. I. Lebedev, *Psikhologicheskie problemy mezhplanetnogo poleta* (Moscow: AN SSSR, 1975).

in Soviet spaceflight from Gagarin and on through the rest of the 1960s. "We showed the world that in space collaboration we could be reliable partners," said ASTP flight director Eliseev, echoing the thoughts of Mozzhorin, who remembered that the Soviets' greatest fear was to be considered an unreliable partner "with whom one cannot do business."[86]

Zero-Sum Games and the Forces of Fear

While there was little public Soviet resistance to détente (one of the advantages of an authoritarian political system, from its own perspective, is the silencing of oppositional voices), there were always US officials eager to roll back the policy. Even in 1974 Soviet engineers were worried, and baffled, by the increasing attacks on Nixon for Watergate and the ominous way that it was connected with US domestic attacks on the policy of détente. As Syromiatnikov put it, "Soviet cosmonautics was communicating with American astronautics through a kind of narrow 'tree hole,' but the hole was expanding." That the Americans would sacrifice a budding and mutually beneficial relationship seemed irrational.[87]

Meanwhile, US opponents of détente viewed the Cold War as a zero-sum game—as illustrated also in the *Playboy* image from the previous chapter— where one side's gain must necessarily be the other side's loss.[88] The forces of fear, such as Senator Henry "Scoop" Jackson, had provided support for the Jackson–Vanik amendment to the trade act of 1974, which denied most-favored-nation status to communist nations. They took it as a matter of faith that the United States had a commanding technological edge over the Soviet Union and that collaboration in any form would sacrifice that advantage.[89] In the mid-1970s, many members of Congress and government bureaucrats were sure that "continued Russian secrecy" would damage the credibility of the United States among its allies and result in the United States giving far

---

86 "Istoriia TsUPa: Trud, radosti, mytarstva," Nauka i zhizn', No. 8, 2005, http://epizodsspace.airbase.ru/bibl/n_i_j/2005/7/istoria-tsupa.html, downloaded June 11, 2018; Eliseev, *Zhizn'*, 106, 109, 110; *Tak eto bylo*, cited from the online version, chapter 6, downloaded June 12, 2018: http://epizodsspace.airbase.ru/bibl/mozjorin/tak/06.html. The official Soviet history of the project also emphasized the point that the Soviets had proven their capitalist critics wrong and shown that they could be a reliable partner: *Soyuz i Apollon: rasskazyvaiut sovetskie uchenyi, inzhenery, y kosmonavty*, 53.
87 Syromiatnikov, *100 Stories*, 456, 515.
88 On emotions in US–Soviet relations: Frank Castigliola, "'Unceasing Pressure for Penetration': Gender, Pathology, and Emotion in George Kennan's Formation of the Cold War," *Journal of American History* 83, no. 4 (1997), 1309–39.
89 "Joint Mission Was a Handout of Our Technical Knowledge to Russians," *National Enquirer*, August 19, 1975, 20; "The Apollo-Soyuz Experiment," *Aviation Week*, May 5, 1975, 7.

more in strategic scientific and technological assets than it would ever get in return. Working with the Soviets on ASTP, they claimed, allowed the Soviets to be seen on a technological par with the United States and to legitimize the Soviet Union as a viable modern state and political system. "ASTP is the bannerhead of this national suicide," proclaimed one détente opponent, "a proud advertisement that we will spare no expense to give away what we have fought hard to create, give it away to those who did not earn it, and could not duplicate it."[90] The Pentagon's director of research and engineering, a staunch opponent of détente and advocate of tight technology transfer controls, said at a defense industry gathering in Detroit in May 1975 that the United States was now in its "late-Roman period" and feared it lacked the political will and technological initiative to compete as a major power; the willingness to collaborate with the Soviets only proved the point, along with "uncontrollable socio-economic programs" in the United States.[91] These attitudes created a dramatic shift in NASA attitudes in the Carter administration. The Soviets advanced numerous proposals to link up the Salyut capsule with the new Shuttle program, but by 1977 there was not a single design engineer at NASA willing to discuss these projects with Soviet colleagues; just three years earlier, NASA and Soviet engineers had been drinking vodka toasts together to world peace.[92]

Neo-McCarthyites received enthusiastic support from the Executive branch following the Soviet invasion of Afghanistan at the end of the Carter administration—and following the exile of Nobel Laureate for peace Andrei Sakharov, also creator of the Soviet Hydrogen bomb, to the city of Gor'kii in 1980. Sure of the superiority of American space technology, and seeing outer space as an arena for national competition rather than collaboration, the proponents of re-securitization found their man in the White House with Ronald Reagan. New regimes of secrecy were reflected in NASA's reluctance to work even with Western Europeans on joint missions and payloads (whose origins went back to Nixon's initiatives), for fear that Western European partners, especially France, might share US technology with the Soviets.[93] In early 1980,

---

90 "What's the Sense of the Apollo-Soyuz Linkup Mission?," *Washington Star News*, October 27, 1974, B3; NASA Historical Reference Collection, "Background and Policy Issues in the Apollo-Soyuz Test Project," Congressional Research Service, January 31, 1975, 39.
91 "Currie Urges Restraint on Technology Exchange," *Defense Business Daily*, May 13, 1975, 8-F; "U.S. Scientific Exchanges with Soviets are Canceled," *Washington Post*, February 26, 1980, A1.
92 Vladimir Syromiatnikov, *100 Rasskazov o stykovke i o drugikh prikliucheniakh, Chast' 2, 20 let spustia* (Moscow: "Logos," 2010), 221.
93 "The Last Frontier for Trust, NASA Shuns Contact with Cosmonauts," *San Francisco Chronicle*, March 27, 1988, 6; "First European Astronaut Criticizes Shuttle Manning," *Washington Post*, December 20, 1983, A4.

one US Air Force official predicted that the new chill would result in an arms race in space and reinforcement of the system of secret science.[94] US scientists and engineers faced new restrictions on contacts with foreign colleagues and draconian new regimes of technology transfer. In February 1980, eight physicists from the Soviet Union, Hungary, and Poland were "disinvited" from a private industry meeting in Santa Barbara, California, to discuss new computer technologies. The Commerce Department forced the remaining participants at the meeting to sign a pledge not to discuss any information from the conference sessions with individuals from 20 communist countries or face federal prosecution, 10 years in jail, and a $10,000 fine. The meeting's organizer told a reporter from the *New York Daily News*: "[The US government] claimed that by talking to anyone we would be guilty of exporting technology. We were told we would have to apply for an export license, which would take two months and would be denied." A Commerce Department official explained that under the law, "oral exchanges of [sensitive] information with foreign nationals constitute the export of technical data."[95]

The decisive end to détente in the sphere of scientific and technological collaboration came in 1982 with the refusal to renew the agreement for widespread collaboration with the Soviet Union in space and other areas, first signed in 1972 in Moscow by Nixon and Kosygin. The agreement had initiated regular exchanges of information in space exploration, physics, biology, computer engineering, and a host of other areas. NASA officials were at the time in the midst of negotiations with Soviet colleagues on joint projects for planetary exploration. The United States disbanded working groups that had met regularly since 1972, on space meteorology, environmental studies, lunar and planetary exploration, and space biology and medicine.[96] Reflecting the new chill, on October 4, 1982, for the 25th anniversary party for Sputnik at the Soviet embassy in Washington, DC, a former NASA official in attendance did not see a single person from the Reagan administration, or from NASA, in the crowded room. NASA employees who had been working regularly with Soviets since Apollo-Soyuz were warned not to go.[97] Finally, Reagan's Star Wars speech in March 1983 announced in dramatic fashion the American intention to re-securitize and militarize space exploration.

---

94 "U.S.–Soviet Chill Is Expected to Speed Space Arms Race," *Washington Post*, January 11, 1980, 1.
95 "U.S. Bursts Technology Bubble for Red Scientists," *New York Daily News*, February 22, 1980, 4.
96 "U.S. Ends Most Exploration of Space with Russia," *NYT*, June 6, 1982, 20.
97 "Chill on Space Front," *Washington Post*, October 11, 1982, A14.

Space Travelers of the World Unite!

The Soviets, meanwhile, were expanding their international missions in the early 1980s, building on the systems of collaboration that had accompanied ASTP. The Soviets saw these joint missions as tangible proof of the Scientific Technological Revolution's promise of friendship and peace forged through scientific and technological collaboration, a mechanical manifestation of the doctrine of peaceful coexistence that dated back to the Khrushchev era.[98] The traditions of cosmism, meanwhile, provided an ideological framework of internationalism, environmentalism, anti-militarism, and a planetary perspective with which many cosmonauts and space industry officials came to understand the meaning of their professional endeavors.[99] The Soviets sponsored joint missions with various countries—involving scientific investigations and human spaceflights—through Interkosmos.[100] Multinational crew broadcasts from space became a public event for Soviet television audiences through the 1980s. Cosmonaut crews chatted with pop stars in front of national and international television audiences, for which Soviet central television devoted an entire studio, further transforming a formerly secret activity into a public activity. Family members also participated in these real-time conversations, which seem to have left profound and positive impressions on both the cosmonauts and television audiences. With every successful mission, the Soviets experienced even more "pride" in being a country "on which others could depend. Of course, nothing develops such strong and friendly relations like collaborative work in dangerous situations."[101]

France was the first Western European country to send a man into space through the Soviet space program (before any Western Europeans had flown into space with NASA) in June 1982. The Franco-Soviet spaceflight took place one month after the Reagan administration had allowed the 10-year-old space-cooperation agreement with the Soviets to lapse. Meanwhile, NASA, in addition

---

98 Syromiatnikov, *100 Rasskasov, Chast'* 2, 55–56. On the Soviet view of science as a transnational factor in creating alliances for peace: Matthew Evangelista, *Unarmed Forces: The Transnational Movement to End the Cold War* (Ithaca, NY: Cornell University Press, 1999); Natalia Egorova, *"Narodnaia diplomatiia" Iadernogo veka: dvizhenie storonnikov mira i problema razoruzheniia, 1955–1965 gody* (Moscow: Akvilon, 2016).

99 During ASTP, the Soviets requested of NASA that they allow the Soviets to take copies of Tsiolkovskii's ideas about space travel and cosmism into space, have them signed by the US and Soviet crews, and then taken back for display at the Tsiolkovskii museum in Kaluga. NASA Historical Reference Collection, ASTP Goddard/Tsiolkovsky Reports, LEK 7/16/3, "Historical Payload for ASTP Mission," Memorandum, July 22, 1975.

100 For a general overview: V. I. Kozyrev, S. A. Nikitin, *Polety po programme "Interkosmos,"* (Moscow, 1980); on the details of these flights and their origins: Eliseev, *Zhizn'*, 115–16, 124–26.

101 Eliseev, *Zhizn'*, 121, 124.

to limiting exchanges of information and technology with other nations, was also working more closely with defense contractors to develop secret SDI payloads for Space Shuttle missions, including the fourth shuttle mission that coincided with the Franco-Soviet launch and which carried sensors to detect missile launches.[102] Soviet news wire reports, with some justice, contrasted their own programs of collaborative scientific investigation, including the study of plankton in the North Atlantic and dust storms over the Mediterranean, with the secret defense payloads on the Discovery Shuttle mission, which one classified Reagan directive (issued on Independence Day in 1982) declared would have priority on all Shuttle missions over open civilian payloads and projects.[103]

In October 1984, the OTA noted the "growing Soviet inclination to cooperate with other countries (outside the Soviet bloc) in space," including India and Sweden. While the United States had terminated nearly all of its collaborative efforts with Soviet bloc countries, and remained wary of collaboration with Western Europeans, the USSR was becoming a "leader in international cooperative ventures in space," taking over the role, according to the OTA, that the United States had "traditionally" played. It was undeniable, according to OTA, that the Soviet Union was becoming a more attractive option for countries interested in space exploration than the United States. At a time when the United States was strengthening its regime of secrecy in science and technology and pursuing an isolationist strategy of space exploration, "space cooperation [was] becoming a competitive tool which the Soviets seem prepared to wield vigorously."[104]

The contrasting attitudes toward information exchange and collaboration across ideological barriers came into sharp relief in July 1985, the tenth anniversary of ASTP. The 10-year celebration of the historic linkup served as a much-anticipated measure of commitment to openness and dialogue. US hostility toward commemorating the event—against the backdrop of Reagan's Star Wars program—stood in stark contrast to Soviet celebrations urging the demilitarization of space. Stafford, the ASTP commander, traveled to the Soviet Union and talked with the Soviet ambassador to the United States, Anatoly Dobrynin, "to placate the Soviets, who reportedly are upset by the administration's apparent lack of interest in marking the historic space flight."

---

102 "Soviet-French Space Shot," *Christian Science Monitor*, June 25, 1982, 2.
103 "Cosmonauts, Scientists Discuss Joint Space Exploration," FBIS, No. 124, 27, June 1985, U1; Reagan Library and Archive, Executive Secretariat, NSC Subject File, National Security Decision Directive 42, July 4, 1982.
104 "Draft Study: The U.S.–U.S.S.R. Intergovernmental Agreement on Cooperative Space Activities: Should It be Renewed?," October 9, 1984, 14, NASA Historical Reference Collection, 10/14/3, Folder 15592.

Leonov, the Soviet commander, noted with some justice that "it is not our fault that the successful dialogue in outer space was not continued." While the US executive branch refused to recognize the occasion, Senator Spark Matsunaga, the main opponent of Reagan's militarization of space, made sure to enter ASTP into the Congressional Record and to urge, once again, a renewed commitment to joint space exploration. Echoing the cosmist rhetoric of the Soviets, he noted that "the unity of planet Earth so evident from space is undermined daily by human conflict, but it survives in our aspirations. [...] But what has proved impossible on Earth will, I am convinced, eventually prove necessary and unavoidable if humanity is to realize its destiny in the cosmic immensity of the heavens" Over in the House of Representatives, Congressional Democrats also filled the vacuum of the Reagan administration's snub with paeans to space cooperation, but the response from Reagan and NASA was ... silence.[105]

Thus, despite the impressive and growing record of international collaboration in the 1970s, beginning with French and Soviet joint efforts and ASTP, the perceived national and strategic imperatives of the Reagan administration had stopped the momentum of international space-cooperation initiatives and moves to declassify space industry activities. Instead, hawks within the administration worked with red-baiting journalists to throw doubt on ASTP and to interpret it as a moment when the United States gave away its strategic technological advantage because of misguided notions of collaboration and information exchange with a supposedly duplicitous and unreformable enemy. Frustrated NASA officials in October 1985, or at least those eager to start up collaboration again and overcome their own resource constraints, complained about DoD sabotaging of cooperative efforts.[106]

The renewed emphasis on the military uses of space exploration also meant ever-tightening controls over technology transfer and information exchange, driven by fears that even collaborative efforts with friendly Europeans (especially the French) might ultimately—through their contacts with the Soviets—give away supposedly decisive American technological advantages, which had saved the United States, through its faith in "high technology," from living like the people "in Bangladesh."[107] Such sentiments had a chilling effect on

---

105 "U.S. May Boycott Space-Linkup Event," *Washington Post*, May 16, 1985, A21; "Space Anniversary Fete," *Washington Post*, July 10, 1985, A17; "Cosmonaut Calls for Weapons-Free Space," *FBIS* 143, July 25, 1985, U1; *Congressional Record—Senate*, July 17, 1985, S9660; *Congressional Record—House*, July 17, 1985, H5767–68.
106 NASA Historical Reference Collection, 10/14/4, 15591.
107 Newt Gingrich, "Space—A Window of Opportunity," Address to the 27th Annual Goddard Memorial Dinner, Ronald Reagan Presidential Library and Archive, Outer Space, 240000–387999, Box 3.

attempts to build on the precedent of ASTP and build bridges across the Cold War divide.

Role Reversals

The newly strengthened regime of information control in Reagan's United States occurred against the backdrop of Gorbachev's policy of *glasnost'*, which by 1987 had produced the attitudes of openness and information exchange on the Soviet side that had so surprised the former NASA administrator Paine, cited at the beginning of this chapter. But so far as Soviet science and technology were concerned, the deconstruction of the Soviet regime of secrecy had begun much earlier than Gorbachev, emerging first through new collaborative science and technology projects with the French, then with the United States during détente, and between the Soviet Union and other nations participating in the Interkosmos program of the late 1970s and 1980s. Gorbachev's policies thus represented a certain amount of continuity with previous practices that had reduced the system of classification and secrecy for joint science and technology projects with socialist and nonsocialist nations.

France played a particularly important role in integrating the Soviet Union into the global system of science and technology, and in the process strengthened the idea in the Soviet Union that science should be international, open, collaborative, and based on freer information exchanges. Under Nixon's leadership the United States also began to promote a more international and open approach to science and technology, transforming technological and scientific assets from an instrument of military power and into a soft-power force for reducing tensions and promoting peace between itself and ideological competitors. This policy also dovetailed with US ideological claims about being an open system, as compared to the Soviet Union. With the invasion of Afghanistan and the Reagan administration, the United States reversed these policies, reinforcing its regime of secrecy and imposing tight controls on technology transfer and challenging its own ideological claims of being a system based on free exchanges of information. Seen in the broader context of the global Cold War, the United States during the 1980s, rather than the Soviet Union, was the major global force for advocating a secret system of science devoted to national security and power in line with its own historical tendencies toward isolationism and xenophobia, rather than in accordance with the belief that the United States represented a bastion of openness and free exchange of information. The Soviet Union, even before Gorbachev and dating back to the 1970s, was the more assiduous and assertive advocate of a collaborative and international model of science, despite its own well-known traditions of secrecy and elaborate system of classification. Its example of openness highlighted the hypocrisy of US claims. Relative to regimes of secrecy and information exchanges in the early 1960s, the United States and the Soviet Union by the mid-1980s had reversed roles.

CONCLUSION: COOPERATION AND ASTP'S ENDURING LEGACIES

The mission of ASTP was to conjoin two nations that were locked in a seemingly unstoppable race toward nuclear Armageddon. It was at once a technical and political project of creating codependency (in the positive sense). The hope was that the hybrid features of the docking mechanism would turn hostile superpowers into a mutually dependent system, thereby challenging a relationship that had been based on a zero-sum game mentality. The former allies and vanquishers of Nazism were walled off from each other; they were separated by iron and ideological curtains which were reinforced with missile silos, barbed wire, checkpoints, secret military complexes, and a mediascape that increasingly depicted the other as irredeemably evil.[1]

Alongside the dehumanizing images each side had pursued a position of domination, engaging in feats of technological one-upmanship in space and on Earth. Real and ritual displays of domination marked the timeline of the Cold War: for Americans, the famous and menacing image of Sputnik flying over and beeping on American territory; for Soviets, the planting of the American flag on the moon. Meanwhile, both sides waged, funded, and supplied bloody proxy wars in Asia, Africa, and Latin America. The very tall mission of ASTP and space collaboration in general was to transform the superpower relationship into something neutral, ambiguous, and based on parity and mutual respect, "a full-fledged and equal partnership," in the words of the Soviet docking system designer Vladimir Syromiatnikov.[2] The key was to collaborate in an engineering project without either side giving up its ideology and unique systemic features—politically, technologically, and socially. Advancing an alternative to the Cold War imaginary, as noted in Chapter 1, ASTP thus involved the idea of the "sociotechnical imaginary"—the projection of ideas

---

1 Interview with Caldwell Johnson, April 27, 1999, League City Texas, NASA Johnson Space Center Oral History Project, 58.
2 Vladimir Syromiatnikov, *100 Stories about Docking and Other Adventures in Space and on Earth* (Moscow: Universitetskaia kniga, 2005), 395.

about social and political progress through scientific and technological projects—which in the case of ASTP conveyed a radical new understanding of Soviet-American relations based on peaceful technical and economic collaboration and the voluntary refusal by either side to dominate the other.[3] Ideally, the engineering of that system would spread from the mechanical and technological spheres of space exploration and into the social, political, and cultural realms of Cold War culture, effectively ending the Cold War and creating a new phase of global development based on the creation of interfaces that would result in the hybridization of opposites (communist and capitalist, Soviet and American, Apollo and Soyuz, male and female). The designing and implementation of ASTP would thus usher in a new age of peaceful collaboration to replace the earlier phase of the Cold War based on ideological struggle and military competition.

The ease with which both sides collaborated and brought the docking project to a successful conclusion made many believe that ASTP had dealt a permanent and fatal blow to Cold War imaginations.[4] That conclusion turned out to be premature, as collaboration was replaced in the late 1970s and early 1980s by a renewed Cold War and the emergence of what one American historian has termed "Fortress America." The term referred to a culture of fear that imperiled democracy and openness in the United States in the 1980s.[5] The Soviets played their part with the support of anti-American revolutions in various parts of the developing world through the 1970s and with the invasion of Afghanistan, which strengthened the arguments of the Cold Warriors on both sides of the ideological divide. Meanwhile, US Russophobia, which limited the US imagination to images and ideas of war, also thwarted Soviet desires for expanded collaboration, in space and more generally. That resistance was evident even when Nixon was president, gaining momentum with the 1974 Jackson–Vanik amendment that restricted trade with the Soviets as punishment for its restrictive emigration policies. Those tensions grew through the Carter administration, enflamed by hawkish democrats such as Senator Henry Jackson and President Jimmy Carter's National Security Advisor, Zbigniew Brzezinski. They were aggravated dramatically by

---

3 On sociotechnical imaginaries: Sheila Jasanoff and Sang-Hyun Kim, eds., *Dreamscapes of Modernity: Sociotechnical Imaginaries and the Fabrication of Power* (Chicago: University of Chicago Press, 2015).
4 That was certainly the hope expressed in the official Soviet history of ASTP, which contains all the expected overlay of Soviet propaganda but also reflects the excitement and hope engendered by the act of technical collaboration that was characteristic of the memories of participants on both sides. K. D. Bushuev, ed., *Soyuz i Apollon: rasskazyvaiut sovetskie uchenyi, inzhenery, y kosmonavty* (Moscow: Izd. Politicheskoi literatury, 1976).
5 Elaine Tyler May, *Fortress America: How We Embraced Fear and Abandoned Democracy* (New York: Basic Books, 2017).

President Ronald Reagan's Strategic Defense Initiative, or Star Wars program, which the Soviets contrasted, with some justice, to their own Space Peace initiatives at Interkosmos. Star Wars constituted a distinctly military imagining of space exploration as a national security enterprise; its attempt to create a laser system that would destroy Soviet nuclear missiles was condemned by the Soviets as a violation of both the spirit and letter of the 1967 International Space Treaty that had demilitarized space, and they were insulted by NASA's repeated insistence, at Reagan's command, that any future agreement on cooperation be contingent on Soviet acceptance of SDI (NASA administrator James Beggs claimed the Soviets were holding cooperation hostage to their desire to stop SDI rather than what seemed apparent to most non-Americans: that it was the United States holding cooperation hostage to its inflexible insistence on pursuing SDI).[6] The relatively short life of détente would therefore seem to support the conclusion that collaborative projects such as ASTP were limited in their ability to affect the Cold War imaginary beyond the few hundreds of engineers, bureaucrats, and politicians that were directly involved and perhaps a few thousand more that participated in one way or another and were impressed and surprised by their ability to get along with a supposed enemy.

But it would be a mistake to dismiss space collaboration as merely a propaganda show with little long-term impact on attitudes and policies. Syromiatnikov noted that despite the seemingly short-lived policy of détente in the 1970s, ASTP's influence and memory in the Soviet Union and Russia endured, suggesting that the Soviets, who after all had lost 30 million of its citizens during World War II, had more of an inclination to imagine peace than their American counterparts. The experience of collaboration set an important precedent of openness in formerly secretive, classified sectors of the Soviet military industrial complex that made it possible to argue, even at the grimmest times of the reemergence of the Cold War in the early 1980s, that the United States and the Soviet Union could work together. "I cannot say that the Iron Curtain was fully destroyed," noted the ASTP docking engineer Syromiatnikov, "but a breach was made in the wall. Although this 'breach was repaired' after ASTP, it was impossible to return to the old ways completely."[7] That view would soon be confirmed by the rise to power of Mikhail Gorbachev in 1985, whose policies of openness and international collaboration drew at

---

6 NASA Historical Reference Collection, "Field Trip Report for the NASA Advisory Council International Relations Task Force, Moscow, USSR April 11–17, 1987," 10/14/4, 15591; "NASA Response to Congressional Proposal for East-West Ventures in Space," September 1984, 10/14/4, 15582; "Interview: Georgii Beregovoi," *Space World*, March 1985, 15.

7 Syromiatnikov, *100 Stories*, 561.

least in part upon the previous practices of détente—and in particular on collaboration in the scientific and technological spheres—rather than representing the radical break that they are often assumed to be.[8]

The Soviets were also inspired by ASTP to expand their Interkosmos program from uncrewed scientific collaborative projects to joint international missions, a commitment that led to joint Soviet flights with the socialist and nonsocialist countries in the 1970s and 1980s, and to the development of the Mir space station and eventually the International Space Station.[9] At the same time, and especially in Russia where the memory of ASTP is much stronger than in the United States, ASTP inspired numerous initiatives in public diplomacy and in popular culture that sustained the idea of cooperation in technology and science as an antidote to ideological and military conflict. ASTP in Russia thus remained a powerful symbol of collaboration and cooperation that inspired would-be collaborators in other areas, as illustrated by the anniversary celebrations of ASTP in Soviet and later Russian mass media and also by the relative preponderance of memoir literature.[10] Following the example of ASTP and emerging from the spirit of the science and technology agreements of 1972 in which ASTP was a centerpiece, Soviet physicists through the 1980s argued and acted persuasively in opposition to war-mongering and the militarization of space represented by SDI, and they reached across ideological barriers to their American and Western European colleagues, invoking the authority of scientific objectivity to strengthen their claims and protect themselves from political attack.[11]

---

8 On challenges to the idea that the Brezhnev era was one of stagnation, in supposed contrast to the Gorbachev era: Dina Fainberg and Artemy M. Kalinovsky, eds., *Reconsidering Stagnation in the Brezhnev Era: Ideology and Exchange* (Lanham, MD: Lexington Books, 2016); Susanne Schattenberg, *Brezhnev: The Making of a Statesman* (London: I. B. Tauris-Bloomsbury, 2021).

9 The issue of *Pravda*, April 12, 1977, on international cosmonautics day, was devoted to the theme of international crewed flights and cited ASTP as a landmark event in ushering in this new phase of space history.

10 For some of the memoir literature from Soviet engineers and managers: N. A. Anfimov, ed., *Tak eto bylo...: Memuary Iu. A. Mozzhorina: Mozzhorin v vospominaniiakh sovremennikov* (Moscow: OAO 'Mezhdunarodnaia programma obrazovaniia, 2000); Syromiatnikov, *100 Stories*; A. S. Eliseev, *Zhizn': Kaplia v more* (Moscow: Aviatsiia i kosmonavtika, 1998); K. D. Bushuev, ed., *Soyuz i Apollon: rasskazyvaiut sovetskie uchenyi, inzhenery, y kosmonavty – uchastniki sovmestnykh rabot s amerikanskimi spetsialistami* (Moscow: Izd. Politicheskoi literatury, 1976); and "Istoriia TsUPa: Trud, radosti, mytarstva," *Nauka i zhizn'*, No. 8, 2005, http://epizodsspace.airbase.ru/bibl/n_i_j/2005/7/istoria-tsupa.html, downloaded June 11, 2018. The newspaper and periodical literature, especially on the anniversaries of ASTP on July 17, is voluminous and continually projects the idea of cooperation in science and technology to the more general population.

11 Matthew Evangelista, *Unarmed Forces: The Transnational Movement to End the Cold War* (Ithaca, NY: Cornell University Press, 1999).

CONCLUSION 153

Figure 5.1 Putin meets the ASTP crew in Moscow in July 2010
Source: NASA

Americans were also affected by the example of ASTP, even if the Cold War imaginary proved more resilient than in the Soviet Union. The astronaut Edgar Mitchell developed the idea of forming a group of astronauts and cosmonauts to work toward collaboration and the peaceful use of space exploration to solve global problems. From his position as director of the Institute for Noetic Sciences, Mitchell explored alternative science, politics, and diplomacy based on the vision of global unity that he experienced in space. In October 1973, he mentioned the idea of an astronaut-cosmonaut group in a letter to the State Department. That was the first step toward what would become, more than a decade later, the Association of Space Explorers explored in Chapter 2, and it included Aleksei Leonov, the ASTP commander, as a leading advocate and peace imaginer on the Soviet side, along with the ASTP flight director Aleksei Eliseev.

ASTP provided a constant source of inspiration for these and other initiatives in the United States, often led by the Esalen Institute in Big Sur, California, which was motivated by ASTP to embark on citizen diplomacy to connect Soviet cosmonauts, astronauts, thinkers, and regular citizens. Carl Sagan in the early 1980s became a powerful public voice for a certain vision of scientific progress that was connected also with global peace and environmentalism, as did John Denver and the science fiction writer Arthur Clarke, all encouraged and inspired by the example of ASTP (Clarke's sequel to 2001 named the space ship in the novel after Leonov). They were joined by the French marine explorer Jacques Cousteau, who had ardent followers in Europe, the United States, and the Soviet Union and who attended the inaugural meeting of the Association of Space Explorers in 1985 in Paris.[12] On the Soviet side of the ideological divide, the cosmonaut and science popularizer Vitalii Sevastianov published numerous books and articles in the 1970s and 1980s, in English and in Russian, on the important role of science and space exploration in saving Earth from violence and nuclear holocaust. He turned the core idea of ASTP—a common docking system that would allow both sides to come to the rescue of the other in the event of an emergency in space—into a metaphor for what the world needed and the title of an extended philosophical discussion of space flight and new political thinking. His 1989 book was entitled *Rescue: Emergency Escape Hatch: Cosmonautics and New Political Thinking in the Thermo-Nuclear Era*. The title was also motivated by a fragment from the Space Shuttle Challenger that had been written in Russian and English: "Rescue—Avariiinyi vykhod". Sevastianov's words convey the post–Cold War imaginary that seems more necessary than ever and which, for a time in the mid-1980s, brought the world as close to unity and peace as it has perhaps ever been in the twentieth and twenty-first centuries.

> Peace, constructive collaboration on Earth and in space, that is the only exit from the emergency situation on the spaceship "Earth." And it is deeply symbolic that the vision of a nuclear-free and violence-free world comes from the country that laid the road to the cosmos for humanity. This vision instills optimism and faith that international collaboration will resolve the dilemmas of the space age, and that the strength will be found to exit from an emergency situation on the spaceship "Earth."[13]

Finally, the International Space Station (ISS) is the mechanical offspring of ASTP's alternative imaginary, connecting adversaries in a common cause in which the ritual of docking is both a technical but more importantly a moral

---

12 On Denver and Cousteau's support of these efforts: "Denver's Soviet Trip: Peace, Not Politics," *USA Today*, December 13, 1984, 2D; John Denver, "Why I want to grasp space's opportunity," *Houston Chronicle*, October 16, 1988, 12.
13 V. I. Sevastianov and V. F. Priakhin, *Rescue: avariinyi vykhod. Kosmonavtika i novoe politicheskoe myshlenie v iaderno-kosmicheskuyu eru* (Moscow: Mezhdunarodnye otnosheniia, 1989), 143.

enterprise that constantly challenges war-mongering back on Earth. If technology is society made durable, ISS represents in microcosm the durable community of peaceful collaboration first engineered in ASTP.

Imaginative Leaps through Space

Depending on one's outlook, new technological capabilities could lead to utopia—a "fantasy about the limits of the possible," according to Jay Winter[14]—or to some horrific dystopia ending in nuclear and ecological holocaust. But paradoxically those two visions were also connected, like two sides of the same coin. The intensity with which Russian cosmists, European Greens, astrofurists in the West, and members of the Association of Space Explorers (ASE) pursued the idea of transcendence fed off the existential threat of mutual assured destruction and the cosmopolitical calculations that drove some of the interpreters and architects of space exploration. That threat had reached a fever pitch during the first Reagan administration—manifested in Western and Eastern Europe over US plans to upgrade its missiles on the continent and to use space technology much more explicitly for purposes of enhancing national military power and strategic objectives. So while the end of the Cold War in the late 1980s seemed to promise new possibilities for collaboration, especially with regard to the future of the European Union (which the European Space Agency (ESA) was partly designed to consolidate), it also removed one of the justifications for collaboration in space, that is, the Cold War itself. The very things that seemed to limit human development in that era—a world divided by ideology, military bases, concrete walls, and nuclear tipped rockets—had stimulated utopian hopes for a renewed commitment to world peace and international cooperation, and perhaps even new kinds of global identities, through space exploration. The head of ESA in 1985 captured the spirit of the long decade of the 1970s: "Space is open and space has no known boundaries," Reimar Lüst wrote: "It is therefore one of the most ideal domains in which to cooperate across national borders, especially across national borders in Europe [...] ESA demonstrates that we can work together very successfully in Europe, and in this way ESA is contributing to building a united Europe." Yet once the European Union expanded to include nearly all of Europe save Russia, space exploration, especially of the crewed variety, was no longer useful, or promotable, as a tool for unification. Or rather, it had outlived its usefulness in that regard.[15]

---

14 Jay Winter, *Dreams of Peace and Freedom: Utopian Moments in the Twentieth Century* (New Haven, CT: Yale University Press, 2006), 3.
15 Reimar Lüst, "Europe's Future in Space," *ESA Bulletin* 5, no. 44 (1985), 8.

At the same time, the late 1970s and 1980s marked a transition from the heroic and romantic phase of space exploration to a more technical and commercial one—embodied perhaps best by the collapse of communism and the passing of the distinctly noncommercial spirit of the early Space Race. The future of space belongs more and more to the private sector and to the Elon Musks of the world. The Soviet newspaper *Komsomol'skaia pravda*, on December 23, 1988, may have observed the beginning of the new era with an article called "Money in Space." The article, written by a veteran Soviet space journalist, lamented that it was time for the Soviets to stop giving free rides into space and charge for their services, just like the Americans. A quarter century after Gagarin's flight, "the flurry of excitement and romance surrounding everything having to do with the cosmos has declined and today public excitement about this once loudly glorified area of our life has become quite calm. Some even angrily call cosmonautics a 'Potemkin Village.'"[16] The days of Interkosmos were over, when the Soviet Union gave "selfless aid to other peoples in exploration and use of outer space for man's benefit."[17]

Yet in other ways the 1970s was the beginning of a new way of imagining human community beyond the nation-state or even a united Europe. Ideas about using space to transcend traditional political divisions marked a critical juncture in transnational history, and they have not given way completely to more traditional conceptions of space as an arena for national competition or private profit. Just as maps, educational systems, and newspapers in an earlier era allowed people to imagine themselves as national subjects, images of the globe from space permitted people to view themselves as transnational subjects, similar to how cyberspace has also promoted new virtual forms of human association. Those images, as they propagate and multiply, will be a constant stimulant to the imagination, as they were for the millions of readers of both *The Home Planet* and Frank White's *The Overview Effect* examined in Chapter 2. At the 1991 Congress of ASE, held in a newly unified Berlin, the theme was "Space Has No Boundaries." The Congress proclaimed: "Space exploration has given humanity a new perspective of the artificial borders that separate nations and the role that international cooperation in space plays in transcending these boundaries."[18] That is perhaps one of the most enduring aspects of the 1970s and its echo in ASE, the International Space Station, and

---

16 S. Leskov, "Den'gi na kosmos," *Komsomol'skaia pravda*, December 23, 1988, 2.
17 V. I. Sevastyanov and A. D. Ursul, "Space Age: New Relationship between Society and Nature," *Space World*, no. 1 (1972), 37.
18 http://www.space-explorers.org/congress/posters/poster7.html, accessed January 5, 2013; the web page with the ASE meeting proceedings, however, is no longer active and has been replaced by images of the posters made for each of the ASE meetings: http://www.space-explorers.org/collectibles.html, accessed October 17, 2013.

other collaborative space ventures: the imaginative leap through space exploration that has infused the exploration of outer space with broader political significance, ideas about the need to transcend national differences and become better stewards of the planet. The broader importance of ISS as a vehicle for both exploring space and rearranging affairs back on Earth had been made clear by enduring tensions between the Russian Federation and the United States. Through the first decades of the twenty-first century, the station was perhaps the major remaining pillar of collaboration between the two. Despite the ongoing tensions and crises, the fraternity of fliers (from Europe, Russia, the United States, and elsewhere) continued to celebrate triumphal conclusions to international missions on the steppes of Kazakhstan, the Eurasian terminus of international space collaboration and a staging ground for experiments in new forms of human association.

The Fate of the Androgynes

While ASTP's message of peaceful coexistence and collaboration was quickly drowned out by the reemergence of the Cold War, the socio-technical imaginary built into the APAS (androgynous peripheral assembly system) design lived on in the global space industry. From May 1973 to September 1974, the two sides built 17 APAS units. Syromiatnikov considered them his "big androgynous family," and could recognize each of his "androgynous creatures [...] personally." Four flew into space and the rest ended up in museums, universities, and military academies.[19] The Soviets continued to refine the design for linking up their capsules and space stations, on through Mir and ISS, and the APAS became the standard for international docking, including for the Chinese Shenzou spacecraft and space station. What is less clear is how the socio-technical imaginary designed into APAS functioned in the social and political arena. Here, the results are far more ambiguous, and this has much to do with the attitudes of domination and subordination that continue to shape political and social relations. The recrudescence of the spirit of Ares and Cold War attitudes in the United States dampened interest in the late 1970s and early 1980s in working with the Soviets to further the use of APAS in future missions. Syromiatnikov pushed for a Shuttle-Salyut hookup with APAS in 1977 and later, but his good friend Caldwell Johnson had resigned and the United States, as noted elsewhere in the book, became insular and uninterested in international collaboration.[20]

---

19 Syromiatnikov, *100 Stories*, 495.
20 Vladimir Syromiatnikov, *100 rasskazov o stykovke i o drugikh prikliucheniakh v kosmose i na zemle, Chast' 2, 20 let spustia* (Moscow: Logos, 2010), 221–22.

While APAS may have had limited success as a technological fix to the problem of the Cold War, it worked wonderfully well as a purely technical fix for making space docking far safer and easier, facilitating more than two hundred dockings and counting. It provided a mechanism by which people could not only fly into space but also stay there, and if need be, in the event of an emergency, have a much greater chance of returning to Earth alive. Despite the frustrated expectations of further work with his American colleagues—the end to détente terminated his visits with his NASA friends and aerospace engineers in the United States from the mid-1970s and until the late 1980s—the ASTP experience convinced Syromiatnikov that he needed to continue broadening his technical as well as philosophical outlook. He continually refined the APAS design for Soviet docking between the Salyut and Soyuz capsules, and then reconfigured the APAS for the Mir, at which point it was possible again to use it for hookups with the American Shuttle (a total of nine dockings with the Shuttle, which were also facilitated in the 1990s by the efforts of the ASTP commander Stafford). In 1984 Syromiatnikov published a guide to space docking, providing the design principles he had developed from the time he began working for Korolev in 1956 for all the world to see, though he had originally conceived of them within the secret world of the Soviet military industrial complex and its strategic rocket forces' command. He highlighted the two main challenges of space engineering—maximizing safety while reducing weight. Translated into numerous languages, the book allowed his colleagues around the world to benefit from his wisdom and to spread the message of androgynous coupling.[21]

After ASTP engineering safety became even more of Syromiatnikov's focus, providing a clear example of the broader kind of humane engineering that many, especially after Chernobyl, did not often associate with the Soviet Union. But it was precisely the focus on safety that helped the Soviets to inhabit space for longer and longer periods of time and with relatively few tragedies. His doctoral work from 1975 to 1979 allowed him to perfect the APAS design; he defended his dissertation on June 22, 1979—the commemoration of the day of the Nazi invasion in 1941. That dissertation laid the foundation for all of his future work on the APAS design, which was guided by a deep moral commitment to safety, which he taught to his students. "The modern automobile," he wrote, "is like the autonomous flying object. It should simultaneously satisfy multiple requirements: it should be light but strong, secure and safe, economical and comfortable, controllable and technologically sound." In 1984 he introduced new concepts about evaluating risk and engineering safety to the Soviet engineering community, translating and arranging publication of

---

21 Vladimir Syromiatnikov, *Stykovochnye ustroistva kosmicheskikh apparatov* (Moscow: Mashinostroenie, 1984).

an influential Western textbook for safety engineering. He had found the book in 1982 during one of his frequent trips scouring books in English at the outdoor summer book market in Moscow. The idea to translate and publish the book was another enduring legacy of ASTP, continuing the process of integration—another word Syromiatnikov borrowed from American engineering—through the continual exchange of Soviet and Western engineering practices and ideas.[22] Syromiatnikov provided annotations for the volume, though he was sad that the effort was not sufficient to prevent the disaster at Chernobyl a year and a half later. The volume quickly sold out, and he noted that at the time there was a real hunger among Soviet engineers for theoretical works "in which safety and reliability had primary importance." Through the 1980s and 1990s he was frequently contacted by engineers from many different fields (including engineers of underwater vessels, who also needed to design escape hatches for an emergency) to talk about safety. He later recalled the important safety lesson he had learned along with American colleagues during ASTP that he preached constantly to colleagues and students: "What you think is going to happen ahead of time never happens, but the more you prepare for likely and unlikely situations the more secure and reliable the system becomes." He kept a database of telemetry data from all of the dockings he had witnessed, Soviet and international, and especially the most harrowing ones, which was invaluable in reducing the risks of future docking mishaps. During the Mir-Shuttle dockings, the accumulated wisdom from these experiences and analysis reassured NASA colleagues of the importance that Russian space engineers assigned to safety and reliability, contrary to some perceptions in the West. Russian space engineers were as reliable as ever.[23]

When the Soviet Union collapsed in the early 1990s Syromiatnikov came to the United States and joined his old colleague and friend from ASTP, Caldwell Johnson, to teach his engineering design philosophy at the American Institute of Aeronautics and Astronautics. His devotion to safety is recognized by an award given every year in his name by the International Association for the Advancement of Space Safety, founded in 2004, in recognition of, "designers and engineers who have made major technical contributions toward systems safety."[24]

---

22 Ernest Henley and Hiromitsu Kumamoto, *Reliability Engineering and Risk Assessment* (New York: Prentice-Hall, 1981), which Syromiatnikov translated into Russian as *Nadezhnost' tekhnicheskikh system i otsenka riska* (Moscow: Mashinostroenie, 1984).
23 Syromiatnikov, *100 rasskazov, Chast' 2*, 105–6, 108–9, 147.
24 Merryl Azriel, "Vladimir Syromiatnikov, Father of the APAS, Honored on Reunion Island," *Space Safety Magazine*, February 20, 2013, http://www.spacesafetymagazine.com/spaceflight/rendezvous-docking/vladimir-syromyatnikov-father-apas-honored-reunion-island/; Vladimir Syromiatnikov, "Hybrid Spacecraft," *Journal of Space Safety Engineering* 2, no. 2 (2015), 82.

The French recognized the enduring yet unrecognized significance of that device by erecting a monument to APAS on its territory of Reunion Island, located in the Indian Ocean, in November of 2012. Syromiatnikov's son was there for the unveiling. His father had visited the island several times in connection with another joint project between French engineering students in the Reunion capital of St. Denis and a Moscow engineering student, to be completed in 1997 to honor the 40th anniversary of Sputnik. The Russians took care of the outer structure of the three-kilogram replica while the French team constructed the interior assembly. The two teams met in Paris for the final assembly and the completed replica then flew on November 3 to the Mir space station from which it was then launched into orbit. As for the APAS monument on the island, it is a scale-version cement structure of the clasping docking mechanism overlooking the island and called, "Le Porte des Mondes." Like the APAS itself, it paid tribute to a mechanical device that was both an escape hatch from mortal danger for an imperiled space ship but also a portal to other worlds and cultures. France, of course, had played a critical role in developing a new conception of space as an international, collaborative, scientific, and peaceful project, with its landmark program of collaboration with the Soviets, signed by de Gaulle and Brezhnev in 1966.[25]

The androgynous docking mechanism is to space exploration in some ways what the invention of the Transfer Control Protocol/Internet Protocol (TCPIP) invented by the US DoD in the 1960s was for allowing computing devices of different design and architecture to communicate with each other. For Syromiatnikov, APAS was all those things but also more. The APAS was not merely a technological device but also the manifestation of a certain attitude and philosophy of hybridity that he hoped the device would both facilitate and embody—much as Internet and computer pioneers associated interconnectivity with the construction of utopian new societies. The APAS would be the start of an era of hybridity, creating connecting points and entry ways between peoples, cultures, and technological systems. His philosophy of hybridity, advancing both the technology and ethos of androgynous docking, lives on through the continuous mechanical act of coupling. Every carefully choreographed moment of mechanical embrace in space renews the promise of collaboration and friendly cooperation back on Earth.

---

25 Merryl Azriel, "Vladimir Syromiatnikov, Father of the APAS, Honored on Reunion Island," *Space Safety Magazine*, February 20, 2013, http://www.spacesafetymagazine.com/spaceflight/rendezvous-docking/vladimir-syromyatnikov-father-apas-honored-reunion-island/.

BIBLIOGRAPHY

Adas, Michael. *Machines as the Measure of Man: Science, Technology, and Ideologies of Western Dominance*. Ithaca, NY: Cornell University Press, 1990.
Anderson, Benedict. *Imagined Communities: Reflections on the Origin and Spread of Nationalism*. New York: Verso, 1991.
Anderson, Walter Truett. *The Upstart Spring: Esalen and the American Awakening*. Reading, MA: Addison-Wesley, 1983.
Andrews, James T. *Red Cosmos: K. E. Tsiolkovskii, Grandfather of Soviet Rocketry*. College Station: Texas A&M University Press, 2009.
Andrews, James T., and Siddiqi, Asif A., eds. *Into the Cosmos: Space Exploration and Soviet Culture*. Pittsburgh: University of Pittsburgh Press, 2011.
Anfimov, N. A., ed. *Tak eto bylo...: Memuary Iu. A. Mozzhorina: Mozzhorin v vospominaniiakh sovremennikov*. Moscow: OAO 'Mezhdunarodnaia programma obrazovaniia, 2000.
Babiracki, Patryk, and Zimmer, Kenyon, eds. *Cold War Crossings: International Travel and Exchange across the Soviet Bloc, 1940s–1960s*. College Station: Texas A&M University Press, 2014: 166–209.
Bacon, Edwin, and Sandle, Mark, eds. *Brezhnev Reconsidered*. New York: Palgrave Macmillan, 2002.
Banerjee, Anindita. *We Modern People: Science Fiction and the Making of Russian Modernity*. Middletown, CT: Wesleyan University Press, 2012.
Bjørnvig, Thore. "Outer Space Religion and the Overview Effect: A Critical Inquiry into a Classic of the Pro-Space Movement." *Astropolitics: The International Journal of Space Politics & Policy* 11, nos. 1–2 (2013): 4–24.
Bushuev, K. D., ed. *Soyuz i Apollon: rasskazyvaiut sovetskie uchenyi, inzhenery, y kosmonavty – uchastniki sovmestnykh rabot s amerikanskimi spetsialistami*. Moscow: Izd. Politicheskoi literatury, 1976.
Cadbury, Deborah. *Space Race: The Epic Battle between America and the Soviet Union for Domination of Space*. New York: HarperCollins, 2007.
Callon, Michel. "Society in the Making: The Study of Technology as a Tool for Sociological Analysis." In Wiebe E. Bijker, Thomas P. Hughes, and Trevor Pinch, eds. *The Social Construction of Technological Systems: New Directions in the Sociology and History of Technology*. Cambridge, MA: MIT Press, 1987.
Casey, Steven. "Selling NSC-68: The Truman Administration, Public Opinion, and the Politics of Mobilization, 1950–51." *Diplomatic History* 29, no. 4 (2005): 655–90.
Castigliola, Frank. "'Unceasing Pressure for Penetration': Gender, Pathology, and Emotion in George Kennan's Formation of the Cold War." *Journal of American History* 83, no. 4 (1997): 1309–39.
Chertok, Boris. *Rockets and People. Volume IV. The Moon Race*. Washington, DC: NASA History Series, 2012.

Cohn, Carol. "Sex and Death in the Rational World of Defense Intellectuals." *Signs* 12, no. 4 (1987): 687–71.
Collins, Guy. *Europe in Space*. Basingstoke: Macmillan, 1990.
Davidson, William D., and Montville, Joseph V. "Foreign Policy According to Freud." *Foreign Policy*, no. 45 (Winter 1981–82): 145–57.
Dickson, Paul. *Sputnik: The Shock of the Century*. New York: Walker, 2011.
Egorova, Natalia. *"Narodnaia diplomatiia" Iadernogo veka: dvizhenie storonnikov mira i problema razoruzheniia, 1955–1965 gody*. Moscow: Akvilon, 2016.
Ellis, Thomas. *Reds in Space: American Perceptions of the Soviet Space Programme from Apollo to Mir 1967–1991*, PhD diss. University of Southampton, 2018.
Eliseev, A. S. *Zhizn': Kaplia v more*. Moscow: Aviatsiia i kosmonavtika, 1998.
Elliott, Gordon. *A History of Antarctic Science*. Cambridge: Cambridge University Press, 1992.
Ellis, Thomas. "'Howdy Partner!' Space Brotherhood, Détente and the Symbolism of the 1975 Apollo-Soyuz Test Project." *Journal of American Studies* 53, no. 3 (2019): 744–69.
Evangelista, Matthew. *Unarmed Forces: The Transnational Movement to End the Cold War*. Ithaca, NY: Cornell University Press, 1999.
Ezell, Clinton, and Ezell, Linda Neuman. *The Partnership: A History of the Apollo-Soyuz Test Project*. Washington, DC: NASA, 1978.
Fainberg, Dina, and Kalinovsky, Artemy M., eds. *Reconsidering Stagnation in the Brezhnev Era: Ideology and Exchange*. Lanham, MD: Lexington Books, 2016.
Feoktistov, K. P. *Sem' shagov v nebo*. Moscow: Molodaia gvardiia, 1984.
Galison, Peter "Removing Knowledge." *Critical Inquiry* 31, no. 1 (2004): 229–43.
Galison, Peter, and Hevly, Bruce William. *Big Science: The Growth of Large-Scale Research*. Palo Alto, CA: Stanford University Press, 1992.
Geppert, Alexander, ed. *Post–Apollo: Outer Space and the Limits of Utopia*. New York: Palgrave Macmillan, 2018.
Gerovitch, Slava. *From Newspeak to Cyberspeak: A History of Soviet Cybernetics*. Cambridge, MA: MIT Press, 2012.
——— *Soviet Space Mythologies: Public Images, Private Memories, and the Making of a Cultural Identity*. Pittsburgh, PA: University of Pittsburgh Press, 2015.
Goldman, Marion. *The American Soul Rush: Esalen and the Rise of Spiritual Privilege*. New York: New York University Press, 2012.
Golovkin, T. A., and Chernobaev, A. A., eds. *Kosmos. Vremia moskovskoe. Sbornik dokumentov*, 2nd ed. Moscow: Russian State Humanitarian University, 2018.
Gourne, Isabelle. "Dépasser les tensions Est-Ouest pour la conquête de l'espace. La coopération franco- soviétique au temps de la Guerre froide." *Cahiers SIRICE* 2, no. 16 (2016): 49–67.
Graham, Loren. *The Ghost of the Executed Engineer: Technology and the Fall of the Soviet Union*. Cambridge, MA: Harvard University Press, 1993.
Hajimi, Masuda. *Cold War Crucible: The Korean Conflict and the Postwar World*. Cambridge, MA: Harvard University Press, 2015.
Harvey Dodd L., and Ciccoritti, Linda C. *U.S.-Soviet Cooperation in Space*. Miami, FL: Center for Advanced International Studies, University of Miami, 1974.
Hecht, Gabrielle. *The Radiance of France: Nuclear Power and National Identity*. Cambridge, MA: MIT Press, 1998.
Henley, Ernest, and Kumamoto, Hiromitsu. *Reliability Engineering and Risk Assessment*. New York: Prentice-Hall, 1981.

Jasanoff, Sheila, and Kim, Sang-Hyun, eds. *Dreamscapes of Modernity: Sociotechnical Imaginaries and the Fabrication of Power.* Chicago: University of Chicago Press, 2015.
Jenks, Andrew L. *The Cosmonaut Who Couldn't Stop Smiling: The Life and Legend of Yuri Gagarin.* Dekalb: Northern Illinois University Press, 2012.
Johnston, Sean. "Alvin Weinberg and the Promotion of the Technological Fix." *Technology and Culture* 59, no. 3 (2018): 620–51.
Karash, Yuri. *The Superpower Odyssey: A Russian Perspective on Space Cooperation.* Reston, VA: American Institute of Aeronautics and Astronautics, 1999.
Kecskemeti, Paul. "Outer Space and World Peace." In Joseph N. Goldsen, ed. *Outer Space in World Politics.* New York: Frederick A. Praeger, 1963: 28–37.
Kelley, Kevin W., ed. *The Home Planet.* London: Queen Anne Press, 1988.
Kilgore, Douglas De Witt. *Astrofuturism: Science, Race, and Visions of Utopia in Space.* Philadelphia: University of Pennsylvania Press, 2021.
Kozyrev, V. I., and Nikitin, S. A. *Polety po programme "Interkosmos."* Moscow: Znanie, 1980.
Krige, John, Long Callahan, Angelina, and Maharaj, Ashok, eds. *NASA in the World: Fifty Years of International Collaboration in Space.* New York: Palgrave Macmillan, 2013.
Kripal, Jeffrey. *Esalen: America and the Religion of No Religion.* Chicago: University of Chicago Press, 2007.
Latour, Bruno. "Technology Is Society Made Durable." *Sociological Review* 38, no. 1 (1990): 103–31.
Leffler, Melvyn P., and Wested, Odd Arne, eds. *The Cambridge History of the Cold War, Vols. 1–3.* Cambridge: Cambridge University Press, 2010.
Leonov, A. A., Lebedev, V. I. *Psikhologicheskie problemy mezhplanetnogo poleta.* Moscow: AN SSSR, 1975.
Leonov, A. A., Lomov, B. F., and Lebedev, V. I. "K probleme obshcheniia v internatsional'nykh kosmicheskikh poletakh," *Voprosy filosofii,* no. 1 (1976): 56–69.
Logsdon, John. *John F. Kennedy and the Race to the Moon.* New York: Palgrave Macmillan, 2010.
Lüst, Reimar. "Europe's Future in Space." *ESA Bulletin* 5, no. 44 (1985): 8–15.
May, Elaine Tyler. *Fortress America: How We Embraced Fear and Abandoned Democracy.* New York: Basic Books, 2017.
Muir-Harmony, Teasel. *Operation Moonglow: A Political History of Project Apollo.* New York: Basic Books, 2020.
Nye, Joseph, S. "Public Diplomacy and Soft Power." *Annals of the American Academy of Political and Social Science* 616, no. 1 (2008): 94–109.
Odishaw, Hugh. "International Cooperation in Space Science," in Lincoln P. Bloomfield, ed. *Outer Space: Prospects for Man and Society.* Englewood Cliffs, NJ: Prentice-Hall, 1962, 105–23.
Oreskes, Naomi, and Krige, John, eds. *Science and Technology in the Global Cold War.* Cambridge, MA: MIT Press, 2014.
Pajala, Mari, and Lovejoy, Alice, eds. *Remapping Cold War Media: Institutions, Infrastructures, Networks, Exchanges.* Bloomington: Indiana University Press, 2021.
Pedersen, Kenneth S. "The Changing Face of International Cooperation: One View of NASA." *Space Policy* 2, no. 2 (1986): 120–38.
Poole, Robert. *Earthrise: How Man First Saw the Earth.* New Haven, CT: Yale University Press, 2008.
Porter, Theodore M. *Trust in Numbers: The Pursuit of Objectivity in Science and Public Life.* Princeton, NJ: Princeton University Press, 1996.
Pratt, Mary Louise. *Imperial Eyes: Travel Writing and Transculturation.* New York: Routledge, 1992.

Puar, Jasbir K. *Terrorist Assemblages: Homonationalism in Queer Times.* Durham, NC: Duke University Press, 2017.

Raleigh, Donald J. "'Soviet Man of Peace': Leonid Il'ich Brezhnev and His Diaries," *Kritika: Explorations in Russian and Eurasian History* 17, no. 4 (2016): 837–68.

Reinke, Niklas. *The History of German Space Policy: Ideas, Influences, and Interdependence 1923–2002.* Trans. Barry Smerin and Barbara Wilson. Paris: Beauchesne, 2007.

Rindzevicute, Egle. *The Power of Systems: How Policy Sciences Opened Up the Cold War.* Ithaca, NY: Cornell University Press, 2016.

Rogacheva, Maria A. *Soviet Scientists Remember: Oral Histories of the Cold War Generation.* New York: Lexington Books, 2020.

Sagan, Scott. *The Limits of Safety: Organizations, Accidents and Nuclear Weapons.* Princeton, NJ: Princeton University Press, 1993.

Schattenberg, Susanne. *Brezhnev: The Making of a Statesman.* London: I. B. Tauris-Bloomsbury, 2021.

Serkova, Natalya. "World Wide Gold." E-flux, no. 93 (2018): https://www.e-flux.com/journal/93/213267/world-wide-gold/.

Sevastianov V. I., and Priakhin, V. F. *Rescue: avariinyi vykhod. Kosmonavtika i novoe politicheskoe myshlenie v iaderno-kosmicheskuyu eru.* Moscow: Mezhdunarodnye otnosheniia, 1989.

Sevastyanov, V. I., and Ursul, A. D. *Era Kosmosa: obshchestvo i priroda.* Moscow: Znanie, 1972.

———. "Space Age: New Relationship between Society and Nature." *Space World.* no. 1 (1972): 31–39.

Sevastyanov, V. I., Ursul, A. D., and Shkolenko, Y. *The Universe and Civilization.* Moscow: Progress Publishers, [1979] 1981.

Sher, Gerson S. *From Pugwash to Putin: A Critical History of U.S.-Scientific Cooperation.* Bloomington: Indiana University Press, 2019.

Sherry, Michael. *The Rise of American Air Power: The Creation of Armageddon.* New Haven, CT: Yale University Press, 1987.

Siddiqi, Asif A. *Challenge to Apollo: The Soviet Union and the Space Race, 1945–1974.* Washington, DC: National Aeronautics and Space Administration, 2000.

———. *The Soviet Space Race with Apollo.* Gainsville: University of Florida Press, 2003.

———. *The Red Rocket's Glare: Space Flight and the Soviet Imagination, 1857–1957.* New York: Cambridge University Press, 2010.

———. "Privatising Memory: The Soviet Space Programme through Museums and Memoirs." In Martin Collins and Douglas Millard, eds. *Showcasing Space.* London: London Science Museum, 2005: 98–115.

Smolkin, Victoria. *A Sacred Space Is Never Empty: A History of Soviet Atheism.* Princeton, NJ: Princeton University Press, 2018.

Steinberg, Mark, and Sobol, Valeria. *Interpreting Emotions in Russia and Eastern Europe.* DeKalb: Northern Illinois University Press, 2011.

Syromiatnikov, Vladimir. "Hybrid Spacecraft," *Journal of Space Safety Engineering* 2, no. 2 (2015): 82.

———. *100 Stories about Docking and Other Adventures in Space, Vol. 1.* Moscow: Universitetskaia kniga, 2005.

———. *100 Rasskazov o stykovke i o drugikh prikliucheniakh v kosmose i na zemle, Chast' 1.* Moscow: "Logos," 2003.

———. *100 Rasskazov o stykovke i o drugikh prikliucheniakh, Chast' 2, 20 let spustia.* Moscow: "Logos," 2010.

———. *Stykovochnye ustroistva kosmicheskikh apparatov.* Moscow: Mashinostroenie, 1984.

Vaughn, Diane. *The Challenger Launch Decision: Risky Technology, Culture and Deviance at NASA.* Chicago: Chicago University Press, 1996.
Vernadsky, Vladimir. *Geochemistry and the Biosphere.* Santa Fe, NM: Synergetic Press, 2007.
Von Bencke, Matthew J. *The Politics of Space: A History of U.S.-Soviet/Russian Competition and Cooperation in Space.* Boulder, CO: Westview, 1997.
Weiner, Douglas R. *A Little Corner of Freedom: Russian Nature Protection from Stalin to Gorbachev.* Berkeley: University of California Press, 1999.
White, Frank. *The Overview Effect: Space Exploration and Human Evolution.* Boston, MA: Houghton Mifflin, 1987.
Williams, Michael C. "Words, Images, Enemies: Securitization and International Politics." *International Studies Quarterly* 47, no. 4 (2003): 511–31.
Winter, Jay. *Dreams of Peace and Freedom: Utopian Moments in the Twentieth Century.* New Haven, CT: Yale University Press, 2006.
Wolfe, Audra J. *Freedom's Laboratory: The Cold War Struggle for the Soul of Science.* Baltimore, MD: Johns Hopkins University Press, 2018.
Worden, Al, with French, Francis. *The Light of Earth: Reflections on a Life in Space.* Lincoln: University of Nebraska Press, 2021.
Young, George M. *The Russian Cosmists: The Esoteric Futurism of Nikolai Fedorov and His Followers.* New York: Oxford University Press, 2012.

ACKNOWLEDGMENTS

A book project produces many debts of gratitude for all the people who have commented on drafts of various chapters, invited me to speak, and who edited my work. My colleagues and administrators at California State University, Long Beach, have made it possible for me to pursue research by providing course releases, sabbaticals, and grant support. My university does an admirable job of nurturing an intellectual atmosphere dedicated to both teaching and research. This atmosphere has continually pushed me to explore new ideas, bring them to conferences and eventually take them back into the classroom. I also want to thank my many students over the years who have read drafts of my work and discussed them in various seminars. They gave me a keen sense of whether or not I was communicating my ideas in a way that nonspecialists as well as specialists could understand. To the extent that this book succeeds in communicating to those interested in space history but not necessarily academics, it is due to the contributions of my undergraduate and master's students. The NASA History Division and its impressive scholars and administrators have always been helpful and encouraging. I am especially grateful to Professor Dmitri Sidorov in the Department of Geography at California State University, Long Beach. He drew my attention to the importance of one of the main figures in this book, Vladimir Syromiatnikov. We often discussed Syromiatnikov from an interdisciplinary perspective that made me understand the spatial and cultural dimensions of space flight and docking in very different ways. Without his insights as a geographer and help in tracking down sources, it would not have been possible to finish Chapter 3 on the androgynous docking mechanism. Finally, I want to thank my many colleagues in space history and Soviet history who have read and commented on my work over the years. Alexander Geppert introduced me to the world of space history outside of the Soviet field by accepting a paper of mine for a conference in Berlin many years ago. I did not know it at the time, but that conference was the beginning of this book. Francis French has provided invaluable advice on matters relating to global space history. Asif Siddiqi and Slava Gerovitch have provided the bedrock foundations of Soviet space history and the history of technology and science more generally. I also want to thank Victoria Smolkin for inviting me to speak at Wesleyan University's College of the Environment where I was able to discuss ideas about space docking with a diverse group of scientists, humanitarians, and social scientists, and also for helping me to understand more deeply the spiritual dimensions of Soviet space exploration. Also noteworthy is the support of the Desert Workshop on Russian History, which allowed me to present the ideas for this book at the University of Nevada Las Vegas in February 2018. Their feedback was transformative for this project.

I am grateful to the following organizations for allowing me to use material from essays that I published previously: "Handshakes in Space and the Cold War Imaginary," *Journal of Cold War Studies* 23, no. 2 (Spring 2021), 100–32; "Transnational Utopias, Space Exploration, and the Association of Space Explorers, 1972–1985," in Alexander Geppert, ed., *Post-Apollo: Outer Space and the Limits of Utopia* (New York: Palgrave Macmillan, 2018), 209–37; Andrew Jenks, "Securitization and Secrecy in the Late Cold War: The View from Space," *Kritika: Explorations in Russian and Eurasian History* 21, no. 3 (2020), 659–89.

INDEX

2001
 A Space Odyssey 127, 154
Afghanistan
 Invasion of 142, 147, 150
Antarctica 7, 22, 49, 50
APAS 74, 85–86, 88–92, 94–96, 106–7,
 157–58, 160
Apollo 11 4, 27–28, 47, 49, 98, 127, 131
Apollo 8 17, 21, 23–24, 27, 41, 58
Armstrong, Neil 46, 49
Association of Space Explorers 41, 57,
 73, 153–55
Astrofuturism 5, 163

Baikonur 72, 126, 131
Bean, Alan 166
Beggs, James
 Nasa Administrator 151
Beregovoi, Georgii 29–30
Blue Marble
 Image of Earth 4, 45, 72
Borman, Frank 17–18, 21–22, 28–29, 31,
 34, 45, 126
Brand, Vance 59, 70
Brezhnev, Leonid 14–15, 18, 21, 32, 35,
 76, 94, 105–6, 108–10, 117, 123, 126,
 129–30, 135, 138, 160

Carson, Rachel 83
Carter, Jimmy 114, 139, 142, 150
Chernobyl
 Power Plant 158–59
Chertok, Boris 38, 78–79, 120
Chretien, Jean-Loup 73
Clarke, Arthur 42, 154
Club of Rome
 Overpopulation fears 48, 55

Cosmism 5, 16, 54–55, 71, 73, 144
Cosmopolitics 3–5, 41, 57
Cousteau, Jacques-Yves 61, 67–69, 154
Czechoslovakia 1, 20, 54, 56, 76

De Gaulle, Charles 18, 56, 160
Denver, John 154
Détente 1, 14, 16, 19, 22–23, 25, 27, 35,
 39, 50, 57, 63, 75–77, 82, 84, 89, 93,
 95, 97–98, 102, 113–16, 118, 124,
 126, 138, 141–43, 147, 151–52, 158

Earthrise 4, 17, 23–24, 35, 41–42,
 45, 50, 58
Eliseev, Aleksei 21, 60, 77, 104–6, 109,
 112, 129, 134, 140–41, 153
Esalen Institute 63–65, 153
European Space Agency (ESA) 1, 63, 155
Export Controls, United States 32, 54
Extrasensory Perception
 Edgar Mitchell 63

Feoktistov, Konstantin 29–30
Fletcher, James
 Nasa Administrator 104
Ford, Gerald 97, 109–10, 139
Franco-Soviet Cooperation 18–19, 24, 27,
 57, 73, 144–45
Frutkin, Arnold 26
Fulbright, William 24

Gagarin, Yuri 12, 20, 27, 31, 43–44, 68,
 78, 97, 141
Gemini Capsule 86
George Low
 Deputy Nasa Administrator 31, 34, 39,
 129, 131

INDEX

Gilruth, Robert 26, 31, 128
Glasnost' 118, 138, 147
Gorbachev 138–39, 147, 151

Harvest Moon Initiative 47–48, 55, 74
Hickman, James 64. *See* Esalen Institute

Institute for Noetic Sciences 153. *See* Mitchell, Edgar
Intelsat 125
Intercontinental Ballistic Missile (ICBM) 9, 11, 44, 94
Interkosmos 1, 19–20, 27, 52, 54, 92, 109, 123, 144, 147, 151–52, 156
International Astronomical Union (IAU) 51
International Geophysical Year 20, 43
International Space Station 1, 16, 152, 154, 156
International Space Treaty 24, 151
Intersputnik 54

Jackson-Vanik amendment 141, 150
Jähn, Sigmund 6, 67
Johnson, Caldwell 35, 86–88, 90, 92–94, 105, 133, 157, 159
Johnson, Lyndon 6, 125

Keldysh, Mstislav 20–21, 25–26, 30–31, 33, 39, 129
Kennedy, John F. 4, 13, 125
Khrushchev, Nikita 94, 123, 129, 138, 144
Kissinger, Henry 21, 25, 29, 34–35, 48, 126, 129–30, 138
Korolev, Sergei 12, 20–21, 78–79, 85–86, 158
Kosygin, Alexei 20, 31–32, 46, 49, 59, 82, 102, 143
Krokodil 115
Kubasov, Valerii 29, 102

Lacy-Zarubin Agreement 125
Latour, Bruno 80, 94
Leonov, Aleksei 8, 16, 23, 30, 32, 39, 45, 57–58, 66, 70, 72, 96, 98–99, 107–8, 110, 135, 146, 153–54
Low, George 31, 34–35, 37, 39, 129, 131
lunar mapping 50–51, 53, 74, 76

lunar rocks
  exchanges 50
Lunney, Glynn 39, 134

Male-female docking systems 36, 76, 85–88, 90–91
Manhattan Project 6, 32, 118
Marooned
  Science Fiction movie 83
Mir space station 1, 152, 157, 160
Mitchell, Edgar 57, 61, 63, 65–66, 70, 153
Mutual assured destruction
  Doctrine of 15, 75, 155
Mozzhorin, Yuri 103–4, 135–36, 138–39, 141

National Aeronautics and Space Act of 1958 22, 27
National Security Council 14, 119
Nixon, Richard 4–5, 14–15, 18–19, 21–22, 24–25, 27, 29, 31–35, 45–48, 50, 54–55, 57–59, 76, 82, 100, 116–17, 126–27, 129–30, 136, 138–39, 141, 143, 150

Ostpolitik 18
Outer Space Treaty 24
Overview Effect 71–72, 81, 156

Paine, Thomas O.
  Nasa Administrator 25, 29–30, 34, 62, 117, 127–28, 147
peaceful coexistence
  policy of 9, 22, 39, 94–95, 124, 129–30, 138, 144, 157
Playboy 113–15, 141
Pompidou, Georges 18

Rand, Ayn 4–5
Reagan administration 59–61, 143–47, 155
Reagan, Ronald 114, 116, 142, 146
risk-taking 32, 83–84, 158–59

Sagan, Carl 68–69, 153
Sakharov, Andrei 142
Salyut capsule 56, 87, 142, 157–58
Schweickart, Russell 31, 57, 59, 61–63, 66, 69, 71–72

science fiction 42
Scientific Technological Revolution 123
Scott, David 28, 37
Sevastianov, Vitalii 15, 31, 54–55, 65
Skylab 76
Slayton, Donald Kent (Deke) 107
socio-technical imaginary 17, 149
Soviet lunar missions 46, 52, 91, 98
Soyuz capsule 1, 36, 46, 113, 158
Space Shuttle 55, 62–63, 70, 145, 154
Sputnik 11, 68, 79, 108, 143, 149, 160
Stafford, Thomas 16, 31, 39, 98, 107–8, 112, 136, 145, 158
Star City training center 126, 136, 139
Strategic Defense Initiative (SDI) 9, 59, 69–70, 116, 119, 151

Syromiatnikov, Vladimir 22, 32, 38, 54, 77–93, 95–97, 111–15, 129, 131, 139, 141, 149, 151, 157

technocratic ideas 19, 27–29, 51, 95, 118, 137
technological fix 9, 75–76, 88, 103, 158
technopolitics 17
Tsiolkovskii, Konstantin 82, 97

V-2 Rocket 2, 6
Vernadskii, Vladimir 42
Vysotskii, Vladimir 80

Welding in space, 102

www.ingramcontent.com/pod-product-compliance
Lightning Source LLC
Chambersburg PA
CBHW021143230426
43667CB00005B/234